The Worker in an Affluent Society

By the same author

MEN IN THE PITS (1948)
LABOUR, LIFE AND POVERTY (1948)
THE BRITISH WORKER (1952)

FERDYNAND ZWEIG

The Worker
in an Affluent Society

FAMILY LIFE AND INDUSTRY

DISCARDED

LIBRARY OF
LAMAR STATE COLLEGE OF TECHNOLOGY

↑ 936426

THE FREE PRESS OF GLENCOE, INC.
A DIVISION OF THE CROWELL-COLLIER PUBLISHING COMPANY
New York, N.Y.

© Copyright 1961 by Ferdynand Zweig

First Published in the United States 1961 by The Free Press of Glencoe, Inc.

All rights in this book are reserved. No part of this book may be used or reproduced in any manner whatsoever without written permission except in the case of brief quotations embodied in critical articles and reviews.

For information, address :
THE FREE PRESS OF GLENCOE, INC.
A DIVISION OF THE CROWELL-COLLIER PUBLISHING COMPANY
60 Fifth Avenue, New York 11, N.Y.

Printed in Great Britain

Contents

Acknowledgements	vii
Introduction	ix
The Sample and Method of Interview	xiii

PART ONE—THE STANDARD OF LIVING, HOME AND CHILDREN

1.	The Standard of Living—Earnings	1
2.	Housing Conditions and Home Equipment	5
3.	The Practice of Early Marriage	10
4.	Planning the Family	14
5.	The Father Image	20

PART TWO—HUSBANDS AND WIVES

6.	Masters or Partners: Husband–Wife Relationship	27
7.	The Housekeeping Allowance	33
8.	Working Wives	39
9.	Divorces and Separations	46

PART THREE—WORK AND HOME

10.	Shifts as a Health and Family Problem	53
11.	Acquisitive Tendencies	65
12.	The Quest for Overtime	70
13.	The Changing Ethos of Work	76
14.	Contacts within the Working Group	80
15.	Home and Work Upsets	84

PART FOUR—CULTURE, LEISURE AND SOCIAL CONTACTS

16.	Cultural Horizons	89
17.	Pastimes, Hobbies and Sidelines	96
18.	Reading Matter	100
19.	The Motor Car as an Instrument of Social Change	104
20.	The Impact of T.V.	108
21.	Contacts with Family of Origin	111
22.	Contacts with Neighbours	116
23.	Contacts with Workmates Outside	117

PART FIVE—SAVINGS AND PROPERTY

24.	Attitudes to Saving	121
25.	The Ethos of House Property	124
26.	The Rewards of Temperance	129

PART SIX—CLASS CONSCIOUSNESS AND RELIGION

27.	Self-placement and Class Consciousness	133
28.	Inter-generation Mobility	139
	A. Sons and Fathers	
	B. Fathers and Sons	
29.	Religious Consciousness	146

PART SEVEN—GROUPS OF WORKERS

30.	Single Young Men	155
31.	Confirmed Bachelors	159
32.	Widowers	163
33.	Men Nearing Retiring Age	167

PART EIGHT—WOMEN OPERATIVES IN MULLARD

34.	The Enquiry in Mullard	171

PART NINE—GENERALIZATIONS AND CONCLUSIONS

35.	The Homeo-static Principle	189
36.	Hedgehog Behaviour	193
37.	'As It Is'	195
38.	Projective Generalizations	199
39.	Ambivalence	202
40.	A New Mode of Life and a New Ethos	205

APPENDICES: LOCAL BACKGROUND OF THE FIVE FIRMS

I.	River Don Works in Sheffield	213
II.	The Workington Iron & Steel Company in Workington	223
III.	Vauxhall Motors Ltd in Luton	234
IV.	The Dunlop Rubber Company Ltd in Erdington	246
V.	The Mullard Radio Valve Company Ltd in Mitcham	257

Index 266

Acknowledgements

ALL THROUGH THE ENQUIRY which provided the material for this book I enjoyed great help and co-operation from union officers and shop-stewards, from managers and foremen, from men and women on the line. All the firms were very generous in their help, providing me with an office and enabling me to interview men and women privately during their working hours, for which those on piecework were compensated. Men and women on the line were generous, giving me their confidence and telling me all about their problems, fears and hopes.

I wish to thank all those who are too numerous to be mentioned by name, and in particular the managers and personnel officers of the following:

The English Steel Corporation Ltd—in Sheffield, especially Mr A. C. Barley, the Employment Officer, and Mr W. B. Kingston, his assistant.

The Workington Iron & Steel Company—in Workington, especially Mr T. S. Kilpatrick, the General Manager, and Mr P. J. Chambers, the Personnel Officer.

Vauxhall Motors Ltd—in Luton, especially Mr R. R. Hopkins, the Personnel and Welfare Manager.

The Dunlop Rubber Company Ltd—in Erdington, especially Mr H. S. Briers, Personnel Manager, Mr Cogswell, his assistant, and Mrs Marshall of the Welfare Department.

The Mullard Radio Valve Company Ltd—in Mitcham, especially Mr J. C. Ross, Plant Personnel Officer, Mr Gogarty and Mr Henderson.

For the initial stage of the study I am indebted to the Institute of Community Studies, with whose co-operation the pilot enquiry in Sheffield was conceived and carried out, and to Mr Michael Young and Mr Peter Willmott who gave me their kind advice and comments.

However, my special gratitude goes to the National Institute of Economic & Social Research, which agreed to administer the main enquiry, and particularly to Mr C. T. Saunders, C.M.G., the Director of the Institute, Mrs A. K. Jackson, Secretary of the Institute and Mr C. St. J. O'Herlihy for their assistance, advice, comments and criticisms. Only I can be aware of the debt I owe to Mrs Jackson, who participated in the planning of the enquiry, took an active interest in all its stages and also helped considerably with editorial work in preparing the manuscript for publication.

The enquiry would not have been possible without the assistance of the generous grant from the Nuffield Foundation to which I am under special obligation. Apart from this I have greatly valued the support of Mr John Beavan of the Nuffield Foundation who has given me encouragement and help throughout.

Mr Donald MacRae, Reader in Sociology at the London School of Economics, read my manuscript, and I benefited greatly from his comments and advice.

However, although I received the most useful advice and comments from these quarters, the responsibility for any shortcomings of the book rests entirely with me.

I should also like to thank the *Twentieth Century* for its permission to reprint part of the article: 'The New Factory Worker' which appears here as 'Concluding Remarks'.

Throughout the study I enjoyed the most generous assistance of my wife Doris Ruth who acted not only as secretary but also contributed findings of her own. It was the most valuable co-operation and I feel I could not have written this book without her unstinted help.

F. ZWEIG

London, 1960

Introduction

THERE ARE A NUMBER of excellent studies devoted to family life and a number of similar studies of industrial life, but there are hardly any studies devoted to the lines of intersection of both areas. Industrial life and family life are studied *per se* as a sort of closed system of industrial and human relations, i.e., as formal and informal relations but within the radius of the workplace. However, industrial life enters family life on many counts, and equally family life crosses industrial life, so changes in one area are bound to affect the other.

The idea of the enquiry was to study the mutual impact of family life and industry, and that remained its central theme. However, the study very soon transcended its original aim, and became a study of social change, an enquiry into working and living conditions of the industrial worker, as they have been affected by post-war development. The change is very deep and far-reaching. Working-class life finds itself on the move towards new middle-class values and middle-class existence. When I compared this situation with what I saw ten years ago when I wrote *The British Worker* (Penguin), the change can only be described as a deep transformation of values, as the development of new ways of thinking and feeling, a new ethos, new aspirations and cravings. It is this transformation which is given priority in this study.

The study had two distinct phases. One was a pilot enquiry sponsored by the Institute of Community Studies. This enquiry was conducted in May and June 1958 in the River Don Works of the English Steel Corporation Ltd in Sheffield (later referred to as 'Sheffield') and was based on open and informal interviews with the employees.

The second phase, carried out under the auspices of the National Institute of Economic & Social Research, consisted of studies undertaken in four firms in this order:

1. The Workington Iron & Steel Company in Workington (later referred to as 'Workington'), a branch of United Steel Companies Limited, in November and December 1958;

2. Vauxhall Motors Ltd in Luton (referred to as 'Vauxhall') in January and February 1959;
3. The Dunlop Rubber Company Ltd in Erdington, Birmingham (referred to as 'Dunlop') in March and April 1959;
4. The Mullard Radio Valve Company Ltd in Mitcham (referred to as 'Mullard') in May, June and July 1959.

For these enquiries a more or less standardized interview schedule was used with small deviations from works to works as the enquiry progressed (see 'The Sample and Method of Interview'). In addition, in Vauxhall, Dunlop and Mullard a simple test for cultural horizons was given, using the formula, 'Have you heard of so-and-so?' (for details see chapter 16). This was a sideline of the enquiry but proved extremely interesting.

In Mullard sets of provocative sayings and proverbs were presented for comments to both men and women, and this line proved most illuminating, revealing intimate ways of thinking and feeling. I regret very much that I did not use this method earlier in previous studies in other firms.

Altogether 672 interviews, conducted personally by me, were recorded, as follows: 161 in Sheffield; 104 in Workington; 120 men and four women operatives in Vauxhall; 115 men in Dunlop; 101 men and sixty-seven women in Mullard.

In addition a considerable amount of qualitative material was collected from departmental managers and foremen, personnel officers, wages clerks, training officers, employment officers, works doctors, officers of various committees, safety officers and so on.

A number of homes of those interviewed at work were visited by my wife. In some cases I asked: 'Do you mind if my wife visits your wife?' and most men consented. Consequently my wife visited their homes and had a friendly and informal chat with the family and in most cases was shown around. In this way sixty homes were visited—nine in Sheffield, seventeen in Workington, fifteen in Birmingham, eight in Luton, eleven in Mitcham. A few homes were also visited by me. Welfare officers, housing officers, probation officers, marriage guidance counsellors and labour exchange managers were also interviewed by my wife or me. In reporting individual cases details which might have led to identification have been disguised.

Records and statistics of firms where the study was conducted were available to me and proved of great help.

The material collected in this way was used both in quantitative and qualitative terms. All through the study I tried to preserve the separate identity of the five groups of workers employed in the above-mentioned five establishments, looking both for diversity and conformity. In many cases there was a clear underlying pattern which repeated itself in all or most of those establishments, suggesting a definite tendency or trend.

The individual is always the despair of science, and I was dealing with individuals only. Although I present them in groups, according to establishment, and also in other groups susceptible to classification, I am fully conscious of the fact that they are still individuals with their diverse modes of behaviour. 'Be sure to study the great diversity of human nature'—I have tried throughout the study to keep in mind Emmanuel Kant's advice, not forgetting, however, that the greatest prize of the researcher is to find out the common measure or the underlying pattern of this great diversity. The search for the 'One' and the search for the 'Many' are as complementary and necessary as both of our legs. However, only a few generalizations have been attempted and only a general trend suggesting a social change is outlined; for the rest I have confined myself strictly to the presentation of my sample data as supplied by the interviews. Hence the purely descriptive character of the study with its self-imposed limitations.

How far the data are representative of a larger class of workers, it is difficult to say. Firstly, I was concerned with factory workers as opposed to other classes of workmen. Secondly, I was interviewing workers in large-scale, well-organized and well-conducted establishments (their local background is presented in the Appendices). Thirdly, the industries from which my sample firms were drawn are on the whole prosperous and expanding industries in which workers' rates of pay and earnings tend to be above average. The industries concerned employ something like a million adult men, which is nearly a fifth of all men employed in manufacturing industry, and about a fourteenth of all adult male employees in the United Kingdom.

I am well aware of the fact that many puzzles in men's behaviour remain unsolved, hence the unavoidable contradictions which may crop up from time to time. However, my first concern was faithful attention to detail, as only in details does the true picture come to life. Therefore, I found it worthwhile to analyse even the smallest groups, sometimes comprising only a dozen or so men, if they presented some special interest.

Throughout the study I tried to keep the balance between the importance of measurements and the importance of common-sense observations made personally by me and a large number of other observers. I have interviewed, apart from the men in the sample, at least 200 to 250 managers, foremen, etc. on their field of observation. Still the approximation to the truth may in fact be found in the compromise made here between depth and scope, between quantitative analysis and qualitative observation.

The Sample and Method of Interview

THE SAMPLE DATA are based on personal interviews conducted in five works, as stated in the Introduction. Men on the line, i.e., hourly-rated men with a sprinkling of weekly-paid supervisors, were chosen at random (except in so far as I asked for the proportion of single men to be kept down) to cover all departments and all grades according to their strength. I moved from department to department, first interviewing the heads and one or two foremen on general conditions, labour relations and work attitudes, and then a few men chosen at random. In Mullard the procedure was a little different as I had a central office to which men, selected at random, were invited.

Foreign labour was excluded as the survey was concerned with the indigenous population, although four foreign workmen did come up for interview in Sheffield.

The interview was always strictly private. I introduced myself by showing my Penguin book with its photograph on the back cover (this was always greeted with a smile), and explained that as this book was written years ago I now wanted to study post-war developments. I stressed the purely voluntary character of the interview, assuring the men that it had no connection with the firm or management. My appeal for help and co-operation was unfailingly successful. Men took great interest in the enquiry and some expressed their appreciation of this type of study devoted to human beings instead of machines. An answer was rarely refused to any question, although in some cases when I felt a certain reluctance to talk freely, I waived questions which might strain patience and goodwill and jeopardize the interviews with the next men. The opinion which is formed by the first interviewees about the interviewer and the nature of the interview spreads like wildfire around the works, and so one has to be particularly careful at the very beginning. If a negative opinion were formed, the researcher might as well pack his bag and try his luck elsewhere. Flock-like behaviour would assert itself immediately. Fortunately the refusals were very rare. It was mostly shy or backward types who refused to come to my office and luckily this happened only when the enquiry was well under way. Altogether such people never exceeded 4 per cent of the sample in any of the works (Mullard 4 per cent, Sheffield 3 per cent, in other places 2 to 3 per cent).

I tried to make the interview informal, personal and friendly, with a two-way traffic in questions and answers and as near to a natural flow of conversation as possible. In Sheffield no questionnaire was used and frequently the data were not recorded during the interview itself but immediately afterwards. In all other places a standard interview schedule was used, with very little deviation from works to works as the enquiry progressed; this schedule is reproduced at the end of this chapter. Consequently the data are less systematic for Sheffield and more so for the other four works. At Sheffield the investigation was in the nature of a pilot enquiry which experimented with various sets of questions, and so on some topics the sample data refer only to four works without Sheffield or only with part of the Sheffield sample, but this is always made clear in the treatment of the subject.

Now we shall look at the sample itself. First let us see the composition of the sample in terms of skill and status. The classification follows that used in the works concerned. Here the break-down of the sample is as follows:

	Labourers		Semi-skilled		Skilled		Supervisors		TOTAL
	No.	%	No.	%	No.	%	No.	%	
Sheffield	23	14·3	72	44·7	62	38·5	4	2·5	161
Workington	27	26·0	48	46·2	21	20·2	8	7·7	104
Vauxhall	4	3·3	71	59·2	38	31·7	7	5·8	120
Dunlop	7	6·1	78	67·8	22	19·1	8	7·0	115
Mullard	6	5·9	54	53·5	32	31·7	9	8·9	101
	67	11·1	323	53·7	175	29·1	36	6·0	601

The higher percentage of labourers in Sheffield and in Workington reflects the special character of 'labouring' in steelworks, where labourers form simply the first rung in the ladder of promotion. In other places the proportion of labourers is very small indeed. The term 'labourer' is avoided as far as possible (nobody wants to describe himself as 'labourer' on a hire-purchase form) and the management try to give each labouring job an attractive name of its own.

Among semi-skilled men there were quite a few (altogether twenty-six in four works, Workington, Vauxhall, Dunlop and Mullard) who were actually skilled in other trades but were attracted to semi-skilled operations by higher earnings. These were especially frequent in Vauxhall (ten) and Dunlop (eight).

We see that in the sample as a whole labourers formed 11 per cent, supervisors 6 per cent, while semi-skilled (54 per cent) and skilled (29 per cent) formed the bulk of the sample. The small number of supervisors may however somewhat over-represent the number in the works concerned.

I then examined the age structure of the sample. I divided the sample into two main groups, the under-forties, from twenty to thirty-nine inclusive, and the forty-plus group. I use this division whenever I want to compare attitudes and behaviour between two generations. The age distribution of the sample shows the following pattern:

	Under-forties		Forty-plus		TOTAL
	No.	%	No.	%	
Sheffield	68	42·2	93	57·8	161
Workington	45	43·3	59	56·7	104
Vauxhall	54	45·0	66	55·0	120
Dunlop	50	43·5	65	56·5	115
Mullard	52	51·5	49	48·5	101
TOTAL	269	44·8	332	55·2	601

In the country as a whole, of the male working population between the ages of twenty and sixty-five, 47 per cent are between twenty and thirty-nine and 53 per cent are between forty and sixty-four.

The particular age composition of the labour force in a given works appears to be influenced by the age of the works itself, a long established firm having more older men than a young firm.

I also analysed the marital status of the men. The sample is divided here into two main streams: single men and family men (i.e., those who are married or were once married); and in many respects the two streams are treated separately.

	Married		Single		TOTAL
	No.	%	No.	%	
Sheffield	150	93·2	11	6·8	161
Workington	89	85·6	15	14·4	104
Vauxhall	107	89·2	13	10·8	120
Dunlop	106	92·2	9	7·8	115
Mullard	96	95·0	5	5·0	101
	548	91·2	53	8·8	601

In the country as a whole single men account for about 20 per cent of the total male population between the ages of twenty and sixty-four. The lower percentage in my sample reflects my request, already mentioned, that the proportion of single men chosen should be kept down, as my main interest was in family men.

I had in my sample, besides seven separated men, eight divorced or widowed who had not married again. Thus in my sample the widowed and divorced were about 1·5 per cent of married men as against about 3 per cent of married men aged twenty to sixty-four in the country as a whole.

Special chapters are devoted to young single men, confirmed bachelors and those who were divorced, separated or widowed.

Sixty-seven married women were interviewed in Mullard on a similar basis and with a similar interview schedule, and four women workers were interviewed in Vauxhall, but they are not included in the general sample, which deals only with men. Women operatives in Mullard are treated separately in Part Eight.

INTERVIEW SCHEDULE

1. (a) Age
   (b) Single, married (first time), divorced or separated, widowed
   Date of marriage
   (c) Number, sex and age of children and their occupations
   (d) Council house or privately rented (with bath or without) own house, company house, parents' home, furnished rooms
   (e) Parents or other members living as part of the household, lodgers

The Sample and Method of Interview

2. (*a*) Present job (supervisory, skilled, semi-skilled or labourer)
   Was he apprenticed?
   (*b*) Previous jobs in other firms
   (*c*) Length of service in firm apart from National Service
   In how many departments and jobs and why left
   (*d*) What he liked or disliked most about the job
   (*e*) Would he change it for another job, especially would he move to another district if he had no job
3. (*a*) Hours of work and shifts
   (*b*) If on shifts do they affect health, stomach, sleep or nerves, or home life
   Does his wife mind his nightshifts
   Would he prefer nightshifts on a weekly or monthly rotation
   (*c*) Does he care for overtime
   Would he prefer regular days with less money
   (*d*) Does he prefer piecework to time rates; individual bonus to group bonus
4. (*a*) Wages (net)
   (*b*) Housekeeping money: Regular or variable Including rent and bills
   (*c*) Savings:
   Does he save for purchases, holidays, rainy day, old age
   Does he prefer to save or to buy things
5. (*a*) Is wife working
   (*b*) Her job
   (*c*) Working hours
   (*d*) Reason for working
   (*e*) Her health
6. (*a*) How many accidents in working life and for how long incapacitated
   (*b*) Period of sickness
7. (*a*) Does he feel happy at home or has he upsets at home affecting his work
   (*b*) How many shifts lost last year and why
   (*c*) How long unemployed For what periods
8. (*a*) Has he T.V., washing machine, car, motor cycle, radiogram, refrigerator, piano
   (*b*) His commitments on H.P.
9. Interest in education or jobs of children at home; ambitions for them
10. Occupation of father:
    Supervisory, skilled, semi-skilled or labourer
    Does he or did he work in the same firm or job
11. (*a*) Do parents and siblings live in the same district.
    Does he keep in touch with them
    (*b*) Is any of his brothers a professional, staff or business man
12. (*a*) Contacts with workmates: Seen outside works Visited or invited
    (*b*) Contacts with neighbours: Just friendly or on visiting terms
13. (*a*) Hobbies, sports and sidelines
    (*b*) Reading
    (*c*) Who are his friends
    (*d*) Gambling
    (*e*) Drinking in pubs and clubs
    (*f*) Crafts and arts
    (*g*) House decoration and gardening
    (*h*) Working or middle class
    (*i*) Religious interests
    (*j*) Test paper

PART ONE

The Standard of Living Home and Children

1. THE STANDARD OF LIVING—EARNINGS

'MEN ARE NEVER SATISFIED with their wages. I suppose it's human nature but on the whole they have achieved a standard of living unthinkable before the war.' This comment came from a shop-steward when the subject of wages was discussed. A similar comment came from a foreman in a steelworks: 'A rise of wages is good only for a fortnight. If they get £12 they want £13, when they get £13 they want £14. They continuously set themselves a new standard. The more money they get the more they want.'

It was interesting to note that men at each end of the wage scale seemed to be more dissatisfied with their wages than men in the middle ranges. Those who earned £10 a week, or less, frequently voiced their grudge, while those who earned £20 or more also often expressed dissatisfaction, but whether it was genuine or on principle it is difficult to say. Shop-stewards, when asked how wage claims originated, said that they seemed to come from the bottom-wage men because they have a genuine grievance, and from the top-wage men because they are the leaders, the best organized and the most conscious of their rights.

While discussing wages I often found that not all men were conversant with the wage structure as practised in the establishment, as it was often too complicated and disjointed. Basic rates, cost-of-living bonuses (as practised in steelworks), efficiency or production bonuses, piece rates, with minimum guarantees, allowances and odd premiums for conditions are so numerous that men are often lost in this maze of items. The nature of national bonus was often misunderstood. As one man in Workington exclaimed: 'Surely national bonus is paid by the government'. In some places the wage system was described as 'antiquated' or 'too cumbersome' or 'more historic than factual' or 'it got out of hand'. There seems to be a case for simplification of the wage system and for bringing it up to date with a more realistic appraisal of wage differentials which are often too low to act as incentives. Also the automatic elements of wage systems, like the cost-of-living bonus in the steelworks, seem to make up too large a part the total wage. None of the works which I visited applied a thorough-going system of job evaluation such as is widely practised in American industry.

However, we are concerned here not with wages systems but with living standards—though these are of course governed by the wage level of the men together with their wives' and children's earnings.

First let us look at the average weekly earnings of adult males at each of the five establishments. I give below figures of average weekly earnings of adult male manual workers, which were kindly provided to me by the firms concerned, not only at the time of my visit, or near to it, but also, in each case, for October 1958 and April 1959. For purposes of comparison, I give weekly earnings for adult males for all manufacturing industry, and for all industry at large, as published by the Ministry of Labour.

	At the time of interviews	October 1958	April 1959
Sheffield . .	Spring 1958 about £15 0s 0d	£13 8s 10d	£13 5s 0d
Workington .	July 1958 £13 2s 1d	£13 4s 10d	£12 1s 9d
Vauxhall . .	January 1959 £17 3s 8d	£15 7s 7d	£19 7s 8d
Dunlop . .	January 1959 £15 13s 0d	£15 13s 5d	£15 10s 6d
Mullard . .	April 1959		
Semi-skilled	See third	£11 13s 0d	£12 8s 7d
Skilled	column	£16 2s 0d	£16 11s 10d
All Manufacturing Industry		£13 5s 5d	£13 11s 9d
All Industry		£12 16s 8d	£13 2s 11d

My enquiry stretched from May 1958 when I started at Sheffield to July 1959 when I finished at Mullard, and during this period the economy as a whole began to move out of a slight recession. We see the upward swing in the figures for Vauxhall and Mullard though Dunlop shows little change and the steelworks had not recovered from the recession by April 1959.

During the period of my enquiry the average wage level was highest in Vauxhall and second highest in Dunlop; the other three firms were close to each other with Workington perhaps a little behind.

The figures illustrate the point that the average weekly wage in a firm can fluctuate considerably in quite a short period. Seasonal as well as cyclical changes in demand for the product can be important and the effect on individual earnings may be even sharper.[1]

The average wage in a firm does not of course reflect the wide range of earnings of individuals on different jobs: for example in Sheffield at the time of my visit a labourer could earn £8 9s 0d for 48 hours, while a first and second hand melter could earn £24 16s 0d. I often found, however, that the differences in earnings were less than the differences in rates of pay because of opportunities of lower-rated men to earn extra through shift allowances and overtime. For example, at the time of my visit to Vauxhall I found a labourer who had made £17 8s 0d for a 59½-hour week, a semi-skilled production worker who had made £18 2s 2d for 57 hours, and a skilled special-grade worker who had earned £16 7s 7d for 42½ hours.

I found that for the big majority in each firm the variations between individuals in weekly net earnings (often called 'bottom-line wages' or 'take-home money') fell within £3 or £4—the variation being, of course, smaller after deductions of Income Tax, National Insurance, etc., than before.

I was interested in the deductions from gross pay, other than Income Tax and National Insurance, which reduced the amount of

[1] I can quote examples of a skilled man in Vauxhall who received £16 in a flat week and in another week £33 for 76 hours; a Dunlop cover maker earned £17 for 44 hours and up to £26 with overtime; a fettler in Sheffield, £17 6s 2d for 44 hours and £24 2s 0d for 58 hours; a skilled man in Workington earned £15 on mornings, £17 on afternoons and £22 on nights; a semi-skilled operator in Mullard £12 10s 0d for 44 hours and £15 to £16 with overtime.

'take-home money', and so in each firm I asked for a list of typical deductions.[1]

Now we come to the family income as augmented by wives' and children's earnings.

Out of a total number of family men, i.e., men married or once married, the number of men who had more than one wage packet coming into the house (including their own) was as follows:

NUMBER OF WAGE PACKETS

	Total family men	2	3	4	5	Total with more than one
Workington	89	28	10	5	0	43
Vauxhall	107	45	10	2	1	58
Dunlop	106	38	16	4	1	59
Mullard	96	40	9	4	3	56
	398	151	45	15	5	216

[1] In Sheffield the list of voluntary deductions included: Hospital Scheme (2d), Sports Club (1d, 2d, or 3d), Save the Children Fund (1d), Dr Barnardo's Homes (6d), British Empire Cancer Campaign (2d).

In Workington a typical list ran: Pension Scheme (3s), Holiday Fund (1s), Sick Club (3d), Social Services (2d), Blind Appeal (1d), Dr Barnardo's Homes (1d), Workmen's Mutual Aid Society (2d), Jubilee Cottage Fund (1d), Trades Hall (1d), Save the Children Fund (1d), Y.M.C.A. ($\frac{1}{2}$d).

At Vauxhall the list of possible deductions (in order of typicality) ran: Group Life Insurance (compulsory), Group Health, Supplementary Pension Contribution, Recreation Club, Manor House, Bedfordshire Hospital Scheme Association, National Savings, Trustee Savings, Charities, Overalls (supply and laundry), safety boots and shoes (repayments), loan repayments, tool club repayments (Apprentices only).

In Dunlop there were three general deductions, namely: Pension (2s per week plus an additional amount if the man wished to contribute more), Sickness and Benevolent Fund (7d per week), Sports and Social Club (2d per week). In addition to this the man if he wished might have deductions made for National Savings.

In Mullard, deductions fell under the heads: National Savings, Hire Purchase of Company Products, Company Supplementary Pensions, Sports Club, Hospital Saturday Fund contribution and purchase of overalls (by instalment). For those who participated in these activities the average deduction was 1s 8d a week for overalls, 6d for Hospital Saturday Fund, 4d for Sports Club, 4s for pension scheme, 10s for hire purchase, and 18s 6d for National Savings.

Further information about contributory and non-contributory pension schemes and other welfare schemes and clubs run by the firms will be found in the appendix chapters.

We see that about 55 per cent of family men in the sample as a whole had more than one wage packet coming into the house; however, a number of them actually had only part of a packet extra, as nearly half the number of working wives were only part-timers. (See Chapter 8.) We have also to remember that children's contributions are usually relatively small.

Five or six per cent of men also had sidelines (see Chapter 17); a few also drew pensions of various kinds or had property income; many of course drew family allowances.

It was my impression that most of my interviewees achieved a relatively high standard of living but not without hard work, with a great deal of overtime and shiftwork. The hard-up ones were mostly young married men with small children who had only one wage packet coming into the house. So it is not surprising that they were regarded by the management as the best workmen, pulling their weight to the utmost.

2. HOUSING CONDITIONS AND HOME EQUIPMENT

THE IMPROVEMENT of housing conditions in the last decade is one of the most potent factors in the transformation of the working man's way of life. A shop-steward, living for two years in his own modern house, observed: 'In the previous house the front door was never meant to be used; we had a settee across it. Everyone, including the postman, called at the back door. Now it is different. We've moved to the front.' That moving to the front has a deeper meaning. It stands for the shedding of the sense of inferiority of the old-fashioned workman. A man's wife on a new estate told my wife how the old kitchen is gradually losing its appeal as the centre of the family. 'In the other house the front room was never used except for Christmas. If I lit a fire in the front room we always seemed to get back into the kitchen. I suppose we were used to it. Now it's different.' Of course the T.V. has also contributed to this; and moves to new housing estates break some of the old habits, as the whole environment is so different, and has changed social perspectives. One can say that the kitchen mentality is gradually being replaced by the living-room mentality.

A steelworker, previously living in an overcrowded area near the works, and now in a new estate, said: 'Where I lived before, I walked straight from the house into the factory. When the heavy presses were going the crockery rattled in the house. You couldn't relax at home. It wasn't a home actually, you were still in the works.'

A workman who had moved into a council house five years before said this: 'When I moved to a council house I became more house-proud and stopped at home more frequently. First because the home was more comfortable, then because the public house was further away.' The fact is that new estates are not well equipped with such amenities as public houses and cinemas, and the demand for them is falling off.

'Here we spring-clean every year, and spring-cleaning in Sheffield means wall-papering and painting', said a workman's wife on a new estate.

'I believe people on the new estates are more house-proud but less gregarious. You can walk for a mile or two before you see anybody on the estates', my wife observed after her visits on new estates. A new pattern of relationship with neighbours is being established there, which I speak about in another context (see Chapter 22).

Moving to a new house, be it a council house or privately owned, starts the suburban drive of status-seeking through the home. The couple get busy decorating their house with bright colours and bold patterns to make it look modern, new furnishings are bought and the home is gradually equipped with modern gadgets. New standards are being set by the neighbours, especially the young ones, and these have to be followed.

Information about house conditions is shown in the table below which distinguishes between: (1) Own property; (2) Council houses or flats; (3) Privately-rented houses or flats; (4) Accommodation with parents or in-laws; (5) Furnished flats; (6) Company houses (one caretaker in Sheffield was counted as living in a company house).

	(1)	(2)	(3)	(4)	(5)	(6)	TOTAL
Sheffield	19	44	41	9	2	5	120
Workington	33	38	16	1	0	1	89
Vauxhall	50	39	11	5	2	0	107
Dunlop	33	45	18	8	2	0	106
Mullard	29	38	12	10	7	0	96
TOTAL	164	204	98	33	13	6	518

We see the strongest contrast in the sample data between Luton as a relatively new town and Sheffield, an old industrial centre with a great deal of old property centred around the works (Brightside). In Luton only 10 per cent of the men lived in privately-rented houses; in Sheffield one third. In Luton about 47 per cent lived in houses of their own; in Sheffield only 16 per cent. The figures for Workington, Dunlop and Mullard come close to each other.

Except for Luton, the council houses represent the standard housing for the greatest number, covering 33 to 43 per cent of my sample. Privately-owned property covers nearly one-third of the sample as a whole and I will deal with it more specifically in another context (see Chapter 25).

Jointly council housing and privately-owned property cover more than two-thirds of the whole sample, reaching, in Vauxhall, nearly 85 per cent, in three of the other centres between 70 and 75 per cent, and only in Sheffield coming down to about 53 per cent. For the sample as a whole, less than 20 per cent lived in privately-rented houses, practically exclusively in old type property.

Less than 10 per cent were not yet settled in permanent housing, living with their parents or in furnished rooms. However, not all those who lived with parents were looking for a house of their own; some were separated or divorced and some lived with a widowed father or mother. On the other hand a certain number of those who lived in privately-rented houses were looking for better accommodation, hoping to get a council house or their own property.

I was interested to know how many lived in sub-standard houses without amenities such as a bath and indoor sanitation. I asked about this in four works, Workington, Vauxhall, Dunlop and Mullard. In these places there were thirty-three family men living in such conditions, mostly in Workington (sixteen) and in Dunlop (ten); in Mullard there were six men and in Vauxhall there was only one. We see here again a strong contrast in sample data between relatively new towns and older districts. In Sheffield, Workington and Birmingham, quite a number lived in slummy conditions. The houses without a bath were occupied mostly by older men; actually there was only one man in his twenties among the thirty-three.

Young men in their twenties were also very infrequent among

council house tenants. Out of 204 council house tenants, there were only nine men in their twenties, out of whom four were in Vauxhall (young men recruited from London have a better chance to get a council house in a new town with a London grant), two in Mullard, two in Workington, one in Dunlop and none in Sheffield. These young men were able to get a council house because they were suffering from tuberculosis or had children suffering from it or had especially large families which required consideration. The average waiting time for a council house varied from place to place and could be anything up to ten years, as in Sheffield, and in some places, like Carshalton adjacent to Mullard, ordinary families placed on the so-called 'B' and 'C' list had practically no chance of getting a council house.

The company houses were more frequent in Sheffield where the Company owns 2,500 houses which were acquired for further development of the works in Brightside. One-fifth of these houses were occupied by men who worked in the firm, but the tenancy was not regarded as service tenancy. There were about 250 men on the waiting list and the average waiting time was two and a half years, although in some cases houses were used for specific grades of workmen.

Now let us pass to home equipment. I asked more specifically in four works about the possession of such items as television sets (T.V.), radiograms or record players (R.G.), washing machines (W.M.), refrigerators (Fr.), pianos (P.), and I give below the figures for family men, i.e., men married or once married.

	TOTAL	T.V.	R.G.	W.M.	Fr.	P.
Workington	89	64	20	34	1	12
Vauxhall	107	91	44	33	30	12
Dunlop	106	95	38	27	3	19
Mullard	96	84	51	23	26	14
	398	334	153	117	60	57

In looking at these figures it must be remembered that half a year elapsed between my visit to Workington and my visit to Mullard—a period during which there was something of a boom in national sales of consumer durables. Other special factors influencing ownership in the different districts were the provision of discount facilities for buying some electrical equipment at Mullard and Vauxhall, the electric-mindedness of men working in electrical engineering, and perhaps the availability of launderettes in the Mullard and Dunlop districts which may have discouraged the purchase of washing machines.

The proportion of families with T.V. sets was uniformly very high, amounting, for the sample as a whole, to nearly 85 per cent. The proportion owning radiograms or record players came next (38 per cent).

Washing machines were owned by 29 per cent of the families. The standard joke of older men who had no washing machine was: 'I don't need one, my wife is my washing machine'. Another frequent answer was: 'My wife wouldn't have it'. Women who went out to work frequently invested their first earnings in washing machines.

About 15 per cent had a refrigerator. There appeared to be a significant difference in ownership of refrigerators between Mullard and Vauxhall and the rest. Those who had refrigerators were full of praise for their uses. It made shopping easier for women who went out to work. The spreading popularity of refrigerators contributes further to the concentration of shopping at weekends.[1]

About 15 per cent owned pianos, though they were regarded as old-fashioned ('We want to get rid of the piano but nobody would buy it') and often treated as pieces of furniture ('Something to put things on').

The possessions often went in clusters, so that some had most of the items while others might have very few of them. The highest standard of home equipment was among house-owners while the lowest was among those who lived in privately-rented houses. But the difference was mainly in washing machines and refrigerators (and also cars), not in T.V., radiograms and pianos. Even the poorest home had a T.V. set and very frequently also a radiogram or record player. In Dunlop for instance, out of thirty-three house-owners two had refrigerators, eleven washing

[1] It may be of interest to compare these figures with those collected from a national sample of housewives in a survey made by Odhams for *Woman* in September–November 1958. According to this 62·3 per cent had T.V. sets, 21·3 per cent had radiograms (record players were not recorded), 28·4 per cent had washing machines and 10·2 per cent had refrigerators.

machines, sixteen record players or radiograms, thirty-one had T.V. and four pianos; besides this ten had cars and one a motor cycle. On the other hand, out of eighteen living in privately-rented houses none had a refrigerator, three had washing machines, twelve radiograms or record players, eighteen had T.V., five pianos, two had cars and one had a motor cycle.

One can say that the majority enjoyed a comfortable and well-equipped home although a fair proportion were still living in poor conditions. They were also very conscious of their home comforts and their attachment to their homes. One might hear such remarks as: 'I have many things which would be unthinkable to my father', or 'I have achieved something which I thought would have been impossible for me'. It is reasonable to conclude that most of the spare money of these people is spent on the home, which assumes a possibly romanticized image of refuge, giving delight as well as status.

3. THE PRACTICE OF EARLY MARRIAGE

ONE OF THE MANAGERS REMARKED about his men: 'The old men grow younger nowadays and the young men mature so much earlier. We will have young old men and old young men. Anyway we have men of forty who are grandfathers.' There is little doubt that there is truth in both generalizations. Some young men were conscious of this process as one can see from the remark of a fitter of twenty-four, married for three years, with a boy of two: 'We grow up so much younger now. I regret that I didn't get married even earlier.' In my sample I had two cases of men in their twenties, who married at the tender ages of sixteen and eighteen, the first man twenty-two with three children, the second twenty-three with two children; all the children were doing well.

Altogether, I had in my sample derived from five works, sixty-one married men in their twenties (twenty to twenty-nine inclusive); twenty men in Sheffield, nine in Workington, eleven in Vauxhall, nine in Dunlop and twelve in Mullard. Out of these, more than one-third, namely twenty-three, had married at twenty-one or earlier, and more than half, namely thirty-three, had married between twenty-two and twenty-five; only five had married later than twenty-five.

It is well known that early marriages are commoner than they used to be before the war. The following table comes from the Registrar General's Statistical Review, Part II, 1955.

PROPORTION OF MALES, IN ENGLAND AND WALES, MARRYING BY AGE GROUP PER 1,000 BACHELORS

	Under 21	21–24 incl.	25–29 incl.	30–35 incl.
1926–30	46	349	392	120
1931–35	44	324	414	136
1951–55	77	432	304	104
1955	89	443	294	97

In my own sample I compared the group of married men in their twenties with a group of married men in their forties who had married in their twenties. In the former group over a third had married at twenty-one or earlier as against an eighth in the latter. More than two-thirds of the married men in the former group had married at twenty-three or earlier as against 48 per cent in the latter group.

I think that the tendency towards earlier marriage is largely to be explained in terms of ability to support a family earlier; social and economic independence comes earlier. Full employment, opportunities for women's work, and good wages are supporting the young man who wants to build his nest early. Young men feel more confident about the future; they also feel that home life has so much more to offer with all the modern amenities and gadgets, while family planning and the facilities of the Welfare State reduce risks.

Family allowances for married men in the National Service may also be an incentive to early marriage in some cases. A married man of twenty-four without children related his experience: 'I married before the National Service to save money. My wife lived with her parents doing a full-time job and getting, during the two years of my service, £2 19s 0d a week as well as her pay. That was put away with part of her wages and from this we bought a house.'

Nearly half of the married men in their twenties had no children, namely twenty-seven out of sixty-one; the remainder had one or two children, except for one man who had three children. The wives of those who had no children worked full-time, except for three of them who, for health reasons, stayed at home. In contrast the great majority of wives with children stayed at home; only six out of thirty-four such wives went out to work and these were mostly those who lived with their parents.

The whole group was doing very well, with their main effort directed towards getting a house and building up a home. Out of sixty-one, twenty-three already had their own houses (ten out of twenty-seven without children and thirteen out of thirty-four with children possessed their own houses).

About one-third in this group saved more than £4 a week, some more, up to £10. Usually wives' wages were put away or banked. Overtime money was invariably mentioned as 'being put by'.

An electrician of twenty-six, married fifteen months previously, living in furnished rooms, said: 'My wife works as a telephonist for £6 a week. We are saving about £10 a week to get a house of our own. My wife would rather have the inconvenience of night-shifts to get what we want. If you have an object in front of you, you can do it easily. I want everything first-class and put in the hours for it. As soon as we get £500 for a deposit we will buy a first-class house.'

Not only were men buying their houses, some were building their houses with their own hands, with the help of bricklayers and other craftsmen. Others formed a co-operative, helping each other in the process of building, each doing the work of his trade, during weekends.

Most men in this group worked very hard, putting in long hours or applying for shifts. Marriage made a great difference to their interest in the job and their drive. I often heard: 'Since I married I take the job more seriously', or 'I am a better time-keeper', or 'I never have a day off', or 'I am more careful about the job', or 'I feel a greater sense of responsibility to the job'.

This group is more promotion-minded than any other group, often being encouraged in this by their wives. I heard such remarks as: 'My wife encourages me to go as high as I can', or 'My wife tries to encourage me to look after the job well because it is a good company'.

It is the most acquisitive, or at least the most money-minded group. As one man of twenty-two, only married two months, put it: 'Since I became married I see everything in terms of money'.

The practice of early marriage affects very positively attendance, attitudes to shifts and overtime, turnover of labour, and promotion-mindedness, but it may affect adversely the willingness to enter or to finish an apprenticeship, unless the period of apprenticeship can be shortened. I quote here two cases out of many others.

A crane driver, twenty-five, married five years before, with a baby of twelve months, said: 'I started as an apprentice steeplejack but when I was courting I gave it up to get a better-paid job. I had five other jobs which I left one after another because I needed more money. When I got married I decided to go on nights permanently to make more money. I worked as a crane driver on regular nights for a whole year, making thirteen hours a shift and getting about £21 per week.'

A fettler, twenty-nine, married for nine years, with two children, eight and five years old, living with his parents, said: 'I served years of apprenticeship as a plasterer. I liked it very much as an outdoor job but when I got married I changed it for fettling which is repetitive and does not agree with me. If I were single I would carry on in my trade. But the money is good. I can earn £5 to £6 more than in my trade, getting £15 to £17 while on piece. My wife works in the canteen part-time. I do weekend work for my neighbours as well. We want money for our house.'

A sideline is often taken up by the young men, sometimes with the idea of gaining independence through a small business. Here again let me quote two cases.

A welder, twenty-six, five years married, without children: 'At first I bought a house from my own savings but soon I came to the conclusion that it is too expensive to pay all that money only for living quarters. So I bought a greengrocery shop with living quarters for £450 cash from the sale of the house. My wife takes care of the shop.'

A coremaker, twenty-two, married one year, with no children, living with his in-laws: 'I take home £11 to £12 and I give my wife £6 housekeeping money from which she buys me cigarettes, and the rest is put away. My wife takes home £5 as shop assistant and most of her money is banked. I would like to set up a small business in a garage. My wife could do the book-keeping.'

The practice of early marriage has a bearing on the mode and habit of life. The young man moves away from his mates earlier, he is not 'knocking about' with his mates as much as men did a generation ago. He settles down to home life earlier and he takes an earlier interest in wife and children, taking them out and pushing the pram proudly, his hobbies and pastimes also centring round the house. So he is becoming more of a home-maker all round, much more than his father was. The practice of early marriage may be the outcome of the Welfare State, but it strengthens in its turn the fabric of the Welfare State, according very well with the new pattern of working-class life. It is a contributory factor in spreading the 'gospel' of prosperity among the working classes.

4. PLANNING THE FAMILY

FAMILY PLANNING is a firmly established and widespread practice. The stock phrases used in this context were: 'We restrict ourselves', or 'We didn't go in for children', or 'We are going in for children next year'. Once the worker has discovered that he can control the size of his family, the conflict between his desire for children and the fear of being over-burdened assumes its full force.

The data for the size of the family are available for all married or once-married men in the sample for five works, and here is the break-down according to the number of children in the family (including step-children and adopted children):

	_ NUMBER OF FAMILIES WITH CHILDREN [1] _				
	0	1–2	3	4 or more	TOTAL
Sheffield	24	93	22	11	150
Workington	13	54	11	11	89
Vauxhall	20	64	15	8	107
Dunlop	13	55	18	20	106
Mullard	17	53	15	11	96
TOTAL	87	319	81	61	548
Percentages	16	58	15	11	

[1] National figures for family sizes based on the census of 1951 are available only for married women under fifty with legitimate children

We see that about 16 per cent of families were childless. Some of them had married but recently, others were waiting or hoping. Married couples who wanted to remain childless were an exception; they were mostly elderly people who knew the bad old days and succumbed to excessive fear ('I was afraid of bringing up children in those conditions', or 'I was one of eleven and I dreaded poverty', or 'I had no money and no job for a long time, but now I regret it'). From my casebook I can recall only three or four cases of childlessness due to a deliberate choice in Sheffield, two or three cases in Mullard, in Workington and Vauxhall two cases each, in Dunlop not a single case. A child is regarded as the fulfilment of a marriage and when the couple cannot have children of their own, they adopt a child who is regarded as the fruit of their marriage. A striking example of this attitude was the case of an electrician's mate, forty-nine, who ten years before had married an elderly widow with seven children: 'My wife was too old to have a child of our marriage, so we adopted a son to have one child who would belong to both of us.' As a matter of fact I can recall from my casebook a fair number of adoptions, mostly of illegitimate children of the family, notably the wife's sister. The most striking expression of the craving for a child came from a crane driver of forty-three: 'Our neighbour's kid comes along frequently to make up for not having any of our own'.

A widespread practice is postponement of raising a family, primarily in order not to lose the wife's wages. A turner of thirty-seven said: 'This is actually my idea not to have kids. The wife works full-time getting £6 a week as a grocer's assistant.' A man of thirty-seven, married for nine years: 'We can't afford at present to have children. My wife works full-time in Mullard getting £7 to £8 a week. We will have children later on.' Actually his statement of not being able to afford a child must be taken with more than a grain of salt as he had recently bought his own house. Another man of thirty-one, with a car and his own house, said:

---

irrespective whether they survive or not (issue of the wife). According to these figures families without children formed 21·56 per cent (in my sample 15·88), families with one to two children formed 56·81 per cent (in my sample 58·21), families with three children, 11·71 per cent (in my sample 14·78), families with four or more children, 9·92 per cent (in my sample 11·13). Of course these figures are not strictly comparable with my sample.

'My wife is on Staff, earning £11. She has no time for having a baby.'

Postponement due to housing conditions was also frequently referred to. A labourer of twenty-six, living with in-laws, three years married, said: 'We have four more years to wait for a council house. We are careful now. No house, no baby. When we get a house we shall raise a family. We are saving now. My wife gets £6 a week in a warehouse.' Here we see how mixed are the motives.

A reamer of thirty-six said: 'We lived, up to three years ago, with in-laws, so we decided to wait until we got a house, but it is too late now. Instead we bought a car.' Not infrequently a car competes with the prospective baby. 'A car carries you while you have to carry the baby', a man said jokingly.

Sometimes the postponement leads to enforced childlessness as in the case of a Vauxhall operative of forty-three with a car: 'At first we didn't want a child, then we wanted it very badly but it was too late'. So not infrequently, when I asked: 'Choice or chance?' the answer was, 'Half choice, half chance'. Usually it is choice at first then chance.

However, the largest single cause of childlessness alleged was the incapacity of the wife as expressed in such phrases as: 'Ill-health of the wife', or 'Bad heart', or 'Wife had an operation', or 'Miscarriage'. Sometimes this was phrased in more general terms like: 'It wasn't there', or 'Impossible'. Cases in which men's incapacity was cited were much rarer. A fitter of thirty-eight, seventeen years married, said: 'My wife has been very upset. It is my fault. I had to have an operation but the doctors finally decided against it. Actually other people upset us more than anything else.' Apparently not having children is not conforming, or makes others suspicious. In Vauxhall, out of twenty men without children, eight referred to incapacity of the wife and two others had had children and lost them.

Marrying late is also a frequent cause of childlessness. In Vauxhall out of twenty men without children there were two cases of men who married too late.

The largest single group in my sample were those with one or two children, namely 58 per cent of the total. Of course they also 'restricted themselves' for a variety of reasons. A man on the forge, fifty-five, with one son, said: 'My father had seven children. A large family is a millstone. I saw a lot of poverty.' A labourer of fifty-seven: 'My father had six children; we have only one. I didn't want more. I was out of work for several years after the general strike.' A labourer of sixty-one with one son: 'My father had nine children and my wife is one of thirteen. We know what it means to have a swarm of children in the house. We didn't want more children, we couldn't afford them.' It looks as if childhood experiences matter most when a decision about children is to be made. A hypothesis worth exploring would be that excessively large families produce small families in the next generation and vice versa.

If the first child is troublesome or an invalid, it discourages the parents from having more. A rough turner of thirty-six with one boy said: 'The boy was ill and crying at night. I was upset for a long time, we didn't want more trouble.' A moulder of thirty-seven, married eleven years with an invalid girl of seven: 'We couldn't think of a larger family. Our girl is blind and paralysed and has to be fed like a baby.' A cleaner of thirty-nine with a boy of twelve suffering from nerves and asthma had to give up a good job as a leading hand on production in Vauxhall on account of ill-health in the family: 'No more children'.

War years and long army service were also mentioned. A truck driver of forty-eight, who had served for seventeen years in the Army, said: 'We have only one boy. Life was messed up with the Army service.' Having only one child is often a matter for regret, as the house seems empty. 'One child is not enough', or 'Not fair for the kid', or 'You need at least two', were remarks I heard. A fitter, forty-four, with one son, said: 'My father had fourteen children and I saw and dreaded poverty. Now we regret it as we feel lonely. The son is serving in the Army.'

A middle-sized family nowadays can be considered a family of three children and about 15 per cent of the sample was of this size. Here also a certain measure of family planning was practised. A miller on a rolling mill, fifty-four, with three children, said: 'My father had nine children; we used to beg for food. I was careful to make sure that our children don't suffer what we have been through.' A family of this size is not regarded as burdensome. It is still a 'nice family' which keeps a man pretty occupied the whole year round.

A large family may be, nowadays, a family of four or more

children and about 11 per cent of my sample were families of this size. These were mostly the families of older men. In Workington all the men with four or more children were forty or more, in Vauxhall only two were under forty, in Dunlop five, in Mullard only one (and this man of thirty-six, with six children, stated boldly: 'I have finished now, that is all I can cope with'). The under-forties were mostly Catholics or had Catholic wives. In Dunlop out of five under-forties with four or more children, four were Catholics, while in contrast out of thirteen men without children, in the same firm, only one was a Catholic and this man had married only four months previously.

The large families are also due to slips ('just bad luck') or to twins (I can recall three cases of two sets of twins) and also to marrying for the second or third time. The largest families in my sample were those of nine children and actually there were only two such families. None was larger. The Victorian families of twelve or thirteen children, to which some men referred as their families of origin, did not appear in my casebook.

Is a large family regarded as an economic liability? Does it cause poverty? Not poverty, but strain. It helps in getting a council house, the family allowances are also of help and when overtime is worked no tax is paid, but all that does not make up for the wife's earnings. And when the wife has to go out to work in spite of the fact that she can ill afford the time, she can do only a part-time job. Shiftwork is more difficult in large families. Long hours are worked to keep the family alive. Too many upsets with ill-health and children's mishaps cause loss of shifts and an inability to concentrate on the job.

Let us see what fathers of large families have to say about this. A stamper of forty-two with seven children: 'I never had a holiday since I got married. Just work to feed the hungry mouths. The work is heavy and home life is also heavy going. When on nights, I can't get the sleep; the youngest one is fourteen months old. My wife is working part-time to help with the cost of living.'

A teamer on furnaces, fifty-two, with five children: 'I can never afford to take a single shift off. Last time I had an accident and the doctor wanted me to stay home for at least a week. But I went to the hospital for treatment every day and came back to work. With a large family you can't afford to be ill.'

A labourer of forty-two, married ten years, with six children, living in a 'cellar-and-kitchen' old house: 'I just manage to keep my head above water. We didn't go in for so many kids. It was just bad luck. They are supposed to be a blessing.'

A loco driver of fifty, married for thirty-two years, with nine children, of whom seven were still at home: 'It was very hard going. Now it is better. My wife works full-time in a canteen, and my three oldest are also working. Four are at school, the oldest, fifteen, looks after the three younger, twelve, eight and six, when they come from school. I've managed now to buy a house of my own.' I congratulated them on their energy and drive, especially that of the mother who could manage a house and seven children and work full-time. But the children can be a blessing later on.

In order to evaluate the impact of large families in economic terms I compared the possessions (house- and car-ownership) of large families, i.e., those with four or more children, with childless families, in four works, and here are the figures:

FAMILIES WITH HOUSES AND CARS

	\multicolumn{3}{c	}{Families with 4 or more children}	\multicolumn{3}{c}{Childless families}
	TOTAL	With cars	With houses	TOTAL	With cars	With houses
Workington	11	1	0	13	3	6
Vauxhall	8	0	1	20	11	11
Dunlop	20	3	2	13	4	7
Mullard	11	1	0	17	5	7
TOTAL	50	5	3	63	23	31

The most striking contrast is in the possession of houses (50 per cent against 6 per cent), which is partly due to the fact that large families have a better chance of getting a council house than childless families. But also in the possession of cars the proportions are far apart (37 per cent against 10 per cent).

The figures may be inconclusive statistically but there is little doubt that large families appear economically handicapped to the worker. Family planning seems to be one of the most important vehicles of prosperity in the working classes, or at least it is so regarded by workers.

5. THE FATHER IMAGE

ONE OF MY STANDARD QUESTIONS for married men with children concerned their interest in the upbringing and education of their children, and from the answers I could gather that the overwhelming majority took an intense, sometimes passionate interest. The standard phrases which came up again and again, were: 'We want to give them a better chance than we had', or 'That is the finest thing—to give them every opportunity', or 'The children—that's my life', or 'We did our best', or 'I help them in every shape and form', or 'They come first', or 'They have everything they want', or 'We gave them everything we could'.

Fathers of babies often push the pram, give them baths, see them to bed; fathers of toddlers often read them stories, play with them, take them for a walk at weekends; fathers of school-children often go to the school for progress reports and supervise their homework; fathers of adolescents try to apprentice them or find them suitable jobs: 'I got a good job for the lad'. Time and again I heard instances of considerable sacrifice for the benefit of the children, such as the following:

> A skilled man of forty-four with two children—fourteen and twelve—both in grammar schools: 'Last summer I spent £25 for the girl's trip to Switzerland with the school.'
> A rubber worker of fifty-one with a boy of fifteen: 'Last year I bought him a bicycle for £27 from overtime money.'
> Again and again: 'I bought her a typewriter', or 'I bought him a tape-recorder because he is very musical', or 'I bought him an expensive encyclopaedia because he is very clever.'

A very widespread wish is to keep the children at school 'as long as they can make it'. To quote a few examples:

> A skilled man of thirty-nine with four children, fifteen, ten, nine and one: 'If they do well at school I will keep them there as long as I can.'
> A moulder of thirty-seven with four children, twin boys of nine and two girls, eight and three: 'I would like them to keep in school as long as it is good for them. I insured the boys for £300 each at fifteen and the girls for £100 each at fifteen for their later education.'
> A skilled man of fifty-five with a girl of fifteen in a grammar school: 'We want her to go to college if she can make it. We are prepared to make the sacrifice.'

A skilled man of forty-four with a boy of fourteen: 'I would like him to go to college if he is good enough, anyway to stay at school up to eighteen.'

A man of sixty-four with a son of thirty-one, a sanitary inspector: 'I spent on my son £300 during his two years at the Royal Technical College in Manchester.'

Men rarely had ambitions for themselves, but a great deal of ambition for their children. ('Of course it is all up to them but personally I would like him to be . . .') The ambitions were mostly for professional or staff jobs or for skilled trades. In Vauxhall out of twenty-six men whose ambitions for their children were recorded eighteen wanted a professional or staff job, saying: 'I want him to be a doctor', or 'A lawyer', or 'To work in a laboratory', or 'On electronics' (a very popular profession), or 'To be a teacher', or 'I would like him to have a profession and security, unlike myself', or 'I would like to push him out of the manual class'. Eight men wanted a trade for their sons.

In Workington, of twenty-eight fathers whose ambitions for their sons were recorded, thirteen men wanted professional or staff jobs, often saying: 'I would like them to make some sort of a grade', or 'I would like them to get into a profession', or 'I would like to guide them into some sort of profession' or 'I wanted him to become a professional man but he wanted to be a fitter'. Thirteen other men wanted to give them a trade, and still two others wanted better jobs for their children than they had themselves. In Dunlop, out of twenty-three fathers, fourteen wanted a professional or staff job and nine wanted a trade for their children. In Mullard, out of seventeen fathers nine wanted professional or staff jobs and seven wanted a trade.

The level of aspiration for the children depended very much on the social position the parents themselves occupied. Those who were semi-skilled or labourers often wanted a skilled trade for their children, while those who were skilled or were supervisors had a higher level of aspiration. (In these four works, out of fifty-four men with professional or staff ambitions for their children, twenty-two were skilled and four supervisors, while out of thirty-seven men with trade ambitions nine were skilled and three supervisors.)

Those who had children in grammar schools were proud of mentioning the achievements of their children, often adding: 'Oh, she is very clever', or 'She is above the average type, not like her father'. And those whose children had failed the 11-plus examinations could not hide their disappointment, saying: 'We wanted it, but unfortunately he failed', or 'I am not worried, he will try again', or 'I sent him to a private school', or 'It was because of her nerves that she failed'.

In Vauxhall out of forty-three children in the age group twelve to seventeen inclusive, eight were in grammar schools, two in high schools and two in technical schools; in Dunlop out of fifty-eight such children, nine were in grammar schools, one in high school and three in technical schools; in Mullard out of forty such children, three were in grammar schools and three in technical schools. The figures seem to suggest a higher proportion of grammar-school children among supervisors and skilled men than amongst semi-skilled or unskilled. Out of twenty children in grammar schools in these three works, twelve had fathers who were skilled or supervisors (actually five skilled and seven supervisors), much above the average for the whole sample.

The ambitions of fathers for their children are often one of the reasons why most young men do not like working with their fathers in the same shop. In Workington where a large percentage of young men worked with their fathers in the same firm, the overwhelming majority preferred working with other men than with their own fathers. Fathers are too critical. As one father suggested, 'Fathers want perfection for their sons. We are less patient with our children than with others. Therefore you can understand someone else's children better than your own.' And his advice was, 'You have to make allowances; if not, they drift away from you'.

Are the fathers still strict with their children? I often heard, when I asked this question: 'I don't boss them', or 'I am not bossy, I try to be friendly', or 'I never use force', or 'I am like a big brother to them', or 'I am like a mother to my children', or 'I am not forcing them in anything', or 'I guide them but I don't push them'.

Is there a social change involved in this attitude? I have no figures to offer here, but from the large qualitative material I would have no hesitation in answering the question in the affirmative. Men often referred to this, saying: 'My father had power over us; I can't boss them', or 'My father never bothered with us', or 'I suppose I am a better father than my own', or 'I never saw, in my younger days, a man pushing a pram; he would have been a laughing stock'. Women in Mullard also referred to this, comparing their husbands' interest in children with that of their fathers.

There is little doubt that the image of the stern, bullying, dominating and self-assertive father or of the absent father who took no interest in the children, leaving them to the mother, is fast disappearing, and the new image of a benevolent, friendly and brotherly father is emerging. The Oedipus complex, for all I know, might have been a myth with the middle classes, but from my previous enquiries I gained the impression that it had been a stern reality with the working-class males. The man whose life oscillated between the works and the public house, or who came home only for his meals, or the man whose authority was used as a bogey to frighten the children, while the mother slaved around the clock, used not to be exceptional. And this was the background for the frequently distorted image of the father in the working-class man's mind. The 'Mum' was the most powerful figure in the mind of the working-class child as, in many cases, she was the only parent who gave full care and full devotion to the child. Now the powerful figure of the 'Mum' is receding and the father assumes a nearly equal place.

There are three main factors responsible for this change: First, the fact that many mothers go out to work, and take greater interest in the world around them, not only in the children; second, the part which the nursery school and the school play in a child's life, which is much greater than a generation ago; third, the growing interest of the fathers themselves in the children, which, in most cases, does not fall behind that of the mother.

More specifically I asked both men and women in Mullard whether the men took an equal share with their wives in the upbringing and education. Of sixty-one men, fifty-two contended that they took an equal share, saying: 'I share fully', or 'Fifty-fifty', or 'Between us', or 'I do more with the boy, the wife more with the girl', or 'I am very keen'. Six men said that they took the lead, or 'I lay down the law', or 'I look after them'. Only three said that they 'leave it to the wife'.

Out of forty-two women who were asked the same question, thirty-six stated that their husbands shared fully, while only six contended that the children were left more to them (see Part Eight).

Another question which I explored in Mullard was the measure of devotion to parents, both as regards their relations to their own parents and their children. Out of sixty-four women in Mullard to whom I submitted the statement, 'Our greatest devotion goes to our mother', asking for comments, thirty-nine agreed with this, stating: 'My father didn't take an interest', or 'It's "Mum" all the time', or 'When I have a problem, Mum will sort it out', or 'Just that little bit more'. Eleven women professed an equal devotion to both parents, while eight preferred the father ('I envied those who had such a mother, but my mother was not worthy of devotion'). Six others did not remember one or both parents or had neither father nor mother, being brought up in an orphanage. ('I never had the love of parents and that is still going on in me.')

Now for the devotion of their own children as the mothers saw it. Out of thirty-five mothers for whom the information is available, twenty contended that the children care more for them ('Just that little bit extra'); ten professed equal devotion or said, 'Girls more for the father, boys more for the mother'. Six others said that the children preferred the father. In the latter category there was an interesting disclosure: 'Before I went to work, equal devotion; now he goes more to his father'.

It was clear that the attachment to parents was thought to differ not only in terms of magnitude but in quality. It was 'a different sort of relationship', or as one woman said, there were 'different kinds of love for different persons'. However, comparing the attachment for each parent only in quantitative terms for two generations, it is clear that the measure of devotion is moving towards a greater balance as between parents. The young man gets more friendship and affection from his father than the latter had from his own. This may often lead to conflicts in adolescence, as the father may be too anxious or too ambitious or too critical. I met a number of disappointed fathers, whose 'do well!' or 'do better!' was not heeded by the children. 'I wanted him to have a trade but he was not interested', or 'I apprenticed him but he packed up', or 'I wanted him to be a technical man but he did not respond', or 'I wanted them all to go to grammar schools but out of seven children only one succeeded', or 'She hasn't done her best', were some of the remarks I heard.

This brings us to an interesting question: do the parents

understand their children? My material is too fragmentary to answer this one way or the other. The question whenever it was asked was not whether they understood or not, only whether they felt they understood. Fathers of teenagers often felt they did not understand their children, saying: 'I can't fathom them', or 'They are a surprise'. However, one man gave me an interesting reply: 'I don't bother to understand them. I want to live with them. They all have their own troubles.'

More specifically, forty-one mothers in Mullard were asked whether they felt that they understood their older children. Out of these, twenty-one answered this question in the affirmative, saying: 'At this young age I think I still do', or 'I have grown up with them', or 'I think they are open-minded', or 'I can always tell what is going on in their heads', or 'We talk a lot, everything is talked out', or 'He is an artist, but I understand him all the same', or 'That depends how you bring them up. If you keep up with them and let them bring their friends into the home you understand them.'

Twenty mothers felt they did not understand their children, or not quite, saying: 'They surprise you as they grow older', or 'It is a job to understand them really', or 'They pass through an age when it is difficult to understand them', or 'Father understands him better', or 'Granny understands him better', or 'Since he married I don't understand him any more', or 'The boy has funny ways; he played truant for a fortnight and we didn't know a thing about it and still don't know why'. Out of those twenty, twelve were mothers of children in the age bracket of fourteen to twenty. Two mothers were highly critical of their children ('A selfish lot', and 'difficult to satisfy, we never had the privileges they have, they take everything for granted and ask for more. No thankfulness.').

Two mothers had the privilege of having children who 'outclassed them'. A mother of fifty-three said, 'When they get education and a good job they get ideas. Whenever I speak they try to correct me. They must have it right. I feel that low.' A mother of fifty-six: 'He is a scholarship boy and he corrects me frequently, he doesn't like my way of speaking. I have to look up to him but I don't really mind.' I believe all the same that many, if not most fathers and mothers, want to be 'outclassed', although they may have mixed feelings about it later on.

PART TWO

Husbands and Wives

6. MASTERS OR PARTNERS
HUSBAND–WIFE RELATIONSHIP

FAMILY BREAK-DOWNS are reported in the chapter on divorces and separations; here we are concerned only with the normal family—which is a functional unit of the first order in workers' lives.

The husband–wife relationships were described by the overwhelming majority as happy. The upsets were reported only in odd cases. To my question, 'Are you happy at home?', the scale of answers ran as follows: 'Very happy'; 'Happy'; 'We have a good carry on'; 'Nothing better to wish for'; 'No worries'; 'Good life'; 'Nothing to grumble about'. Very few men referred to tiffs of any consequence, perhaps one in twenty or less. Of course one realizes that such accounts may not be accurate, but I had the impression that they were truthful.

I probed a little deeper into the husband–wife relationship in Mullard where I introduced several provocative statements, asking for comments based on personal experience. One of these was: 'Love is the sweetest thing in life'. Out of seventy-four men, fifty-one agreed most readily, some very outspokenly, but most of them added that they meant by this home and children. 'It's the finest thing; something to work for, to look to and to look after'. 'Everything I do is for my wife and children', said a young man of twenty-five. 'It is an essential thing. Happiness is a mixture of love, contentment and good living'—said a man of twenty-eight. A man of thirty: 'That's my life, wife and children'. A man of thirty-six: 'My love, that is my wife and children'. A man of thirty-one: 'All my life is centred around the home'. A man of thirty-nine: 'My children and my home, that is my love'. A man of forty: 'One of the three essentials, work, health and love'. A man of forty-four: 'Children and home, that's my life'. A man of forty-six: 'Love is the sweetest thing but not confined to age'. A man of fifty: 'My wife proved herself, she never grumbles'. A man of fifty-six: 'We get on tops'. A man of fifty-nine: 'Something to live for. If you have no-one to love you live like a rabbit in your hole.' A man of sixty-five: 'There is life in the old man yet'.

Six or seven others agreed with this statement but qualified it in this way: 'Not exclusive love', or 'In the broadest sense, for everything, that is the only way to beat the Devil', or 'Love not only for a woman but for birds and plants', or 'Love with freedom'.

'It's companionship more than love', or 'It's more mutual understanding', or 'Love, but not of a sexual kind'—contended ten men, mostly in the over-forties, adding often: 'Love at first, then more companionship', or 'The process of cooling off is a natural thing', or 'Not the same thing as when you are young'.

Six or seven others contended that love is rather a bitter sweet, saying: 'It tastes rather sour', or 'bitter', or that it was all right 'If you have the right partner', or 'If you have a proper bank account'.

So it is obvious from these reactions that the overwhelming majority enjoyed a loving relationship or a relationship based on good companionship with their wives.

In the same firm thirty-nine women were presented with a similar question: 'Is love the sweetest thing, or is it a bitter sweet?' Thirty of them subscribed whole-heartedly to the statement that love is the sweetest thing, amplifying it with 'Home and children'. I heard: 'We are all happy together', or 'We are very happy', or 'Without love you are lost'—and from the older women: 'It goes on all the time', or 'Not confined to youth'. Five other women, mostly in their late thirties or older, contended that companionship, or mutual understanding, or friendship counts more later on. Only four regarded love rather as a bitter sweet.

Some men in the same firm were asked about nagging: 'Is nagging the greatest curse? What is your experience?' Most agreed, but out of fifteen only one said: 'I have been nagged a bit', and another, 'In one period of my life that was true'; but all the others said: 'Not in my experience', or 'Not in my home', or 'I have never been nagged personally'. Some referred to friends, sisters or mothers or in-laws ('Mother started nagging when father walked out', or 'My mother-in-law was a great nagger').

'When we are married all the company we need is at home': fifty-nine men in Mullard were asked to comment on this statement. Twenty-four men agreed, saying: 'We are quite happy at home, just the two of us', or 'Just the three of us', or 'We rarely go out, we prefer to stay at home', or 'There is no need to go out nowadays'. Many repeated the familiar phrase 'We keep ourselves to ourselves'.

The remainder, i.e. thirty-five, objected to this statement, often very emphatically, saying: 'It's silly', or 'You stagnate and become stale', or 'You get into a rut', or 'We always arrange holidays with another couple', or 'You have to go out and meet other people'. But out of those only three referred to something suggestive of an unhappy experience at home, saying: 'You are fed up at home', or 'Things I am interested in my wife is not', or 'It is too dull at home'. All the others, although they needed outside company, appreciated home and family life.

The same statement was presented to sixty women in Mullard for their comments. Out of these twenty-two women agreed with it, saying: 'We are complete in ourselves', or 'Homely types', or 'Happy at home with husband and children', or 'I prefer my husband's company to anyone else's', or 'Why go out if you have everything at home you need', or 'When you are happy you don't need anyone else', and many again reiterated the phrase 'We keep ourselves to ourselves'. The remainder, thirty-eight, did not agree with this statement, saying: 'You need outside company', or 'It's nice to have friends', or 'It's right for the first three years of married life but not afterwards', or 'If you have children it is all right'. But only four out of those who did not agree with the saying expressed their view in such a way as to suggest a not very satisfactory relationship: 'I like to be out', or 'You are fed up', or 'You need a break from each other'. Again it was clear that the overwhelming majority had satisfactory relations with their husbands.

Does the relationship tend to be, on the whole, more satisfactory now than it used to be a generation ago? I have no quantitative material to go by but from the qualitative material I would answer this question in the affirmative, and I would give the following reasons for this change, to which many referred in one way or another.

A marriage without conflicts is as inconceivable as a man's

mind without conflicts, so I often asked about 'tiffs' and their nature. It came out that most tiffs occur about children, money, about getting things done at home to make the home more comfortable, or when one of the partners is tense or tired, or about relations. The children nowadays are fewer, so tiffs on their account should be on the decline. The home is nicer, more comfortable; that, too, should provide less material for conflict. The money position is easier, the wife is not so hard up, so this, too, should account for less conflict. Upsets at work are, on the whole, on the decline as the work is not as heavy as it used to be and the worker is treated much better by his foreman than a generation ago, so this again should account for less tenseness. On the other hand the wife often goes out to work, and this may make for greater tenseness: but there may be some truth in the pronouncement of working women that they are too busy to develop arguments. T.V. fills most of the time at home, which means less opportunity for argument. Cars take the family out, and away from home tiffs are most rare. But the single and most potent reason for more satisfactory relationships is the decline in heavy drinking, and many women referred to this as the most important factor.

Is the husband–wife relationship still under the dominance of the male, or is the relationship moving towards greater equality of sexes? A manager with whom I discussed this subject put his view in a most pungent way, linking this with the social change in the factory: 'The age of authority and its abuse has passed. Men were bullied at work and they bullied back their wives and children. Now you cannot order your men about, you have rather to coax and humour them. You cannot say: do this, or do that. You have to ask: would you like to do that, or could you do this, or what about doing this or that. The same change is reflected at home. There is not the same authority at home as there used to be.'

There is, of course, nothing new in this idea of linking authority in the workshop with authority at home. It reminded me of the French social thinker of the last century, Frédéric Le Play, who linked the authority of the master in the *atelier* with that of the father in the household at home. The link between the two kinds of authority has a deep psychological foundation as the attitude in one sphere is often transferred to the other: instances of this could be seen most clearly in the attitudes of foremen. But in fact both attitudes have a deeper background in the general decline of authoritarian behaviour. Ours is not the age of authority, the age of absolute values. There are also other reasons for the decline of the authority of the *pater familias*. The husband is not the paymaster who can call the tune, to the same extent as he used to be. His wife may be working, or may have been out to work at one time or another, contributing to the family income. The Welfare State, with children's allowances, Welfare Services, and Assistance Board in case he fails to support his family, also supplements a man's wages. The phrase describing housekeeping money as 'Wages for the Missus' is very rarely used nowadays.

Sixty-three married men in Mullard were asked more specifically about this aspect of male dominance in their relationship with their wives. They were presented with the statement: 'Man is master in his own house' and asked for comments. Out of these thirty professed equal status with their wives and expressed this in such terms as: 'Old-fashioned idea of being a master', or 'We share responsibility', or 'Fifty-fifty', or 'Full partners: we must agree together in everything', or 'Equal when the wife goes out to work', or 'Combined operation', or 'Two heads are better than one', or 'One leg of trousers for each of us', or 'Share the burden'. Out of the thirty, two men said that their wives made them think they were masters but in fact they were not.

There were seven others who stated that they were equal but in big decisions the man had the final word. Again seven others claimed a status which can be best described as *primus inter pares*, saying: 'A little bit over', or 'One up', or 'To a certain extent', or 'Wife is a junior partner otherwise we wouldn't get anywhere'.

A substantial minority, i.e. eighteen, still claimed definite superiority of the male, in such terms as : 'I am the master', or 'There must be only one master in the house', or 'You are the leading hand by virtue of greater intelligence, greater strength and greater contribution', or 'It's natural there should be one head in a family', or 'Man is more conversant with the world', or 'The last word is with me', or 'When I say yes, it stays yes', or 'It is recognized that I am the master'. One man acknowledged the superiority of his wife who 'wore the trousers'.

So in fact three-quarters of the sample claimed absolute equality or near equality; only one in four claimed absolute superiority of the male.

Among those men who professed a full equality of status, half, i.e., fifteen out of thirty, had wives going out to work, while among those men who professed superiority of their status in absolute or relative terms, less than one in three, i.e., nine out of thirty, had working wives. My sample, here, is too small to prove the point, but it was certainly my impression that there was some correlation between working wives and feelings of equal status; and also the profession of full equality was a more prevalent attitude amongst the under-forties than the older couples. The frequent reference to: 'Victorian', or 'Old-fashioned ideas', of those who professed equality was a characteristic feature, pointing to social change.

Similar results were obtained in interviews with married women in Mullard, with even stronger emphasis on equality of status (see Part Eight).

It seems to me that we are witnessing a considerable social change in husband–wife relationships in the working classes, and that this has a bearing on the world of man's values. The more he accepts his wife as an equal partner, the more he acquires, mostly unconsciously, her values and standards. He is no longer contemptuous of women's ideas as he used to be. They may differ from his, placing greater value on domesticity for example, but are more frequently nearer to his own. Once his was the specifically masculine world standing for self assertion, sturdiness, force and pungency. Now he tends to find room for softer and more feminine values.

There is a conflict in every man's mind between the desire to dominate and master and the desire to serve and please. But in this conflict the desire to serve and please seems to be on the ascendant in the working man's life.

La Rochefoucauld's saying: 'There are some good marriages but no perfect ones' is often quoted with approval. But since I made this enquiry I am not quite sure whether there are not some perfect marriages too, as some men depicted their relationships in the brightest and warmest colours.

7. THE HOUSEKEEPING ALLOWANCE

THE WORKING MAN is quite willing to talk freely about his personal relations but somewhat less freely about his money matters. Somehow this is regarded as the most private and intimate aspect of his life. Consequently the data about housekeeping money or savings are less complete than other data. My standard question concerning the housekeeping money was about the type of arrangement, whether regular and fixed, or variable; whether the money was pooled, or the whole wage packet handed over to the wife. Those who, I felt, would have no objection to answering further questions about the subject, were asked about the amount of their allowance. Some volunteered, quoting of their own accord the exact figure. However, whenever I felt a certain reluctance to speak freely about it, I did not press the question. The man's reluctance was not necessarily related to the inadequacy of his allowance. A man who pays an inadequate allowance is rarely conscious of his unfair treatment; he justifies his behaviour by his personal needs or by his wife's ability to supplement his allowance by her own earnings.

It is very difficult to explore this subject satisfactorily by asking questions. What is called 'housekeeping money' covers various items: it usually includes rent, rates and bills, but sometimes certain bills are excluded, such as rent, or mortgage payments, rates, electricity, gas or coal, or children's pocket money, or clothes, or school expenses. The husband's personal expenses such as clothes or his cigarettes and beer are normally excluded but I came across cases where a daily quota of cigarettes came out of the housekeeping money. Three men in Sheffield gave me a figure for the housekeeping allowance and then it came out that out of this the wife had to provide twenty cigarettes a day. Unless the whole budget is known, the true picture cannot be revealed to the full.

The material is more complete as regards the type of arrangements about housekeeping than about the level of housekeeping allowance. But even here I recorded the information as supplied by men from their own description, and my classification follows closely the distinctions as made by men themselves.

The material for the type of arrangements is available in Sheffield for sixty-nine men, in Workington sixty-nine, in Vauxhall seventy-one, in Dunlop seventy-two, in Mullard fifty-six. Before proceeding further I shall present this material in the form of a table which gives eight different types of arrangement, subsequently explained in the text.

	Sheffield	Workington	Vauxhall	Dunlop	Mullard
I.	37	29	33	50	27
II.	9	8	5	5	0
III.	14	1	7	4	3
IV.	1	13	9	5	5
V.	3	12	2	0	3
VI.	0	2	2	0	0
VII.	1	3	0	2	1
VIII.	4	1	13	6	17
TOTAL	69	69	71	72	56

ARRANGEMENT NO. I: *The Regular and Fixed Housekeeping Allowance*

This is a standard arrangement for covering all or nearly all items of the normal housekeeping, including bills or most of the bills. It is usually based on the regular wage without overtime earnings and often without the shift allowance. There is a great deal of give and take between the husband and wife and I often heard: 'I help her out when she is stuck', or 'It's really more', or 'I never let her go short', or 'I give her housekeeping but for the rest I act as the family benefactor'. About half of the sample for whom the information is available practised this arrangement.

ARRANGEMENT NO. II: *The Variable Housekeeping Allowance*

This also includes all or nearly all items of the housekeeping, but it fluctuates from week to week.

To quote a few examples: 'When on days I pay £7 10s and when on nights, £8 16s'; 'I pay £10 on days and £12 on nights'; 'It's not rigid; when on short week I pay less, when on full week £12; now £8'; 'I share overtime earnings and shift allowance half-and-half'.

The variation was in the range of £1 to £2 but more frequently £1.

ARRANGEMENT NO. III: *Housekeeping Allowance plus bills*

Here the allowance is mostly for food, cleaning materials, etc., while all the bills, or most of them, such as rent, gas, electricity, coal, are paid by the husband. Men who practise this arrangement refer to it in such terms as: 'It is only for food. I pay the bills'; 'I pay all the overheads. The housekeeping is only for day-to-day expenses.' When bills are paid by the husband the allowance is in most cases between £5 and £6. For instance, out of four such cases in Vauxhall where the figure was quoted, three were £5 or £5 10s.

ARRANGEMENT NO. IV: *The Whole Wage Packet*

The whole wage packet is handed over to the wife, while she gives the husband something back, each day or for the whole week. Those who practised this referred to it thus: 'The lot', or 'All the money', or 'The whole packet', or 'I have only silver in my pocket', or 'I have no confidence in myself', or 'She is the Chancellor of the Exchequer', or 'She can handle money best', or 'That is the best place for a wage packet'.

The practice appears to have a strong regional background. In some regions it is practised more than in others. Three Welshmen who practised this in Vauxhall referred to this as the Welsh way, the Irish in Workington referred to it as the Irish way. It was practised most widely in Workington where there is a large sprinkling of Irish population, and in Vauxhall where there were a number of Welshmen and Irishmen.

ARRANGEMENT NO. V: *Wage Packet Minus Pocket Money*

This is another variation of the previous arrangement. Men hand over the wage packet minus a specific amount of pocket money. Here the pocket money is fixed while the allowance follows the fluctuation of earnings. Any excess of earnings goes to the home, but if the man falls on short time the allowance also suffers. In Workington the pocket money mentioned in this connection was between £1 and £2, in Sheffield up to £3. This practice was most prevalent in Workington. We saw that in

Workington about one-third of men hand over the whole wage packet or the wage packet minus pocket money.

ARRANGEMENT NO. VI: *Percentage of Earnings*

Here a specified percentage of total earnings, including overtime and shift allowance, is handed over to the wife. In Workington two such cases were mentioned, one man paying four-fifths, another two-thirds of his earnings. In Vauxhall again I recorded two such cases, both paying three-quarters of their earnings. In other firms no one mentioned it.

ARRANGEMENT NO. VII: *In the drawer*

Men refer to this as 'putting the money in the drawer'. I heard remarks such as: 'It is there', or 'She can have as much as she likes', or 'Everyone has a dip in the kitty'. Only a few cases were recorded, mostly in Workington and Dunlop.

ARRANGEMENT NO. VIII: *The Pooling of Earnings*

This is a very popular arrangement with young couples when both are working. Men refer to it as: 'Share and share alike', or 'We pool our wages'. They budget, save and each take their pocket money on an equal footing. This was most practised in two firms where the incidence of full-time employment of wives was the highest. In Mullard there were seventeen such cases with fifteen wives working full-time, in Vauxhall thirteen cases with eight wives working full-time.

One of these men in Vauxhall mentioned a peculiar arrangement which actually made placing him very difficult: 'What she makes is hers, what I make is mine. She earns nearly as much as I do, namely £10 net, while I earn £12. We have a house and a car.' I believe the arrangement of pooling wages is spreading with young couples.

Now we come to the level of housekeeping money. Here we are concerned with the fixed and regular allowance (Arrangement No. I). The information for this arrangement is nearly complete for Sheffield, while it is nearly entirely lacking for Mullard, as in Mullard my time was occupied with other enquiries. It is also fragmentary for Workington and Vauxhall.

The Housekeeping Allowance

The information is available for thirty-five men in Sheffield, for thirty-eight men in Dunlop, for nine men in Vauxhall and eight men in Workington as shown in the table below:

	Sheffield	Dunlop	Workington	Vauxhall	TOTAL
£5	3	0	1	0	4
£6	1	1	1	0	3
£7 or £7 10s	9	5	1	0	15
£8 or £8 10s	9	6	0	4	19
£9 or £9 10s	7	8	3	3	21
£10 and over	6	18	2	2	28
TOTAL	35	38	8	9	90

We see that the big majority, nearly three-quarters of the sample for whom the information is available, paid £8 or more, and only 10 per cent £5 or £6—and those mostly in Workington and Sheffield. The figures, although fragmentary, seem to suggest that the level of housekeeping allowance follows closely the level of wages.

I made an estimate of the percentage of wages which goes into the housekeeping, irrespective of the type of arrangement, for Sheffield where the data for housekeeping allowance are most complete. Out of sixty-six men for whom the information is available, only three men paid as little as 40 per cent of their 'take home' wages; five paid 50 per cent, twenty-nine between 55 and 60 per cent, nineteen between 60 and 75 per cent, ten above 75 per cent.

While the absolute level of the housekeeping allowance goes up with the higher standard of wages, the percentage is dropped in higher wage brackets, when 'The wife is satisfied with what she gets', or 'She doesn't need any more'. The residue is released for the husband's personal needs, for savings and investments, for house purchase, cars, or what are called luxuries.

Were there any cases of hardship, caused by insufficient housekeeping allowance? Let us examine closely those seven cases where the lowest housekeeping allowance was paid, i.e., £5 to £6 a week, four in Sheffield, two in Workington and one in Dunlop.

CASE NO. 1. Man of twenty-two, no children, living with in-laws, earning £12 net, paid £5 housekeeping (actually £6 but £1 went for cigarettes out of this allowance). He had a car. His wife worked full-time, earning about £5. He saved a great deal, out of fear that 'the work would not last'.

CASE NO. 2. Man of forty-four, with a girl of eight, living with father-in-law, earning between £11 and £12 a week net. Housekeeping allowance £5. Father-in-law paid for his keep. Wife worked full-time. How much she earned he wouldn't know: 'It's up to her, if she wants more money she can make it as she is on piece in the cutlery trade.'

CASE NO. 3. Semi-skilled operator of forty-three, with two children, one married daughter who lived apart and a boy of nine. His regular wages were £8 plus overtime. He gave his wife £6, from which he expected twenty cigarettes a day, which meant roughly speaking an allowance of £5. He drank nearly every night, with a drinking bill up to £5 a week if he had a good week. His wife worked part-time, cleaning, making £2 10s a week. He saved about £1 a week, mainly for holidays. Recently while coming home after a bout of drink he knocked down his wife and she left with the boy to join her parents. He discovered that he could not manage without her, so he went to fetch her, promising to behave himself.

CASE NO. 4. A semi-skilled operator of fifty-eight with two married daughters living separately. His regular wage was £10 net plus overtime. Housekeeping allowance £5. His wife worked part-time, five hours a day, cleaning. How much she earned he never asked; he presumed that it all went into the home. He saved for a fortnight's holiday and always had a fortnight's wages in front of him.

CASE NO. 5. Man of fifty-four with two married children living separately. Regular wages about £11 10s net. Housekeeping allowance £5 10s; savings £1 or, if overtime was worked, £2 a week. Wife didn't go out to work. He helped her out if she needed more but said 'she is satisfied'.

CASE NO. 6. A skilled man of fifty-seven with two married children living separately. Regular wages approximately £12 net. Housekeeping allowance £6 a week. Savings £3 a week. Aggregate savings more than £1,000. 'She doesn't need more.' Wife is not working.

CASE NO. 7. A labourer of sixty-two with five married children living separately and three children, twenty-seven, twenty-four and twenty-one at home, working and paying for their keep to the mother. His gross wage was £10 9s 8d. His wife was not working. Housekeeping allowance £6. Savings £1 a week.

The cases of hardship caused by insufficient housekeeping money are very rare, anyway as far as my material goes. There were only odd cases. The working man somehow finds it easier now to satisfy the fair demands of the home, without sacrificing his personal needs.

How does the employment of the wife affect the level of housekeeping money? Often I came across cases where a lower allowance was paid when the wife was working and as soon as she stopped working the allowance was raised considerably. For instance to quote two cases out of many more: 'Up to recently up to £8, now £12'; 'Up to recently £7, now £9 for housekeeping'. But sometimes a lower housekeeping allowance drives the wife into employment.

8. WORKING WIVES

THE PROBLEM of working wives is dealt with more fully in the survey of women operatives at Mullard, which is based on personal interviews with sixty-seven women. Here I deal only with the problems of working wives as reflected in the minds and behaviour of men, on the basis of personal interviews with the husbands. First let us look at the figures derived from my samples in five works.

The percentage of working wives varied considerably from works to works. In Workington it was lowest with about 28 per cent; Sheffield with 39 per cent and Dunlop with 41 per cent occupied the middle ranges, coming very near to each other; the highest level was reached in Vauxhall with 43 per cent and in Mullard with 49 per cent.

The main reason for this wide range was the character of the local labour market (apart from differences in the age composition of the samples). Where opportunities for women's work are largely lacking, as in Workington—a centre of heavy work—the proportion is rather on the low side; where opportunities for women's work are great as in Mitcham the proportion tends to be on the high side. Tradition for women's work, such as in Luton or Sheffield, or lack of this tradition, as in Workington, may also play its part.

Family relations, especially family planning, may have an influence over women's employment but it is very difficult to unravel the mutual impact of both phenomena. The percentage of childless couples was lowest in Dunlop with 13 per cent; Sheffield with about 15 per cent and Workington with 16 per cent occupied the middle ranges, while the two places with the highest incidence of women's work showed also the highest percentage of childlessness, namely about 18 per cent in Mullard and 20 per cent in Vauxhall. Family planning may be a factor in women's work, on the other hand opportunities for women's work are also a factor in family planning.

Is part-time work affected in the same way by the local labour market as full-time work? To a very large extent, yes. The outstanding feature brought out by the enquiry is that in each place the number of full-time working wives nearly equals that of part-timers. There were twenty-seven full-timers and twenty-seven part-timers in Sheffield, in Workington twelve full-timers and twelve part-timers, in Vauxhall twenty-two full-timers and twenty-two part-timers, in Dunlop nineteen full-timers and twenty-two part-timers, in Mullard twenty-four full-timers and twenty-three part-timers.

The typical full-time jobs were factory work, clerical work, work in distribution and shops, and nursing. The wage level rarely fell below £6.

The typical part-time jobs were cleaning, serving in canteens, schools, shops, and half-shifts in factories. The range of wages varied greatly; some worked only one day a week, or two hours a day, and others six or seven hours a day. The earnings might be as low as £1 but usually oscillated around £3 to £4. There were some wives who worked at home; two in Luton for the hat trade; two in Workington, one running a public house and one teaching music; two in Sheffield, one running a public house and the other a grocery shop, and so on. For the purpose of this enquiry these women were classed as part-timers.

Is there a typical age structure of working wives? Apart from the Mullard study of women reported elsewhere, I have no data for the age composition of working wives but only for their husbands.

Age of husbands with working wives	Sheffield	Workington	Vauxhall	Dunlop	Mullard	TOTAL
under 29	9	4	4	3	8	28
30–39	14	6	10	12	15	57
40–49	20	9	18	15	12	74
50–59	8	4	10	9	8	39
60 and over	3	1	2	2	4	12
TOTAL	54	24	44	41	47	210

We see that in four works the peak is reached in the age bracket of forty to forty-nine. Mullard is the only exception where the peak is reached in the age bracket of thirty to thirty-nine. Women with babies stay at home, but they come back when the children are at school or are grown up. They start retiring in their fifties.

As might be expected, however, the age composition is different for full-timers and part-timers. The overwhelming majority of wives with husbands in their twenties worked full-time, namely twenty-five out of twenty-eight. The trend towards part-time jobs is already well under way amongst the wives of husbands in their thirties; there were, in this group, twenty-seven part-timers against thirty full-timers. The trend towards part-time is accentuated amongst wives of husbands in their forties, where the part-timers increase rapidly at the expense of full-timers (there were forty-four part-timers against thirty full-timers), and even more so amongst the wives of husbands in their fifties and sixties.

Young children are an important factor in determining whether the wife goes out to work, and whether she works full-time or part-time. Out of 210 working wives, fifty-five were women without children and forty-five women with grown-up children (fifteen plus). Another forty-six were women with older school-children (ten plus), so about three-quarters of the working wives either had no children or no young children up to and including ten years of age, and these were mostly full-timers.

There were fifty-two mothers with young school-children (aged five to ten inclusive); They had all made some arrangements for the children: the younger ones were taken care of by grandmothers or relatives or neighbours; the older ones were simply given keys. The majority of these mothers worked only part-time, as the following figures show:

	Full-timers	Part-timers
Sheffield	4	10
Workington	2	3
Vauxhall	4	5
Dunlop	2	10
Mullard	4	8
TOTAL	16	36

We see that nearly three-quarters of working mothers with young children worked part-time.

Now we come to mothers with toddlers, children aged three to four inclusive. There were only five such mothers in my sample, two in Sheffield, none in Workington, one in Vauxhall, one in Dunlop and one in Mullard. Let us examine those five cases more closely.

CASE NO. 1. A toolmaker of thirty-two with two children, three and five. Wife worked as dressmaker at home. They had their own house, car, refrigerator, washing machine, telephone. He was taking home £14 and saved regularly up to £2 a week.

CASE NO. 2. A semi-skilled operator of thirty-seven with a girl of three, taking home £13 10s and paying £7 housekeeping allowance. His wife worked four hours in a café. He worked three shifts and was able to take care of the girl.

CASE NO. 3. A semi-skilled operator of twenty-seven with a girl of four. He took home £15 and saved regularly £5 to £6. He had a house of his own, a car and a washing machine. His wife worked part-time from 1 p.m. to 5 p.m., making £4 a week. During midday break he took the girl in his car to a cousin and collected her afterwards.

CASE NO. 4. A fettler of thirty-six with three girls, three, seven and eleven, making £16 to £17 net and allowing £8 for housekeeping. His wife worked only for 1½ to 2 hours in a school kitchen, earning about £1 a week, while the youngest girl was taken care of by her grandmother living near by.

CASE NO. 5. A moulder of twenty-nine with a girl of three, earning about £13 net and allowing his wife £8 for housekeeping. The wife worked as a machinist from 9 a.m. to 3.30 p.m., while the child was taken care of by the grandmother who lived with them.

We see that in every case the mother of a toddler worked only part-time, and the children were taken care of by grandmothers, relatives or the husband.

Finally we have mothers with babies (from birth to two inclusive). There were in my sample seven such mothers, three in Sheffield, none in Workington and Vauxhall, one in Dunlop, three in Mullard. By the way, we see that in Workington there was not a single case of a working mother with a baby or toddler. Where the labour market for female labour is restricted, mothers with babies and toddlers are simply not taken on by the management.

Now let us examine those cases of mothers with babies, one by one.

CASE NO. 1. A semi-skilled operator of forty-two with seven children: a baby of fourteen months, and children four, six, ten, twelve, fourteen and fifteen. He took home £15 and allowed his wife £10. The wife worked part-time from 5 p.m. to 9 p.m., getting £2 9s. The oldest girl was baby-sitting for a neighbour, getting her food there. The baby was taken care of by her sister of twelve or the husband who worked shifts.

CASE NO. 2. A semi-skilled operator of thirty-three with a baby of two, working long hours (about 65 in the week), taking home £13 to £14 and allowing £7 10s for housekeeping. The wife worked part-time as a machinist from 7.30 a.m. to 12 a.m., getting £3. The baby was taken care of by her grandmother who lived with them.

CASE NO. 3. A bricklayer's mate of twenty-six with a baby of one year. He took home £11 and allowed his wife £7 plus £1 for mortgage and rates. He had a house of his own but of the old type without bathroom. His wife worked three nights from 5.30 p.m. to 9 p.m., getting £3 10s. The granny looked after the baby. They had a washing machine, and a T.V. of course.

CASE NO. 4. A semi-skilled operator of thirty-five, previously a clerical man, with two children, a baby of two and a girl of five. He took home £15, had his own house of modern type and a washing machine. His wife worked as full-time shorthand-typist. The children were taken care of by the grandmother.

CASE NO. 5. A skilled engineer of thirty with a baby girl of five months. They have a modern-type house, a car, a refrigerator, a radiogram, washing machine, telephone and T.V. The wife did a part-time job as window dresser; the baby was taken care of by her grandmother.

CASE NO. 6. A charge-hand of thirty, earning £14 net, with a girl of two, living in the parents' home. The wife had a part-time job in a stationer's. The baby was taken care of by grandmother. The reason for working: 'Nothing to do at home as she lives with her parents.'

CASE NO. 7. A semi-skilled operator of twenty-eight, living in an old-type privately rented house without a bath, with a girl of two. The take-home money was £11. The wife worked full-time as a progress clerk, earning good money. The girl went to a nursery. They had been married only three years and they were saving hard to get things for their home. They hoped to buy their own house.

We see that the majority of mothers with babies (five out of seven) worked part-time. The majority of babies (five out of seven) were taken care of by grandmothers, one went to a nursery school, the other was taken care of by the older sister and the husband.

I tried to detect whether there were any cases where women

worked under duress, under the whip of sheer economic necessity, simply for survival. I assumed that women without children or with grown-up children, or families owning a house, or a car, refrigerator or washing machine or with adequate housekeeping money would not fall into this category. After scrutinizing all my cases carefully, I came to the conclusion that two or three such cases may have existed in my Sheffield sample; one in Workington (a mother with four children of seven, ten, eleven and twelve, getting £9 housekeeping money, apart from family allowances, who worked full-time—I classed her as such a case but it is doubtful whether she should come into this category); one case in Mullard (a wife of a labourer of fifty with six children at home of whom three were already working); one doubtful case in Vauxhall and one in Dunlop. There may have been other cases which escaped my attention or which were covered up by husbands. But I firmly believe that such cases are rare occurrences.

The motives for wives' employment are very complex and it is impossible to do them justice by asking a few questions. In most cases the answers to my question: 'What is the reason for your wife's work?' ran as follows: 'To help with the cost of living', or 'For company', or 'Lonely—sooner be at work', or 'Nothing to do at home', or 'For the children—to give them extra comforts', or 'To make things easier for the kiddies', or 'To keep them longer at school', or 'To pay for the car', or 'To pay for the house', or 'To pay for the furniture', or 'To pay for a good holiday', or, as one man put it jokingly, 'To build up my bank balance'. A number of men simply answered: 'It's a help'. A few said: 'On doctor's advice—to keep her mind occupied', or 'For her peace of mind': there were two such cases in Mullard, two in Dunlop, and one in Vauxhall.

Of course if the wife keeps her job for any length of time they both get used to a higher standard of living and they would miss her wages. There were a few cases where the wife wanted to retire but the husband viewed it with dismay: 'She wants to retire, of course on me. Pity that we men cannot retire on our wives.' But those cases were rare.

The forces governing men's attitudes to their wives' employment are very complex and conflicting. On the one hand the man wants to keep his wife at home. His status, his prestige, his comfort, the proper care of children are involved in this. On the other hand he wants the extra money and the extra money can smooth out many of his troubles. And he often finds that his wife does not really mind going out to work and often enjoys it. In some instances the need for extra money arose some time in the past, when the husband had an accident or was laid up for a length of time (there were two such cases in Sheffield): the wife had started to work and had kept on ever since.

In most cases the initiative for women's work is with the wife herself, and the man often professed: 'I don't interfere—she does as she pleases', or 'It's all up to her, I don't mind'.

Where the wife has a sort of vocation such as nursing, teaching or welfare work, or a well-paid skill, both partners may feel that it would be a pity to waste it, and they make a proper effort to give the wife the opportunity to lead a fuller life.

There are two generalizations one could make about attitudes to wives' employment. First, whenever the wife is happy in her job, the home and the husband–wife relationship are better for it; on the other hand when the wife is unhappy in her job and feels she has to do it because the money is needed and the husband expects it, the home and the personal relationships are at a disadvantage. Some husbands referred to this, saying, 'She is a better wife since she left the job'. Second, by and large those whose wives go out to work are happy with this arrangement, and those whose wives stay at home are again happy and content. The complaints of men on account of their wives' work were very rare, one could say exceptional. 'It's against my advice', 'I believe it's too much for her': such remarks were the exception. Invariably the men with working wives regarded it as their duty to give them a helping hand in the home.

On the other hand I heard from those husbands whose wives stayed at home a whole spate of arguments against the employment of women. To quote only a few: 'I don't believe in it'; 'The woman's place is in the home'; 'Plenty to do at home'; 'I like my warm meal and a clean house'; 'When a man marries a woman he has to keep her'; 'It's a poor man who cannot keep his wife'; 'I don't think it is right'; 'Enough money for two of us'; 'It's only greed that makes men send their wives out to work'; 'More earned, more spent, no profit'; 'Sensible sort of a girl, not bored at home'; 'If you can keep your wife, that is the best'; 'I like my wife feeling and dressing well. I encourage her in this.'

Are the men whose wives go out to work better off? The figures for ownership of cars in all five works seem to suggest that it may be so. As for houses—only in Dunlop, Vauxhall and Mullard did those with working wives own proportionally more houses; in Sheffield and in Workington there was little difference in this respect between the group of men with working wives and the group of men whose wives stayed at home.

An additional reason for the fact that families with working wives may be better off is that amongst the wives who stay at home we find a higher percentage of ill-health or disability, and this is often the reason why the wife does not go out to work. Time and again, when I asked: 'Does your wife go out to work?' the answers from those whose wives stayed at home ran as follows: 'She has been ill for a long time'; 'Invalid for years'; 'Semi-invalid'; 'She had an accident'; 'She had an operation of the womb'; 'High blood pressure'; 'Suffering from change of life'; or 'Nerves'. In Sheffield fifteen such cases were recorded, in Workington eleven, in Vauxhall nine, in Dunlop ten.

If we take account of such cases and bear in mind women who have retired or are nearing retiring age, or have babies and toddlers or specially large families, we may come to the conclusion that, where the labour market permits it, the big majority of wives who are in a position to seek employment are actually at work.

9. DIVORCES AND SEPARATIONS

DIVORCES AND SEPARATIONS are not frequent in workers' lives. The worker needs his wife to keep him steady, to help him in his struggle against poverty or ill-health and to provide the comfortable living conditions which make his work so much easier.

My casebook in five works recorded twelve divorces and seven separations, among which there were two concubinages and two or three other estrangements which might have ended in separation or divorce. These men often felt that they were trapped; some were still under stress and affliction, others already sailing under a better wind were able to speak of the past almost objectively, even with a sense of humour. Some were monosyllabic and morose, others quite willing to oblige with a full story, feeling a sense of relief from laying open the wounds.

The reasons for divorces and separations centred around a few set patterns which were constantly recurring: 'I was in the Army, posted abroad, and she was carrying on with another man', or 'She had a baby by another man', or simply 'Another chap'; less frequently: 'After stillbirth she went to pieces with a flying temper', or simply 'Ill-tempered woman, a terror', or 'Refusal of sexual contact', or 'We were living with in-laws and her mother interfered'. It is characteristic that all of them presented themselves as the innocent party. In fact no one thinks of himself or herself as a guilty party, as I learned again in Mullard, interviewing divorced and separated women.

However, if the length of service in the firm were taken as a measure of reliability and steadfastness, most of them could be so characterized, having a long service record. Eleven out of nineteen men divorced and separated had between twenty-one and thirty-four years' service, four between ten and eighteen years, four between six and nine years. Is this coincidence, or more than coincidence? Had the long stay in the firm dulled their attractiveness as partners, or were they neglecting their partners for the sake of work? Were they solely good workers? Anyway it was obvious from their remarks about the job that they liked it and took great interest in it.

One characteristic story which may throw light on this nexus of work and love came from a young welder, married for three years and separated for nine months. The couple lived with his in-laws and badly wanted their own house. He took on permanent nights and worked very hard, with a good deal of overtime, to get the money for the house, but when he had saved £500 for the deposit his wife told him she was not interested and walked out on him. He had to leave the house, and went to live in a furnished flat, consoling himself with a car. He did not realize at that time that he had been neglecting his wife, who had found in the meantime another attachment.

This was not an isolated story. A foreman said: 'Young men, thinking only of money to please their wives, often over-reach themselves and neglect their wives in other ways. Women expect from their husbands something more than money. Often they drift apart as a result of too much overtime and shiftwork.'

One man attributed his broken home to the many accidents and nervous rashes he suffered in his work. But since his wife had left him, his condition had become still worse. Nearly every year he was laid up with one disease or another; gall bladder, stomach ulcers, skin diseases. But actually that was not the whole story. His wife had a very good position as owner of a grocery shop; she was earning about three times as much as he did and the trouble was that she always felt superior to him as he was only a labourer.

Neuroses or nervous breakdowns were common in this group. Emotional trouble affected the men's productive performance during the time of strain and stress. 'It preyed on my mind for a long time. I couldn't concentrate, I lost shifts, I had to take an easier job with less responsibility' were remarks which I noted.

One man recounted the following story: 'My wife shouldn't have been married, she was cold, one of those forbidding characters—a sort of Catholic recluse. We were married for thirteen years and had three children but the last ten years I spent in chastity like a monk. She refused any sexual contact. I believed there was something wrong with me, I felt despised and rejected, lived on dope pills and moved like an automaton. There was a sense of general futility and senselessness, a feeling of emptiness in me. I worked very badly, often taking off shifts and walking around aimlessly. I couldn't concentrate, everything was a problem. Now I live with another woman who also cannot get a divorce and I work very much better. I am happy, although at times it is trying with her children and our own child growing up who will soon ask questions.'

Now let us divide our cases in three groups: (1) Those who were divorced and married again; (2) those, whether divorced or separated, living alone; and (3) concubinages.

Eight out of twelve of the divorced men had married again, and one other was courting. Most men do not get discouraged from a second try. All of those who married again confided: 'Very happy', or 'Happy with my present wife', but they were never quite sure whether their happiness would last. The shadow of the first marriage was always upon them and they could not shake off the 'remembrances of the lost time'.

They had fairly big families although not as large as the remarried widowers. Out of the eight divorced men who had remarried, one had five children by two wives, one four children and step-children, two, three children, three, one child or step-child, and one had no children. They were not well off (only one man with no children and a wife on the staff was well-off, with a new Vauxhall car). They had spent a great deal of money on getting a divorce in spite of legal aid (one spent £145 of his own money out of £500 total costs, another £125); they paid maintenance, and lost furniture and houses which they left to their wives or children. None owned a house; only two had cars; every second wife in this group went out to work. They gave their wives housekeeping money, but none of them gave all their wage packets like the majority of remarried widowers did; a sort of suspicion still lingered on.

Closely related to this group were two cases of concubinages. Both men were Catholics with large families; one had three sets of children, numbering eight in all; the other, two sets of children numbering seven in all. In one case both partners were separated and unable to get a divorce, settled in an old dilapidated house which they had bought very cheaply with the help of their friends, and by pretending before the neighbours to be married. The other case was that of an Irishman who had a large family tucked away in Ireland. He had left his wife and four children but continued to send them £3 a week regularly while living with another woman in the house of her father who was a widower. By her he had three young children, the eldest seven and the youngest four. He paid her regular housekeeping money of £8, so he did not have much to spare as pocket money. He described his life, in a mood of understatement as 'a bit complicated', especially as his lady worried him, moaning, 'What will become of me and my children if you happen to die?' Another trouble of his was: 'With so many bastards of my own I cannot go to church, but I send them to Sunday School. What I will say to them when they grow up, I don't know.'

Now we come to a group of nine men divorced or separated, and living alone. Most of them had been left by their wives who had gone off with other men. Their families were very small or childless (seven out of nine had no children, or one child only). four lived in the same house as before their wives left them, while five lived in lodgings or with parents. Only one paid maintenance: £2 5s 0d. They were not very well off; none had a house of his own, only one had a car, and three had motor cycles.

Only two men were courting or had an attachment; the remainder were very lonely. Two other men would have liked to have had their wives back, and would have accepted them in spite of everything. Most of them were suffering from emotional disturbances, often developing symptoms of physical disorders or inviting accidents above the normal quota. Among the nine cases, one had tuberculosis, one had a slipped disc, one was suffering from diseases of the skin and gall-bladder, another suffered from permanent catarrh, another from nerves and headache. 'One wears oneself out getting no sleep'—some of them would say. They lost shifts more than others. Asked whether they cared for overtime they would answer: 'Not now as I am a single man' and some would add: 'and I got rid of nightshift as well'.

They were conscientious workers, trying to forget themselves in work, but the sense of defeat often followed them. When they recounted their story they often cast side glances at me, and their faces had a lethargic expression, seeming to be caused by their misanthropic solitude: they often have the feeling of being wronged. However, asked whether they were happy now, they would answer: 'Quiet, happier than previously'. They had developed their own compensations. They were conscious that they were not as well off as previously, but probably they thought that austerity with peace was better than prosperity in a trap.

There were two cases of estrangement in my sample. A labourer of fifty-four, father of seven children, for thirty years in the firm, had been for the last ten years living in his own house as a perfect stranger, shut in his room. Sexual contact was refused by his wife, and he was brooding over this, suffering from insomnia and all sorts of disorders. He intended to change his job, to go into another town and lose his identity by changing his name.

Another man estranged from his wife was a skilled man of thirty-five with one boy. He had a lodger and suspected him of having an affair with his wife. His nightshift, he thought, offered the opportunity, as the lodger was alone with the wife in the house. Maybe he imagined that to live under one roof with his wife and not to fall in love with her was beyond the power of a normal man, and the gossip of malicious friends did the rest. Twice during his nightshift, in the middle of the night, he had asked the foreman for his pass and rushed home to catch the perfidious couple, but discovered nothing. But all the same this became an obsession with him: so much so that he went to a psychologist for treatment. How many men on nights are torn by suspicion when their wives have friends among neighbours or lodgers, or go out—as they often do—to sleep with their mothers or sisters?

PART THREE

Work and Home

10. SHIFTS AS A HEALTH AND FAMILY PROBLEM

SHIFTWORK IS SPREADING all over the country and invading more and more industries as the tide of re-equipment and modernization rises. Recently it has also invaded office work in connection with the introduction of computing machinery and other expensive equipment. So it is not surprising that the exploration of attitudes to shiftwork and its impact on family life became one of the main themes of the enquiry.

The exploration of the problem of shiftwork is extremely difficult as the subject is very complex, resembling a jig-saw puzzle; even its presentation is far from easy. Before we proceed to a detailed analysis of the factors involved, let us start with a few generalizations based on the sample data.

The highest turnover of labour is, generally speaking, in shiftwork, especially when a man starts shiftwork later in life, let us say in his forties. He must start young in order to adapt himself fully and take it for granted. Also the highest figures for absenteeism are for shiftwork—I think, because of certain attitudes, as well as the effect on health, especially in winter time. Those two factors—the higher turnover of labour and absenteeism—speak clearly for the general attitudes as well as the strain involved in shifts.

The data for attitudes and impact of shifts are available for 322 men, namely seventy-nine in Sheffield, sixty-eight in Workington, seventy in Vauxhall, eighty-three in Dunlop and twenty-two in Mullard. I divided them in four main classes: (1) Those who accept shiftwork, seeing no harm in it, taking the rough with the smooth, and not contemplating any change, often simply taking it for granted. Not all of them would choose it but most of them tolerate it well. (2) Those who reckon that their health is affected—stomach, sleep, nerves, chest and so on—and feel upset or disturbed by shifts. (3) Those who reckon that their health is affected but only to a small degree, who feel very tired or weary or very irritable, but only during part of the shift period. (4) Those who enjoy shiftwork, preferring it to daywork, not only on account of money but in itself.

The distribution of these four classes in five works presents the following pattern:

	Upset	Lightly disturbed	Accept	Prefer	TOTAL
Sheffield . .	19	9	45	6	79
Workington .	15	10	24	19	68
Vauxhall . .	24	11	32	3	70
Dunlop . .	32	10	37	4	83
Mullard . .	7	1	13	1	22
TOTAL . .	97	41	151	33	322

We see that the highest ratio of acceptance of and preference for shifts occurs in steelworks, both in Sheffield and in Workington and the lowest in mass production firms, namely in Vauxhall and Dunlop. The incidence of shiftwork in Mullard is very small.

The most important single problem in shiftwork is its impact on health, and we see from the data presented that roughly speaking one in three believes himself to be affected in his health by shifts to a larger or smaller degree. The intensity of the impact on health is very difficult to assess as this could only be accomplished by a thorough medical survey. In my view such a survey would be a most valuable contribution to the subject. Anyway a more stringent medical screening in selection of shiftworkers would be advisable in order to reduce the impact of shiftwork on health.

Health, vigour and adaptability are the most important factors and assets in attitudes to shiftwork. Healthy, vigorous men, placid and well-balanced emotionally, can adapt themselves easily to the requirements of shiftwork. However, any weakness, especially of stomach, chest or nerves, shows up in shifts and puts an additional strain on the men affected. Stomach disorders stood out as complaint number one, but very frequently they were mentioned together with disturbances of sleep.

The second most important problem is the impact of shiftwork on family life. There is a mutual interdependence between family life and shiftwork. A shiftworker can stand the challenge of shifts well only if his wife is willing to make proper adjustments in her routine and be helpful rather than adding to his strain by making difficulties. A man's attitude to shifts is actually a resultant of two attitudes: his own and his wife's. He must adjust himself, and his wife must do the same, but they influence each other very closely. In practically every case where a man was affected in his health by shifts his wife's attitude was reported also as strongly negative, and described often in such terms: 'She detests them', or 'She loathes it', or 'She keeps telling me I should change my job'.

The data for wives' attitudes to shifts as reported by the husbands are available for 221 men in five works, namely, thirty-five in Sheffield, thirty-seven in Workington, fifty-three in Vauxhall, seventy-five in Dunlop and twenty-one in Mullard. Here are the answers divided in two classes: (1) Wives upset or minding the shift; (2) not minding.

	Upset	Not minding	TOTAL
Sheffield	20	15	35
Workington	17	20	37
Vauxhall	37	16	53
Dunlop	45	30	75
Mullard	9	12	21
TOTAL	128	93	221

We see that the majority of wives, namely, fifty-eight per cent, are alleged to be upset by shifts, although of course in varying degrees. Again the best acceptance of shifts by the wives occurs in steelworks and in Mullard (while interviewing women operatives in Mullard I found confirmation of this), while the most negative attitudes prevail among women folk in Dunlop and Vauxhall.

Those of a nervous disposition, or young wives without children —who often go to the mother or sister for the nights—or those with babies who must be kept quiet while the husband sleeps during the day, or those with large families where there is always hustle and bustle, have a specially poor view of shifts. Shifts, generally speaking, upset the normal routine of housework. Men seem to be most irritable when on nights. The current expression which I often heard was: 'My wife tells me: "When you are nights you are the most irritable man in Sheffield" ', or 'The most irritable man in Birmingham', or 'in Luton', and so on. Irritability following nightwork is a big factor in home upsets. Most men confess that they try to keep their tempers under control, but: 'We are only flesh and blood'. It is very difficult to assess the intensity of the impact on family life on this score, but I would say, on the basis of my material, that the family 'tiffs' caused by shifts are not very serious and I heard of only very few more serious cases. Shifts are troublesome for family life but in most cases with the goodwill of both partners they can be coped with and mastered. But there are a number of cases which need special consideration and this is rarely taken into account by the management.

Now let us proceed to a more detailed analysis of specific factors in men's attitudes to shifts. I shall present this by means of question and answer.

(1) Where is the shift system best tolerated, or even appreciated?

I would say primarily where shiftwork means promotion. For instance in steelworks shiftwork means better jobs which men acquire in time by promotion from lower grades. Men join the steelworks as labourers, they move to production jobs on days, and then to still better jobs on shifts. There is a strict seniority on those jobs. So to move on to shifts means promotion, and only few refuse it for one reason or another.

Shiftwork is also best tolerated in areas where it is a general and long-established practice, as for instance in Workington where most jobs in this area are on shifts. In Workington shiftwork has a long tradition behind it, not only in this works but also in the district generally. It has been carried on from father to son and is simply taken for granted. In such places shiftwork becomes a way of life, so much so that shiftworkers develop a different mode of living from dayworkers. Men on three shifts have three different routines, one for each week in a three weeks' period. They move in cycles of three weeks. A month means little to them; instead three weeks represents a full cycle of working and living. In this cycle each week is characterized by its own ways. Some enjoy the constant changeability, the constant variation which brings a greater richness in living, granted good health and adaptability. 'I like the variety, life is never dull for a moment', many would say, and most enjoy a long weekend, or at any rate longer than dayworkers. The big majority of men in those areas simply take the shifts for granted; they do not think about them. The problem does not actually exist for them—it only flares up when an investigator comes and asks questions.

An entirely different situation occurs in places where shiftwork is relatively new, and in addition irregular. In Vauxhall for instance, the shifts in many departments are irregular; in some departments men work nights one month in two, in others one in three or one in four, five or six months. When, for instance, nights are worked once in three or four months, the shiftworker does not develop a regular habit or regular ways of adjustment. He has not built up strong defences against the onslaught of nightwork; he just takes it as a troublesome nuisance. There shiftwork is not a way of life but a deviation from normal living, an anomaly. There one can hear such pronouncements as: 'It's unnatural', or 'It's against human nature'.

A similar situation arises where the obligation to work shifts is less definite and less firm and where there can be an escape from shiftwork. If the worker feels that he has no escape and there is no vacillation about it, his process of adjustment is more effective.

Very much depends, also, on the standards of selection of shiftworkers. In firms such as Mullard, for instance, where shiftwork is needed only to a small extent (about 17 per cent of males work shifts), shiftworkers can be selected more thoroughly and only those workers go on shifts who are most suitable and willing.

(2) Is there a significant difference in attitudes between skilled, semi-skilled, and labourers, and has the nature of jobs any influence on attitudes?

Definitely yes. Skilled men with few exceptions have a very negative attitude to shifts and they word their opposition to shifts very emphatically. This is because of the complexity of the work ('We are not so alert at night') and the difficulty of maintaining proper standards of performance ('It isn't fair to the job'). It is a greater strain for them to work on nights than for semi-skilled men.

I have found in general, not only on this enquiry, that the greatest tolerance to nights is shown by labourers, especially light labourers on cleaning, servicing, or watching.

As to the nature of jobs, whenever the work is very exacting or strenuous or linked with hazards, the nightshift is an additional strain. In some departments I came across a widespread acceptance of the nightshift, and when I probed more deeply, it came out that on those particular jobs one could relax at night and even snatch a nap. Generally speaking, whenever the work is disliked by a man for any reason, the nightshift imposes an additional strain, while a positive attitude to the job itself lightens the burden of the nightshift.

There appeared to be a significant difference in attitudes for mass production as compared with other work. Usually between three and four a.m. a man finds his energy at a minimum, at what is often called dead time; when he is on piecework he can ease up and make up for it later on, while a man controlled by a conveyor has to maintain his output all the time, which imposes greater strain. It might be advisable for the production engineers to take into account this period of nightwork, and adapt the speed of the conveyor accordingly.

However, it should not be surmised that nightwork brings only inconveniences. There are also some compensations. Most men interviewed stated that the team spirit is better on nights. 'We cling together more on nights', they said, or 'A better carry on', or 'A sort of a forgotten family feeling, being all in the same boat. It is more like an army unit in a forlorn village or position.' Supervision is often more lenient, often lacking altogether. No one shouts about not keeping the floor tidy, the afternoon shifts often leave things easier for the nightshift and the morning shifts often have to clear up the mess from nights. Management interference is largely non-existent, and for this reason the junior foremen often prefer nightshifts. 'Not so many bosses running around', I heard, and 'I can get things done easier on nights'.

(3) Which shift systems are more and which are less popular?

There are so many shift systems; two shifts, days and afternoons, or days and nights, based on a two-weeks, monthly or two-monthly cycle; three shifts in a three-weeks cycle with Saturday and Sunday off, or a continuous working week with changing days-off based on a four-weeks cycle; the rotation may also vary from a week to a month; moreover the hours vary considerably both in regard to starting-off time and the length of shift. Which of those systems are preferred?

Generally speaking those systems where nightshifts are excluded (for instance mornings and afternoons), or those where nights are at a minimum both in terms of number of shifts and hours; but otherwise the principle of 'as it is' prevails. The most popular are those systems which are in actual operation in a given plant, the more so the longer they have been in use. The percentage of men who would like the previous system or any other system is small. A man can adapt himself to anything if he is given time, so the most frequent answer I received to my question: 'Would you prefer a change in the shift system?' was 'No'. Once a man has adapted himself to a set of conditions, he does not feel that another set will suit him better. Of course there are good and bad points in every single shift system. In a shorter cycle the nights are suffered only for a week; in a longer cycle self-adaptation and force of habit come into their own.

(4) What is the best sequence of shifts in a three-weeks' cycle?

Again 'as it is' was the answer for most men, but those who had the experience of working with the sequence: nights, afternoons and mornings, instead of the usual sequence: mornings, afternoons and nights, put forward a very cogent argument in its favour. They contended that after nightshifts a man is tired and needs a longer rest which he can get by a longer weekend (from Friday night to Monday afternoon) and that there is a better opportunity to sleep when on afternoons. While going on from nights to mornings he has no chance to catch up on his sleep. This suggestion seems worth considering.

(5) Is any shift regarded as entirely satisfactory?

When we speak about shifts, we seem to concentrate unduly on nights, but the other shifts also have their handicaps. None is regarded as entirely satisfactory. Morning shifts usually start at 6 a.m. which, for men living far out, often means rising as early as 4.30 a.m. or 4.45 a.m. A number of men contended that knowing that they have to get up so early they cannot sleep properly the whole night. Some men, especially those of a more nervous disposition, stated that this was their worst shift from a sleeping point of view. Being tired out from the previous week on nights they move straight on to another week of sleepless shifts. When they come home from their morning shift they have their dinner and go straight to bed, not being able to do very much for the rest of the day.

The afternoon shift interferes with their hobbies and leisure-time activities. A man on afternoons gets up late and potters around the house. He has nothing to do at home, he is only in the way while the wife does the cleaning. He wastes his time and waits for the clock. The time moves slowly, it is monotonous. Again when he returns home from work, usually after 11 p.m. or so, he cannot eat much if he is to avoid going to bed with a full stomach. He cannot fall asleep for a long time because he is still keyed up from working: his mind has had no time to unwind itself from the strain and stress of noise and bustle at work. He gets into the habit of going to bed late and getting up late. He does not see much of his children or friends. Nevertheless, this shift has its compensations and many called it a 'saving shift' as there is little time in which to spend money.

(6) What is the influence on shift attitudes of the two most important gadgets in modern life: the television and the motor car?

They both affect shiftwork in more than one way. Men on afternoons and to some extent those on nights miss the T.V., and they dislike this immensely. On the other hand T.V. helps them to keep their wives quiet, and the first thing a shiftworker would do if he has no set already would be to get one for his wife. 'My wife doesn't mind my shifts: she has a Telly', or 'She is not alone; she has the children and the Telly'—this was often heard from the men. Not being able to go out is nowadays not such a handicap as previously, as 'the picture house is at home' as one man has put it. T.V. has, undoubtedly, eased the pressure and strain felt on the wife's side on account of missed outings.

A car presents a different set of questions. A regular shiftworker is more likely to be able to afford a car than others, and the highest percentage of car owners among semi-skilled men will be found in the ranks of shiftworkers. This was especially true of men in Dunlop and Vauxhall. The car is particularly useful to the shiftworker as the hours are not very convenient for catching a bus, being either too early or too late. Many shiftworkers in Vauxhall or Dunlop contended that they could do their shiftwork only because they had a car.

Actually a car would be an answer to the shiftwork problems of many firms. Some firms would consider running two dayshifts instead of a day- and nightshift, as for instance I was told by the management of Vauxhall, but the main reasons for not doing that was the difficulty in arranging proper bus services. These could be overcome if the firms were able to provide a car service for shiftworkers living a good distance from the works. Shift hours could be much better arranged than at present, making some shifts attractive and not all shifts burdensome. I believe the shiftworker's car is a general answer to many troubles at present connected with shiftwork.

(7) Is age a significant factor in attitudes to shifts?

Yes, in the sense that younger men are more adaptable, more vigorous and suffer less from ailments of deterioration linked with age, which are the qualities necessary for the shiftworker. Also it is more difficult for men to start working on shifts at a later age. Men of fifty would say: 'I am too old to start working shifts', and when promotion to better paid jobs involving shiftwork comes at that age they refuse to take it. In some firms, like Vauxhall, men over sixty are excused from working shifts. Some younger men may dislike nightwork more than older men but they would not be affected in their health as much as older men are. Generally speaking, a higher percentage of younger men may show greater tolerance to shifts on the score that if they cannot adjust themselves to shifts they can leave and find another job, while for older men this avenue is closed. The latter have too much to risk, in the way of seniority rights and other fringe benefits, in finding an alternative job.

But if a man is healthy and he started shifts early he may enjoy shifts more in later years than when he was younger. He is, so to say, already broken in, and knows all the tricks of the trade. In that sense age is not a significant factor in attitudes to shifts.

I divided the classes of those who reckoned they were upset or lightly upset (affected in their health) into two age groups (under forty and forty plus), and found that there was hardly any difference between them, as many contradictory factors were at work. However, younger men were more frequently found among those who expressed a preference for shiftwork, i.e., out of thirty-three twenty belonged to the under-forties.

(8) Do single men like shiftwork more than married men, or vice versa?

There is a very complex set of factors in operation, often contradictory; its outcome is very uncertain, and changes with each situation. Single men have less incentive to work shifts and they are more highly taxed, so they do not get the full benefit of the shift allowance. On the other hand they have no family commitments and no wife to reckon with. They are not disturbed by the fact that the young wife sleeps by herself, or that she is afraid of sleeping by herself, or that she goes out for the night to her parents or sister—situations which start a whole chain of restless thoughts.

On the other hand, single men, when they are courting, need the money very badly, so they are very keen on getting on to shifts; but they have also to cultivate their courtship and not to neglect their fiancées while they are on afternoons. The afternoon shift is the worst shift for single men courting and for single men in general.

(9) How do housing conditions affect shift attitudes?

Housing conditions which deny privacy are not conducive to shifts. Slummy houses, overcrowded or furnished rooms, part houses, noisy streets, houses near factories, or flats in a block, may produce such conditions. In Dunlop many men live in flats in Council blocks and they complained about the noise preventing their sleep. Single men living in furnished rooms often find difficulty in obtaining accommodation as the landladies do not like shiftworkers. Men living with in-laws feel that they are upsetting the routine of the household, and even more so when other members of the family are on different shifts.

(10) Is the need for money a significant factor in attitudes?

Very much so. If the man needs the money very badly he will try harder to adjust himself to shift requirements, and he can count on greater help from his wife on this score. A man who has done shiftwork for a long time is not only used to shifts but he is also used to the standard of living to which he managed to rise because of his shift allowance. Young, newly-married men, who are building up their homes, often apply for shifts. By and large one can say that shiftworkers form, among semi-skilled men, the cream of the labour force. They are, on the average, more enterprising, more adaptable and, I would say, also more acquisitive. They are prepared to go to great lengths in order to improve their standard of living and they are proud that they are able to endure the discomforts for the benefit of their families. On the whole they have better equipped homes, as they want to show something for their labour.

So the question: 'Do you like shiftwork?' is an abstract question if it does not bring the money side into it. The men would say: 'Money comes into it'; 'Money is the main object'; and if one asked: 'Would you prefer regular days?' the answer would be: 'That depends how much less money I would get' and the difference usually amounted to a round figure, sometimes 10s, sometimes £1 or £2, but rarely coming up to the whole shift allowance. Only those who suffered seriously in health would say, 'Money doesn't come into it, as health is the overriding factor'. But these were few and they belonged to a class of people who had no real alternative to shiftwork. It must also be remembered that shiftwork often consists of more interesting work, often serving complex machinery and rated higher than other semi-skilled jobs, apart from the shift allowance.

(11) Is the nature of family relations an important factor in shift attitudes?

Very much so. But the influence is very complex and goes through many channels, which may run in different directions.

When there is a good husband–wife relationship, the wife will make a great effort to adjust herself to shift requirements, and in such cases the man would say: 'My wife is very reasonable about shifts. She knows that we need the money', or 'My wife tells me "That is your job, and we must make the best of it." Anyway my routine is not the most important thing.' On the other hand an affectionate wife might feel more lonely at night, and she might not be able to refrain from complaining.

If the couple is already estranged, they may both feel that the nightshift is for them the better one. In some cases men ask to be put on nights permanently as that helps to ease the strain at home. In cases of mistrust and jealousy shifts cause a big worry, especially if there is another man in the house or close neighbourhood. One man described to me his pangs of jealousy while he was on nights, and how he had made a fool of himself. When the marriage finds itself under stress already, the shifts may bring it to breaking point. Another man described to me how he had lost his wife, while doing nightshifts in order to make more money quickly.

(12) Do children have any effect on shiftwork?

A big effect—but it is very varied. Here again, according to the degree of her success in controlling the children, the wife can be a great help or a nuisance. Men with small babies who cry during the day, tend to complain that they cannot sleep. But even older children, when they come from school, can be very noisy. By and large, men with big families find it more difficult to get their sleep or even rest during the day. They have another job to do at home with the children. True, they need more money and they are the ones who would apply for shiftwork, but the shifts tend to wear them down unless they are very strong and adaptable and have understanding and efficient wives. I came across cases where men did not know where to turn, finding themselves in a quandary. I feel that men with large families should be excused from doing shiftwork; and also men with invalid children.

(13) How does the wife's work affect attitudes to shifts?

Shiftworkers are on the whole the better-paid men, so they can better afford to keep their wives at home. In my Dunlop sample the ratio of men with wives working was smaller for shiftworkers (39 per cent) than for dayworkers (45 per cent), but in other work-places there was hardly any difference. There are so many factors which come into the question of whether or not the wife decides to go out to work. The shiftworker's wife may feel lonely and upset and she may like the company of others in a place of work. The attitudes of shiftworkers themselves are very divided. Some men, just because they are on shifts, want to keep their wives at home; they feel that they are slaving quite enough, and they therefore expect better service when they come home, for instance with meals at odd times. Others, more enterprising and more independent, prefer their wives to go out to work precisely because of their shifts. When he is on afternoons, the shiftworker with a working wife has the house to himself in the morning, not being disturbed by and not disturbing his wife's routine; when he is on nights he can sleep the whole day undisturbed. I came across some cases where the wife went out to work specifically in order not to disturb her husband's sleep while he was on nights. Rest-times between shifts may also be convenient for taking care of children while the mother is at work, or for shopping, or for helping around the house, and so may actually enable the wife to go out to work.

However, there is little doubt that shiftwork in conjunction with women's work cuts down the time that husband and wife can spend together, and it often happens that men on nights come home after their wives have left for work. Some feel the better for it; most men accept it as a matter of course. 'There is nothing wrong in that, is there?' they would say—and they would add 'Long weekends make up for it'.

(14) Do hobbies, pastimes and 'sidelines' affect shift attitudes? Very much so. But this depends on the nature of the pastime. A regular pub-goer or club patron hates the afternoon shifts more than anything else. The same applies to those whose social life is fairly developed. Generally speaking, men with interesting hobbies which require a good deal of time prefer shiftwork to daywork because it gives them more leisure. Those who have a 'sideline' (and a small percentage of men in every single workplace dabbled thus), appreciate shiftwork for the same reasons, as often a sideline is possible by virtue of varying hours of work.

We have seen, in this short review, the enormous complexities of shiftwork which resemble a jig-saw puzzle. Shiftwork has its dark side, but it also has compensations. Some of the most happy men I interviewed were on shifts, with an excellent record of work and family life; there were also instances of family upsets and complications added to by shiftwork. However, these were few; one could say only odd cases. The overwhelming majority of men come to terms with shiftwork and make proper adjustment to it and arrangements for it. In this the following factors are of the greatest help: a certain regularity of shifts, in whatever system; health and vigour; a consenting wife; not too many children; a good house; T.V.; and a car. The modern trend, actually, by virtue of a better health service, smaller families, improving housing conditions, T.V., and cars, favours the acceptance of shifts.

11. ACQUISITIVE TENDENCIES

THE VARIETIES OF MEN, jobs and situations are so numerous that we would search in vain for an over-all formula which, in a few simple terms, would cover the main features of workers' attitudes to their work. We have to distinguish here between personal attitudes and the general and social trends which can be discerned in the attitudes.

The attitude to work is amongst the most complex of all a man's attitudes, often involving not only strong ambivalence but also side-thrusts in all directions, and links with his way of life, home and family. Work transforms his entire being, imposes certain ways of living and introduces him into a whole network of compelling human relationships. Work provides both a supplement to and contrast with the other side of his life and supplies it with a necessary equilibrium. It releases a considerable discharge of a whole range of human emotions, both positive and negative, both creative and destructive, narcissistic and aggressive.

The personal attitude to work is governed by innumerable factors such as temperament, character, age, health, life experience, marital status, skill, nature of work, wages and working conditions, industry and place of work, nature of comradeship at work—and the enquiry shed light on many of these. However, I would like to concentrate here on a few generalizations, suggested or brought out strikingly by my enquiry.

There is a basic diversity in attitudes to work between skilled and semi-skilled workers. The skilled men, in the overwhelming majority, took a great interest in the work itself. The nature, tone and intensity of interest differed very greatly from that of semi-skilled men. They would say: 'I was always interested in metals'; 'I like fiddling with machines'; 'It is in my blood'; 'You can always learn something new'; 'I like making things'; 'It is the right type of work for me'. The skilled man has a trade which he follows no matter which firm he is working for; the semi-skilled man looks for a job whose nature often changes from one firm to another. The skilled man often said, 'If I had my time over again, I would do the same'. The skilled man showed a longer service record than the semi-skilled. The majority of them disliked piecework, regarding it as conducive to scamped work, while the semi-skilled on the whole preferred it. They disliked nightwork much more than semi-skilled men, regarding nightwork as not conducive to a good piece of work. In all the firms I visited I found the same gulf between the interest of skilled and semi-skilled men; though it was a little stronger in the engineering works than in steelworks, where the dividing line between skills and semi-skills is often blurred.

Another striking feature is the impact of comradeship on attitudes to work. Comradeship or companionship played a big part in governing men's attitude to work. Comradeship is often a compensation for the dullness of the work. If the human relationships are satisfactory, much of the monotony of work can be relieved and even not noticed. The net of relationships at work is very complex but what count most are the relationships between the men themselves, which are more important than the relationships between man and foreman. Very rarely did I hear 'I like the foreman', but very often 'I like the fellows'; 'All good mates'; 'Good crowd to work with'; 'Good job, good company'; or 'Happy crowd'. The atmosphere of a work-place depends primarily on the nature of human relationships, especially between the men themselves.

That atmosphere varied considerably from work-place to work-place; even from department to department. I can safely say that most men in the works I visited liked their work or even enjoyed it—of course in different degrees; although some only tolerated it and a few merely endured it. However, the relative strength of those who enjoyed their work as compared with those who tolerated it or endured it, varied from works to works and from department to department. Disregarding personal characteristics, one could say that a certain basic attitude to work is representative for a whole works, department or section, so that the differences in relative strength of positive and negative responses would follow these divisions. The place of work could be very interesting, interesting, monotonous, or forbidding. There was a flocklike behaviour not only in having cars or T.V. sets, but also in the evaluation of the job. Somehow, the interplay between personal attitudes of men in the work-place led to a common reaction. 'This is an interesting job' or 'This is a monotonous job': everyone would repeat such phrases whether they really thought they were true or not; perhaps the individual thought so because common opinion made him think so.

Another striking feature was the difference in attitudes to work between single men and married men. Married men often transferred their interests in their home to their work, regarding the job as the foundation and the sustainer of the home. One could hear, from young married men: 'Since I married I take my job much more seriously'; 'My interest in the job grew with my family'; 'When you get married you settle down and take a lot more interest in the job'; 'Since I married I tried to better myself';

'Since I married I took up a steady job and want to stop here'; or 'I don't get bored; I need all the money I can get for my home.'

More security, better financial prospects, or 'to better oneself' were the most frequent reasons given by young married men for changing their job. Often, when I asked young men newly-married whether they regarded themselves as settled in their jobs, I got the answer: 'I have to, I am married now', or 'I can't play with the job now'.

We should also not forget the enormous influence of age in shaping attitudes to work. There is a constant age-conditioned shift of interest between home, work and outside activities. At first the outside interests predominate, then home, when a family is raised, then the interest shifts more to work ('The work has grown on me'), then again the interest in work fades out ('I gradually slowed down and the interest faded out'), then man retreats into his home 'keeping himself to himself'. After forty or so a man stays put if he can as it is more difficult for him to find another job. 'So I have to like it as I can't change now', or 'I am just staying put', they say.

Now we come to the more general trends and attitudes to work encountered in post-war conditions.

The most striking trend is the rise in acquisitive instincts as expressed in shop-floor behaviour. Money-mindedness plays an ever-increasing part in a man's attitude to his work. Frequently an applicant for a job would ask about the wages a job carried, but not about the nature and conditions of the work. Some skilled men take up unskilled work if they can earn more money at it. Men with long service often give up security of tenure and pension rights to earn more money. 'Ninety-five per cent of all grievances, complaints and squabbles on the floor are about money. It's money, money all the time'—both supervisors and shop-stewards agreed on this point. This is expressed also in the constant quest for overtime with which I deal in another context (see Chapter 12).

The other important and notable trend is the growing measure of satisfaction with work. Many more men are now satisfied with their work and working conditions than before the war. Many men whom I interviewed referred to their bad past. 'I enjoy my work now, but if you had asked me the same question before the war I would have said definitely not', or 'In my life I had jobs to endure, believe me. It was different in those days', or 'Compared with now the pre-war days were slavery. It is comfortable now, you can please yourself'; such were typical comments.

In many departments which I visited on my rounds I asked the supervisors: 'Have you any misfits here, somebody unhappy or out of place?' That made them think hard, and then usually, after a long while, they answered: 'No, not really; I can't think of any'. Sometimes a man suffering from nerves or a former inmate of a prisoner-of-war camp was mentioned. More often than not the man was a war or health casualty or the victim of a broken home. Some jobs were of course highly strenuous and their continuous performance required extra strength, or extra fitness and vigour. But they were usually sugar-coated in one way or another, and through the operation of the homeo-static principle to which I refer throughout this study, they ended up by being as desirable as the 'better' jobs. Somehow an equilibrating force seems to operate in such matters, equalizing the strains and stresses with rewards and inducements.

I often asked men whom I interviewed: 'If you had your own way, what improvements would you introduce in the works or in the department, apart from money of course?' Only on very rare occasions could I get any answer, and then only on very trivial things. 'No, I can't think of anything; the conditions are good.' Often the same answer came from the shop-steward and supervisor.

In the five works I visited I could say that there was very little sign of what is often called the 'alienation' of the workman from his work, or 'estrangement from society'. I had no feeling that the worker was estranged from society, or from the firm employing him. The tendency is, I think, for the worker to be brought nearer to the firm which gives him good treatment, a relatively good livelihood and a measure of security, and—this is perhaps the most significant development—for him to loosen the sense of identity with his own class, to which he is bound no longer by the links of common hardships, handicaps and injustices, and the constant call to arms in class-warfare.

12. THE QUEST FOR OVERTIME

OVERTIME WORKING has become a very important issue in British industry, with full employment on the one hand and a marked trend toward shorter standard hours on the other. The greater the scarcity of labour, the greater the call for overtime. This is especially true of skilled labour. Seasonal industries, like the motor industry, rely on regular overtime over longer periods.

The overtime problem has many facets; overtime can act as an incentive or a disincentive to taking and keeping a job, as a correction or distortion of the wage structure, as a stimulus, or as a drag on efficiency. It also presents a health and family problem.

The general attitude of men to overtime is governed by a set of contradictory forces. On the one hand they like, ask, or even clamour for overtime, on the other hand they hate it, object to it, or try to avoid it. Every individual strikes his own balance between those two contradictory forces. The prevailing attitude can be described in a generalization made by one foreman: 'If no overtime is worked they complain and some leave; if too much or too long overtime is worked, they complain again. They claim a right measure of overtime at the right time.'

From keen overtimers one can hear the general pronouncement 'Everybody cares for overtime: the extras make all the difference'; from those who object to overtime comes an opposite statement, 'Nobody really likes overtime: it's a social evil'. Both statements may be true, but they do not refer to the same thing; the first refers to extra money, the second refers to extra work.

The overtime behaviour is a most puzzling phenomenon but it becomes less puzzling if one or two facts are kept clearly in mind. The general or prevailing attitude to overtime differs from work-place to work-place according to innumerable institutional and personal factors, about which more will be said later, but one of the biggest factors is the regularity or sporadicalness of overtime. If regular overtime is worked over a longer period, overtime working becomes not only a habit ('I am used to it') but, what is even more important, overtime money becomes part of the regular wages, the standard of living is raised and the family soon becomes accustomed to it and takes it for granted. Then any fall in overtime becomes a shock and a bitter disappointment. Men on regular overtime buy houses, cars, and enter other long-term commitments, and when overtime suddenly stops they are in a quandary. In such cases one could hear such comments as: 'The men are extremely unhappy because there is little overtime now'. The management often warns the men: 'Do not count on overtime; do not take overtime for granted; arrange your standard of living on ordinary wages'. But in prosperity few men heed the warning, and when overtime is stopped there is a general outcry, and many go in search of jobs with overtime. The employment officers record that one of the first questions an applicant for a job asks is: 'Will I be able to work overtime?'

On the other hand some people do not like overtime for this very reason. As one man put it philosophically: 'If you get more money, you spend more. You get used to spending more money and when overtime is suddenly dropped you feel you have lost part of your wages and you become discontented.'

The other important institutional factor is the reduction of standard hours. Where standard hours have been recently reduced, men used to working longer hours are ready for more overtime. Men who are used to working six days a week, when five days a week becomes the standard practice, do not mind putting in an extra day for extra money. One can say that the general rule prevails: 'Shorter standard hours, longer overtime'. In full employment more overtime is a natural outcome of the trend for shorter standard hours. More overtime does not necessarily mean longer hours, it often means simply higher earnings with unchanged hours.

The Union allegiance, when strong, affects the overtime attitudes, but more in terms of lip service than of actual behaviour. The keen Unionist would say 'Overtime is a social evil', or 'It's a disease', or 'It's a disease with some people', or 'I'm against it on principle', or 'It should not be necessary'. Union-minded men often added: 'I like overtime provided it doesn't take away other people's jobs'. The Union officers regret the present scramble for overtime which they believe often goes against men's solidarity. Clamouring for overtime is regarded as 'money-grabbing'. 'Those men who are never satisfied with what they make' is the description of keen overtimers by Union officers. Fair shares in overtime is one of the principal pre-occupations of the men and a constant subject for Union intervention. In spite of the policy of fairness to which most foremen adhere, overtime is often used openly or in an underhand way as a bait and an incentive to do better, or as a reward.

There is one factor of a traditional nature which must be taken into account, that is, the distinction between housekeeping money and pocket-money which is usually made. In the large majority of cases overtime is not used for housekeeping money. Some men give a share of overtime money to the wife, but mostly as a treat or extra which is not included in the housekeeping allowance. 'It's pocket-money, and what I make on overtime is mine' was a remark I noted. This is the time when a man works for himself in the strictest sense, so when overtime is stopped men's pleasures are affected and they feel it badly. But it would be wrong to assume that overtime goes only for pocket-money; it is often used for short-term savings, especially for holidays. Cars are also a favourite target for overtime working.

There is one more reason why most men welcome overtime. As one foreman said: 'They feel more secure, when overtime is worked. As soon as overtime is stopped, they start worrying whether or not employment is falling off, and who will be the victim of the coming redundancy. Give them plenty of work to do, that is the general background for a good atmosphere.'

The willingness for and resistance to overtime varies with seasons, days and shifts. By and large shiftwork is not conducive to overtime working, and shift allowance is often meant also to compensate for loss of overtime earnings. Overtime is more often appreciated in winter than in summer, and on Saturday mornings more than on weekdays. Not by all, however; some, especially if they live far out, prefer weekday overtime, and they would say: 'If I am already here, I don't mind working longer hours.' Amongst weekdays, Monday overtime is not very much liked, as most men feel 'mondayish'. The best weekdays are Tuesday, Wednesday and Thursday. Friday night overtime is thoroughly disliked, not only because Friday is pay-day and there are social activities to take part in, but also because the men feel particularly tired. Sunday mornings are appreciated and refusal to work Sundays on religious grounds is practically unknown. As one manager put it: 'In all my twenty years' experience I can remember only one case of refusal to work Sundays on religious grounds.' Even Catholics do not object to Sunday work, but they invariably say: 'I do it but I don't like it; it is allowed, if it is a real necessity.'

The strongest objection is to Saturday afternoon, and this can be, in some places, a big issue, as was the case in Vauxhall. The management, American-inspired, contended that double time on Sunday should be paid only after a whole shift on Saturday had been worked; but the British worker loathes Saturday afternoon work more than anything else. In most work-places this is accepted as a matter of fact and Saturday afternoons are worked only as a last resort.

Now let us look more closely at the overtime behaviour at the personal level, as the outcome of personal and family relations.

Men can be classed here in four main groups: (1) Those who object to overtime; (2) Those who clamour for overtime ('I like overtime very much', or 'As much as I can get'); (3) Those who take their turn, but are glad to have it ('I like my share', or 'I am not grabbing. I take my turn'); and (4) Those who take their turn, but do not like it ('I am not fond of it, but I am ready', or 'If it is there, but not specially', or 'I never ask, but I never refuse').

There are two other special categories: (5) Sporadic overtimers—those who care for overtime only from time to time. They would say: 'When I need the money', or 'When I have something to clear'. (6) Those whose job requires regular overtime. These would answer, 'Overtime is part of my job; it can't be helped'. Maintenance men often belong to this category.

Most managers prefer the groups (3) and (4) to groups (1) and (2) as the latter are regarded as a liability. In most cases the moderate ones are more appreciated: those who clamour for overtime are regarded as a nuisance because when the management cannot provide them with overtime they become troublesome and often leave.

The distribution of these groups varies from works to works and from department to department, but in most cases the first two groups form a small minority, let us say between 10 to 15 per cent each, while the big majority is made up of groups (3) and (4).

To the first group belong the following examples:

A single man who pays high Income Tax ('I gain little by overtime').

A man without children, whose wife goes out to work ('If I had children it would be different').

A man who has strong hobbies or sidelines ('I keep pigs'; 'I conduct a choir'; 'I teach ballroom dancing'; 'I am a publican'; or 'I am a Scout leader').

A man whose wife is expecting a baby and he has to help her, or a man whose wife is ill, or a man whose wife works on Saturdays ('I have to do the shopping on Saturdays').

A man who is not well physically and whose work is already imposing a strain on him ('It's too long to be on your feet', or 'I am too tired').

A man getting on in years and approaching retirement ('I liked overtime when I was younger', or 'I would sooner have the weekend, it gives you a rest').

The second group is made up primarily of young married men who have just started building up their homes ('I want overtime to buy a house'), or by those with large families. 'With a family like mine,' said a man with five children, 'I want every bit of overtime I can get hold of.' Labourers or other low-rated men who can make a living wage only by working long hours, belong also to this category. I came across labourers who worked 60 to 70 hours regularly. There was also a sprinkling of very money-minded men who would say, 'I am a glutton for overtime. The more the better', or 'I love overtime; I was able to achieve so much through it'.

In group three men do not depend on overtime for their standard of living. They may say, 'I make a living wage', or 'Our standard of living is based on five days' work'. However, they welcome the extra and use it mostly for saving. When the question about saving was asked, often the answer was 'The overtime money'.

Group four comprises men who do not need the overtime money. Some are getting on in years ('Not at my time of life', they might say) and have few needs as their children have left them and their wives are working. 'We make enough as we are', or 'I don't need overtime; my wife is working as well' were typical comments from this group.

Women's work often restricts the demand for overtime as more money is coming into the house, but, on the other hand, it often whets the appetite for more possessions when a house has been bought or a car acquired.

Both the two last groups qualified their willingness to work overtime according to its duration. I heard the remarks: 'Not too much'; 'Up to a point'; 'In moderation'; 'I want one weekend in three free'; 'Every other weekend free'; 'One day in the week free'; 'Too much gets you down, you are ready for a break-down'; or 'Not too long spells of overtime'.

How does a rise in wage rates affect overtime behaviour? It releases two contradictory sets of forces. On the one hand the need for working overtime declines as more money comes in the regular wage packet, but on the other hand the incentive for overtime increases as the overtime rates are based on the new wage rates. The interplay between these two forces, combined with the number of situations sketched above, is actually governed by the changes in standard of living. If the standard of living is raised in a permanent way as a result of the increase in wage rates, then the need for overtime continues; on the other hand, if the traditional standard of living is maintained, the need for overtime declines. On the basis of my material I would say that the need for overtime continues: in most of the works I visited the quest for it was stronger than ever.

How does overtime affect home and family life? My material would suggest that about 10 per cent of men in most of the works I visited worked consistently long hours, in excess of 50 hours a week. I quote a few examples. A man of fifty-eight worked 66 hours; weekdays from 7.30 a.m. to 7 p.m., Saturdays from 8 a.m. to 5 p.m., Sundays from 8 a.m. to 1 p.m. He owned a car and apparently these long hours were paying for the car. But actually his only free time was Sunday afternoon, and he was so tired that he had to go straight to bed on that day. Another man of thirty-nine with one boy worked 63 hours, two hours longer than the normal time, three times a week, Saturday, 8 hours and Sunday, 5 hours. A number of skilled men worked 62, 60, 58, $56\frac{1}{2}$, 54 hours and so on.

Young men working long hours in order to secure a house or a car often over-reach themselves, leaving their wives too much alone. Weekend work in addition to women's work does not leave much of a home life. Fathers of young children hardly ever see them when they work long hours.

One frequent qualification put forward by the men, where irregular overtime was worked, was the demand for proper warning in advance. They wanted notice of overtime one or two days earlier so that proper arrangements could be made at home, as the wives objected to irregular overtime more than anything else.

'I like my home life too much to care for overtime', or 'I wouldn't like to spend my whole life in the factory', some men would say. But it looks as if some of them are spending practically their whole life in their work-place, having only one afternoon a week free. For them the long working week of nearly a century ago still obtains.

13. THE CHANGING ETHOS OF WORK

IN ORDER TO EXPLORE the ethos of work I asked a number of questions and I submitted provocative statements, asking the interviewees for their comments. The points involved were also discussed with managers, foremen and shop-stewards.

(1) *Does the job give you anything else apart from money?* This question was asked in one of the steelworks and one motorworks, and from time to time also elsewhere.

There seemed to be a difference in response between steelworks and motorworks. In the steelworks two in three answered 'yes', citing primarily comradeship, company, or sense of achievement, or saying, 'You learn something', or 'Passing the time', or 'Pleasure to earn your own living', or simply 'Interest'. Only one in three contended that the work gives only money, nothing else.

In the motorworks the relation was nearly reversed. The majority answered, 'Only money', the remainder quoted similar motives to those previously mentioned. This discrepancy may be partly explained by the greater strain caused by the speed of mass production and also by the fact that the labour force was recruited from young, energetic workers with a big carrot dangled under their noses.

But even amongst those who answered, 'Only money' one could detect a hesitant note; they were not quite sure about the other benefits derived from work. I am inclined to think that although they do not admit it, they are aware of those benefits.

(2) *Would you carry on in the job if you won thousands on the*

pools? This question was asked again in one of the steelworks and the motorworks.

In the mass-producing motorworks very few would have been willing to carry on in the job, although most of them said, 'I would have to do something', or 'I am an active sort of fellow, I can't sit idle'.

In the steelworks one in five contended that they would carry on with the job all the same, some adding, 'Perhaps not exactly the same, I would get rid of shiftwork', or 'I would get rid of dirty work'. The older men in their fifties or sixties would have retired altogether. A large number would have bought a shop or garage, a smallholding or some other small business of their own, or 'A hobby job', or 'Something that pleases me', or 'A gentleman's job'. A very interesting note was struck by a few men when they reasoned 'It would be selfish to take another man's job when you don't need the money'.

But the big majority reiterated that they couldn't 'Sit idle', arguing: 'If a man knocks off his work he may as well be dead', or 'You have to have a routine', or 'The job helps you to keep fit'.

(3) *Some people enjoy work, others tolerate it, still others endure it. What is your experience?* This question was asked in one of the engineering works. What came out was the general conclusion that although work is mainly for money, it has to be enjoyed and it can be enjoyed. The big majority said: 'It is a natural thing to enjoy it', or 'If I didn't enjoy it I would be miserable', or 'If I didn't enjoy it I would change my job', or 'It helps you if you enjoy it'.

A number of men qualified the statement by saying that the ability to enjoy one's work depends very much on the frame of mind: 'It depends how you feel', or 'I can't enjoy it always; the sun doesn't shine always either', or 'It is enjoyable most of the time', or 'I enjoy 90 or 80 per cent', or 'Sometimes work goes wrong and you have to endure it'. Some stumbled on what I regard as general truth about most men's jobs: 'It's a mixture of all three', or 'It's a very mixed bag; sometimes you enjoy it, sometimes tolerate it and sometimes endure it'. Only a very small minority contended that they merely endured their work.

So one can say that ethos of work demands that although one works for money that should not prevent one from enjoying the work one does.

(4) *'Better sit idle than work for naught'*: Would you agree with that? This provocative statement was submitted for comments in one of the engineering works. Most people disagreed with this saying, some in violent terms. 'Oh, no'—they would say, 'I would sooner do some work'. A number of reasons were given for this attitude: 'I can never sit idle'; 'Better to keep yourself busy'; 'It can't be any good to sit idle'; 'Retired people die quickly'; 'I do a lot of work for naught'; 'I like to do a little work for others'; 'I have worked many a time for nothing'; 'Better help others than sit idle'; 'Better to work for naught than to rot'; 'It is awful to sit idle'; 'I never like doing nothing'; 'I would say most emphatically no, you've got to keep your hands in working order; you can always keep working if only for yourself'. Some quoted a proverb: 'Idle hands work for the devil'.

Only a small minority agreed with this saying.

(5) *Work lends dignity to man:* this was submitted for comments in one of the engineering works.

Most men regarded this saying as far-fetched or untrue, when it was submitted to them in its positive formulation: 'Work has nothing to do with dignity', they said. Work is the essential factor in man's life, he would lose all interest in life but not dignity or self respect. 'I have no dignity by doing a piece of work.' Another man: 'To a Spanish peasant or an Italian pauper, yes, but not to an Englishman who takes his work for granted and expects to carry on his work day in day out.' Another man stressed the class aspect of this problem: 'If you have the money, you don't lose your self-respect if you don't work'.

However, a number of men agreed to this saying, arguing: 'It is man's nature that he should be working. It is not a natural thing to be out of work', or 'You have to do something to repay for what you are getting'.

It is interesting to note that when I formulated the question in this way: 'Can a man keep his self-respect if he is out of work for a considerable time?' the big majority agreed that it would be difficult for such a man to keep his self-respect. They said: 'He is more likely to be down in the dumps'; 'You are fed up with yourself and it is most difficult to keep the respect of your family and friends'; or 'When I was out of work I could keep my self-respect because at that time many were in the same position as me, through no fault of their own'. One man related his experience

'I was only eight weeks out of work, but how many times people asked me: "You are still out of work?" During that time when I stayed home I had more squabbles with my wife than we ever had during our whole married life. A man, to be a man, has to work and earn his living.'

In answer to my question: 'Does the work give you anything else apart from money?' not infrequently I came across a very curious remark: 'The passing of the time'. This remark gave me a good deal to think about. A number of men related their experience of sitting at home when they were not working, and most of them found that their wives do not want them at home when they have to attend to their routine, and they themselves are bored and dissatisfied, getting in trouble with their wives. They find that the job is necessary not only for their living but also for their mental health and emotional balance, that a certain routine 'is all to the good'. 'I was glad to be back', or 'It was good to be back', one heard from men who had been staying at home sick—or even after a holiday.

What conclusions can one draw from all these probings? It is clear that the idea of 'the natural human aversion to work' of which Sigmund Freud [1] and many others speak gives only one side of the picture. The syndrome 'Unhappiness and work' may have been a fact in the past and it may still occur here and there, but there is very little of it in modern, well-organized and well-run industrial establishments. Work has been since immemorial times both a curse and a blessing but in all those places which I visited it had very little, if any, of the character of a curse and a great deal of the character of a blessing.

One can definitely say that the ethos of work is undergoing a change for the better, and is assuming a much more positive valuation than before the war. In all those work-places I visited the big majority were doing well, pulling their weight and in most cases enjoying or liking, or good humouredly tolerating their job; only the odd ones were out of harmony with the place. This, I think, was partly achieved by improvements in the works and partly by the adjustment of the workers, who are becoming more

---

[1] 'The great majority work only when forced by necessity, and this natural human aversion to work gives rise to the most difficult social problems'—*Civilization and its Discontents*, Institute of Psycho-Analysis, London, 1930, p. 34.

and more adapted to the smooth running of factory life. One could say that the workers in these places were part of the smoothly and efficiently-running pieces of industrial machinery. The pessimist would speak about the de-humanizing effects of a thorough-going process of industrialization, and perhaps there is some truth in what he says. The optimist would point to the process of adjustment which has taken place on both sides, meeting half-way. The process of de-humanizing human beings by the impact of industrial machinery is partly offset by the process of humanizing the machine itself, as the factory pays an ever greater attention to the personal and human needs of its workers.

14. CONTACTS WITHIN THE WORKING GROUP

I OFTEN ASKED MEN working in a team: 'Who are your mates, and how many do you work with?' And often men on the same job gave me a different answer. When a craftsman worked with his mates permanently or when men helped each other as one team, sharing in one bonus, the answer was simple, but the majority of cases were much more complicated. Most men were very uncertain in answering this question. Some said: 'All the men in my department', others: 'Those who work nearest to me'; still others: 'Those who are on the same job'. So on the same job the number of workmates quoted could be anything from one or two to fifty or so.

Let us take a specific example from a steelworks. In one department, the Bessemer, there were three teams of men, fifty-four men in each, serving one or two furnaces on each shift and sharing the same tonnage money. Among them thirty-five men had a definite place in production, while eighteen to twenty men who had no definite jobs were assisting generally as required. There were groups of jobs, as for instance three vesselmen, No. 1 to No. 3 according to seniority with different rates of pay, three pitmen, three or four ladlemen with their assistants, four crane drivers and so on. The most senior post was that of the blower who was in sole control of the process. When I asked a vesselman who his mates were, one would answer: 'All men on the shift', another: 'The two other vesselmen', still another: 'The vesselman who releases me on the next shift' (he cannot go home before his mate on the next shift takes over); still others might include the crane driver who served him or the slinger.

The question: 'Who is your leader?' asked in the same department was also answered differently by men on the same job. One would say: 'The blower who is actually in control of the process', another might say, if he were a vesselman: 'The first vesselman', or if he were a pitman: 'The first pitman'; still others might say: 'The foreman', or 'The shift manager'—who holds the position of the highest authority on the shift. Authority, as far as men are concerned, is actually split between the blower, the foreman and the shift manager, even if one disregards the Union delegate who would have a great deal to say if something unexpected happened or a change were required. Apart from these there may also be informal leaders who may work hand-in-hand, with or against the managerial set-up.

In this particular instance out of three teams working in the Bessemer, one team, let us call it No. 1, was the best team, both in terms of quality and quantity performance, and whenever the manager had special orders to fulfil, he entrusted them to this team. The team spirit in this group was very strong, there was pride in the performance of the team, the blower and foreman always held a very united front, and there was no disrupting personality among the informal leaders, who worked hand-in-hand with the management.

In many instances the working group was even more complex and more difficult to determine. Actually a worker entering a modern factory becomes a focus of a whole web of group relations, not of a single group. We can distinguish as least four types of groupings, basically different, partly competing and partly co-operating with each other, crossing each other's path and often overlapping.

One would be the strictly bureaucratic grouping devised from above by the management, let us say a unit under one foreman. From the example just quoted we can see how the authority in this unit can be split. In an engineering factory of any size the authority is actually split between a foreman, personnel manager, rate-fixer, chaser, inspector and maintenance engineer. This group may be further sub-divided into smaller units under charge-hands, leading-hands and so on.

There is another grouping, which we may call semi-formal, where men are on a collective bonus (often called 'pools') or where men, although not on a collective bonus, work in close proximity under one informal leader. This group may not be homogeneous, it may comprise skilled men and semi-skilled, sharing the same bonus, or men on two shifts, sometimes it may comprise everybody working on one floor, producing one type of product, or completing one cycle of operations in a phase of production, or linked by specific working conditions or by targets of output.

The third type or grouping is the Trade Union operating at the level of a plant or its department. The department in which a man works under a foreman may have its own labour unit represented by a shop-steward or Union delegate, and often the foreman cannot undertake many changes without consulting the shop-steward.

Finally we have a whole net of informal groupings, such as tea and dinner groups, faction groups of different kinds, length-of-service groups, craft or job groups, regional groups, age groups and so on. Sometimes men, when asked about their mates, would answer: 'I haven't what you might call a mate in my own department but I have one in the next building'.

The behaviour of the industrial worker can never be satisfactorily described in terms of any one of these groupings above. There is no one single group which can claim to be in full control of his behaviour and attitudes. Management only or management and Union jointly cannot claim that they are or can be in full social control of the worker. The behaviour of the worker must be described in terms of all these four types of grouping in their mutual relationship and interplay.

One of my standard questions was: 'How do you get on with your mates?' and the answer was, in the overwhelming majority of cases, 'Very well', or 'The finest lot', or 'We have our ups and downs but it's never serious'. Actually the comradeship as revealed in the answers seemed cordial but not intimate. It entailed helping one another during the work and conversing during the break, mostly on such topics as sport or T.V. programmes or other leisure-time activities, or girls in general, but very rarely on their own home life.

I would describe the trend as a widening of contacts but at the same time with a definite decline in intensity. With the growing size of factories, the specialization of functions within the factory and functionalization of management, the working groups have multiplied out of all proportions and the group life has become extremely complex and varied. But with the growing complexity of the group life, the integration and cohesiveness of the group has declined practically at the same pace. The workman is less centred and less focused in one single group, he is more 'floating' as he has links with many groups, but of a more ephemeral character. The foreman has become an administrator; he is rarely a leader of the group as he used to be, and he is no longer the centre or focus of group interests. Even in regard to the works as a whole, the process of identification of the worker has become more difficult and more complex. Who is the real manager for the workmen? He often does not know. In a firm of some size there are departmental managers, functional managers, a works manager, general manager, general director, and finally, the members and chairman of the Board.

This multiplication and atomization of working groups has many effects on the position and the mind of the worker. On the one hand there is little doubt that men are sheltered from the abuse of power and authority to which they were exposed previously in a more concentrated group with one leader of real authority. If the foreman was a bully, tending to abuse his authority, the position of men under him was much worse than nowadays. The divided authority constitutes a defence against abuse and maltreatment.

The divided authority also provides the worker with a wider range of choice between groups. In a sense he can choose the group with which he wants to identify himself. On the other hand he is left more to himself, which may affect his sense of security. He feels more of an individual, as the cohesion of the group has declined and the number of groups multiplied. But he may feel also lost in the amorphous, gigantic mass of circles of authority, groups, equipment and men called the Firm or Company.

The multiplication and atomization of the working groups is a very important process, of far-reaching implications for modern society.

15. HOME AND WORK UPSETS

'HOME AND WORK DON'T MIX.' This is a phrase which often circulates among working men. It means that 'You should leave home at home, and work at work', or 'Once you leave work, forget it'. As one man said: 'When you clock out, clock out your mind'. Others said: 'It is a mistake to carry your work home'; 'Enough time is spent in work without taking it home'; or 'I try to keep home and work separate'.

Work matters are rarely mentioned at home. Men would say when I asked about it: 'My wife never asks me and I never tell her', or 'I never talk shop at home', or 'My wife asks when I come home, "Have you had a good day?" and I answer, "All right" and that's all', or 'Only if something extraordinary happens I mention it', or 'My wife doesn't pretend to know about my job so she doesn't ask'.

Work means tension, and home is for relaxation. Men would say: 'I never mention work at home otherwise I would never relax', or 'Home is entirely different, it's for relaxing', or 'You have to refresh and renew yourself. Home should give you strength for the next day.'

Only a small minority carry their work home, mostly those who have a leading position or do a very skilled job. A foreman would say: 'It is impossible not to carry your work home although I try not to', or 'I carry the usual foreman's worries with me'. That is one of the reasons why some men do not care for promotion.

Whenever the wife is conversant with the kind of work her husband does, if for instance she was on similar work during the war, or she has a similar job, as was often the case in Mullard, or when the wife is especially affectionate and concerned about her husband, talking shop occurs more frequently. In these cases men would say: 'My wife is very interested in what I am doing', or 'My wife takes an intelligent interest; she knows all about the job', or 'When I have a bad day, she knows at once and I have to tell her'.

In Sheffield when the works were opened to the families of the work-people during the so-called 'Open Week', one in three wives visited the work-place. The remainder did not avail themselves of this opportunity. One of the characteristic answers came to one husband who asked his wife whether she would like to visit the works: 'Don't you think it's enough if *you* have to go to that place?'

Although 'home and work don't mix' in the normative sense, they do in fact influence each other in more than one way. A man cannot help comparing his home and his factory, the two places where most of his time is spent. Men with clean homes demand clean and tidy work-places, and men working in clean and tidy factories demand also a higher standard at home. There is a subconscious connection between the standards in each place. At one time standards in both places were not very high, but now they are rising rapidly.

Formerly, the men who were bullied at work bullied their wives and children in turn. The authoritarian system at work was linked with the authoritarian system at home—I have already referred to this in another context. The type of discipline which is imposed at work may not be directly transferable in full measure to the home, but has a definite bearing on the type of discipline which a man tries to impose on those under his authority. This is most clearly seen in the case of foremen who are often reminded by their wives: 'You're not in the factory; you can't be a foreman to your children'. Some foremen, when asked about this, denied this transfer: 'I have enough men at work to order about. I don't need to order my children about.'

Work and home intermingle also under the head of worries, troubles and upsets. A good home background makes a good worker while a bad home is the root cause of many difficulties at work. Many foremen stated this as an undeniable fact: 'Whenever the quality of work deteriorates I come up and ask the man what is the matter, and in most cases it's a family upset which causes it'. Or as another foreman put it: 'When they have troubles with their wives, they are embittered, they lose interest in their job. They don't do a clean piece of work and don't seem to pull with their mates.'

Speaking about home and work upsets, we can distinguish three basic situations:

(1) A man has troubles at home as well as at work. This is, of course, the worst situation, as one aggravates the other. Troubles

at work do not necessarily mean upsets, but they may lead to situations which impose a great deal of strain and worry. Foremen, charge-hands or leading-hands in responsible positions often find themselves in such situations. I came across cases where foremen or potential foremen had to give up their positions as they could not stand the combined weight of worries at home and at work. In typical cases a wife had to have an operation, or was suffering from heart attacks, or a child was dangerously ill, ot there was an emotional upset with the wife and the foreman felt that he was heading for a break-down.

(2) A man has home upsets while the work is straightforward, not presenting special strain or worry. We have to distinguish here between major upsets such as those caused by estrangement from a wife or separation, or by the death of relatives (I report them in special chapters), or ill-health in the family on one hand, and minor troubles and worries on the other. The first kind finds expression in loss of shifts and inability to concentrate. 'The work becomes harder, your hands are not steady,' men with such experience would say. Or as one man put it: 'If a man cannot sleep and relax at home, of course it affects his work. Many accidents happen through home worry. A man's mind is not there.'

A man of fifty-seven said: 'My daughter was partly paralysed and ill for many years. For eight years I lost practically ten to twelve weeks in shifts yearly, and in one year twenty-two shifts. I contracted many illnesses, all through worry.' Several years previously his daughter had recovered, and so had he. It is little realized that illnesses may not only be psycho-somatic but they may also have a social dimension. One illness in a family may bring in its wake other illnesses.

A man of fifty-two, a widower who had married again, had a wife with a weak heart, who had suffered two strokes and partial paralysis over several years. He lost many shifts and could not concentrate on his work. He lost a job on the machine where he was working. 'You can't be a good workman if you have lost a good home, if your mind is not at rest.'

A man of fifty-three had a wife who had suffered a nervous break-down after her last baby and, on the advice of her doctor, had left home for a while to join her mother. 'It was very hard to get on with my job during that time—although you can't afford to let your mind run away with you.'

In the case of small troubles and worries at home, work is more often a help, providing a balancing factor. Men often referred to this and women even more frequently. Out of sixty-two women operatives in Mullard, to whom I submitted the statement: 'Those unhappy at home cannot be happy at work', for their comments, twenty-four contended that they often forget their troubles and worries while at work if they were not too great. These women said: 'Little things are forgotten at work, they come back when you get home'; 'You can keep your mind off your troubles'; 'I forget myself, I lose myself here'; 'When my son was stationed in Cyprus it helped me to forget'; 'Better off at work with small worries'; 'You can forget if your worry is not too great'; 'Here, I get away from my troubles'; 'When I had a nervous break-down, following a series of deaths at home, I went on short time; the doctor did not let me stop working and I felt better for it'; 'Instead of nagging the husband we let off steam at work'; and even 'I am happier at work than at home'.

These women often referred to the possibility of confiding in their workmates as the main factor in bringing relief. 'I confide and I feel better for it,' they said, or 'I am one of those who cannot keep their troubles to themselves', or 'Women confide more than men, they relieve their mind'. On the other hand there were those who said: 'I don't confide', or 'I don't display my feelings; those who can are better for it'.

(3) Some men have upsets at work while their home life is normal. This affects their home life to a certain degree but to a much smaller extent than home upsets affect their work life. One man put it in the following way, comparing home upsets with work upsets: 'While I cannot help bringing my troubles from home to work, I don't take my work troubles home. You can't switch your mind completely from your home because it is so much deeper than the work.' Another man said, 'It is easier to leave work at work than home at home'. Most men would deny that upsets at work have an effect on their home life to any extent, unless they are very bad. However, a number of men confided: 'When I have a bad day, naturally it affects my mood and behaviour. We are all flesh and blood'; or 'After nights I am irritable'; or 'If you are not careful it can affect your home'; or 'If I have a bad day at work I feel niggly and snappy at home'; or 'It does happen at times that I feel grumpy after a bad day'.

As for social change, I believe the separation between work and home is in fact greater now than formerly in the sense that the home is now more insulated against the adverse effects of factory life. Previously a man used to bring work home in the form of dirt in his clothes; now more often he has a bath provided by the firm. He used to bring work home in the form of anxiety, perhaps as to whether he would be able to hold his job; now security of employment is much more general. He also used to have more frequent conflicts with his workmates with whom he was competing, or with his foreman who told him 'to get on or get out'. He used to be more tired, working longer hours under more strenuous conditions than now. Now when he gets home he not only wants to forget about his work but is also more able to do so as the job rarely carries a great load of frustrations, anxieties and conflicts. He is rarely pushed and driven, he is rarely offended in a way which could involve his self-respect. He does not need to keep his resentment or grievances, he can voice them freely, and can lodge his complaints. He still, so to speak, wears a mask while at work, but wearing it is not such a strain as it used to be. He feels better adjusted all round, so when he comes home he is not so 'bottled up' as he used to be.

PART FOUR

Culture, Leisure and Social Contacts

16. CULTURAL HORIZONS

THE STUDY OF CULTURAL HORIZONS was one of the most fascinating sidelines of the enquiry. In fact it opened up a new line of investigation in its own right, which may throw light on the question of how far the working classes take part in the cultural activity of the nation. Has progress in prosperity been accompanied by progress in culture? Are cultural values absorbed from the new media of mass communication? Is there any real desire to acquire knowledge beyond the immediate range of utility, or to enjoy art and learn to appreciate it more? What are the lines of most fruitful contact with the culture of the nation?

To help to answer those questions, however fragmentarily, I devised what I called 'tests for cultural horizons' based on sixteen names derived from literature, science and learning, art and religion. The question was asked: 'Have you heard of Byron, Shelley, Sir Walter Scott, Rudyard Kipling, Sigmund Freud, Karl Marx, Albert Einstein, Charles Darwin, Michelangelo, Rembrandt, Picasso, Buddha, Mohammed, Confucius, John Wesley and Martin Luther.'

A sheet of paper containing a list of these names was given to the interviewee to read, and I read out the names one by one. When Sir Walter Scott was mixed up with Robert Scott the explorer, or Einstein with Epstein the sculptor, or Karl Marx with the Marx brothers, the name was repeated.

This test, on a strictly uniform basis to make comparisons possible, was given to 115 men in Dunlop, 101 men in Mullard and sixty-seven women in Mullard.

Previously I had experimented with various sets of other

names in Vauxhall where 114 men were tested in this way. The names were, apart from Freud, Marx, Einstein and Darwin, already mentioned, Bach, Beethoven, Mozart and Chopin, Dickens, Bernard Shaw, H. G. Wells, Tolstoy, Dostoievski, Gandhi and Albert Schweitzer.

The interviewees took a fancy to this part of the interview. They regarded it as a sort of a game and we always had a laugh about it. 'You take me right back to school', some of my interlocutors said with a smile. Only a few knew all the names listed, and there was a great deal of guessing about the unknown names, as apparently most men want to pass for more knowledgeable than they are. There was a fair amount of exchange of questions between me and the interviewees and usually some discussion followed about the nature of ideas and values connected with the names. I have to explain that the question was not whether the interviewees knew anything about the works, ideas, theories or values of those listed, or had read their writings or about them, but only whether they had heard their names and could identify them as writers, men of science and learning of one sort or another, artists or religious figures.

If they said, for instance, as many did: 'Marx—the Communist', or 'The great Russian bloke', or 'Something to do with the Russian revolution', or 'Darwin—the monkey bloke', or 'Shelley and Byron—writers', or 'Buddha—an Eastern idol', or 'Eastern God', or 'Mohammed—an Egyptian God', or 'The bloke they pray to in the Middle East', or 'John Wesley—the Archbishop', or 'Walter Scott and Rudyard Kipling—something to do with writing'—a credit was given to them.

But if they said: 'Einstein the singer', or 'Writer of detective stories', or 'Buddha the Indian ruler', or 'Indian cricketer', or 'Mohammed an Egyptian something', or 'Michelangelo the horse in the Grand National', or 'Rembrandt the greyhound', or 'Picasso the boxer', or 'Darwin the T.V. personality' (maybe they heard the name of Darwin mentioned in a T.V. programme), or 'Sigmund Freud a song writer'—a failure was recorded.

The answers often revealed their interests more than anything else. A boxer took everybody for a boxer, convinced that all famous names must come from sport; a dog- or horse-racing fan said the same about racing, and a T.V. addict about T.V. personalities, and so on. There was also a fair amount of guessing by some who did not know a single name. They disposed of the whole list by a single phrase such as: 'Actors, aren't they?' or 'Comedians', or 'T.V. personalities', or 'High-ups, I don't care'. These felt that any great names worth mentioning must come from the world of entertainment—the world of splash and glitter, the modern Olympus on which the high-ups dwell in splendour.

A number of men said: 'I know the name but I can't place him', or 'It's a long time since I heard those names', or 'I heard such names on T.V. but it is a job to remember them all'.

Now let us look at the results. Certain regularities emerged which held good in all places of enquiry.

In Vauxhall, where I asked about the names of Bach, Beethoven, Mozart and Chopin, out of forty-two only one man did not know the names of Mozart and Chopin. I discontinued this question as obviously the names of great musicians are known to practically everyone. This is probably due to the effect of Radio and T.V.

As to the rest, the pattern of knowledge repeated itself in all firms: writers were the best known, then painters, religious figures, men of science and learning, in that order.

In Dunlop and Mullard where a uniform test was given the following pattern emerged:

Out of 115 men in Dunlop (averaging the answers in specified groups):

    82 knew the names of writers
    63 ,, ,, ,, ,, artists
    46 ,, ,, ,, ,, religious figures
    29 ,, ,, ,, ,, scientists and men of learning

In Mullard out of 101 men:

    87 knew the names of writers
    70 ,, ,, ,, ,, artists
    48 ,, ,, ,, ,, religious figures
    37 ,, ,, ,, ,, scientists and men of learning

Women in Mullard showed a similar gradation, although on a lower level. Out of 67:

    46 knew the names of writers
    38 ,, ,, ,, ,, artists
    17 ,, ,, ,, ,, religious figures
    8 ,, ,, ,, ,, scientists and men of learning

In these groups (in both firms) there was also an astonishing similarity in gradation of knowledge of single names. Among writers Kipling came first and Byron second, among artists Rembrandt first, Picasso second, among religious figures Buddha and Mohammed were leading, among scientists and men of learning the gradation in all three firms, including Vauxhall, was the same: Marx came first, then followed Albert Einstein, Charles Darwin and Sigmund Freud in that order. Out of 329 men in three firms, 132 knew the name of Marx—which is roughly speaking 40 per cent; Einstein was known by 127 men, Darwin by 113 (although only 320 were asked about Darwin), Freud by fifty-five.

Women showed a similar gradation, but the range was sharper. Out of sixty-seven women, Marx was known to eleven, Darwin to nine, Einstein to eight, and Freud to three.

A marked regularity, apparent in all three firms, concerned the gradation in standards of cultural horizons between skilled men and non-skilled (semi-skilled and labourers). In Dunlop, out of twenty-two skilled men twelve scored 10 plus (10 or more), while out of eighty-five non-skilled only twenty-three scored 10 plus. In Mullard out of thirty-two skilled men twenty-three scored 10 plus, while out of sixty non-skilled, twenty-five. Men who had a skill of their own, but had discarded it, being at present on non-skilled operation, scored above the other non-skilled men (in both firms out of thirteen such men six scored 10 plus).

Women operatives in Mullard scored below the level of non-skilled men in Mullard; out of sixty-seven women, seventeen scored 10 plus. This was not, however, below the level of non-skilled men in Dunlop.

The supervisors in Dunlop scored much above the level of skilled men; practically all of them scored 10 plus, though in Mullard they scored somewhat below the level of skilled men.

In Vauxhall, although no uniform test was given, I could see the superiority of the standard of cultural horizons among the supervisors over skilled men and that of the latter over non-skilled.

The greatest gap between the standard of skilled and non-skilled men occurred in the tests for names from science and learning. Out of twenty-two skilled men in Dunlop, three or four names in this field were known to eight men, while out of eighty-five non-skilled men they were known only to eleven. The same pattern also occurred in Mullard.

However, the greatest surprise came from the comparison of scores between age groups, and here again the same gradation in scores repeated itself in both firms, Dunlop and Mullard. The most knowledgeable were men of the age group thirty to forty-nine. Out of 131 men in this age group, sixty-nine scored 10 plus. The standard declined sharply with age. Only thirteen out of fifty-six in the age group of fifty or more scored 10 plus. The age group twenty to twenty-nine was also below that of the middle age group. Out of twenty-nine in this age group only ten scored 10 plus. Actually the outstanding group as far as cultural horizons were concerned were those between thirty-five and forty-nine. I wonder whether the deficiencies in war-time education were partly responsible for these differences.

I also asked myself whether property owners were not scoring higher as they often struck me as brighter—not simply because they owned property but because they were often more daring and enterprising, more inclined towards self-improvement. In fact their score was higher than for non-skilled men and closely approached the standard of skilled men.

Objections might be made to the method of scoring, which was based on an unweighted point-system in which all names were given equal value. However, I believe that any other method would lead to similar results, and this system of scoring is the simplest and least controversial.

I shall now give an account of my experimental tests in Vauxhall. I wondered whether famous foreign writers of international standing were known to any extent, and in Vauxhall I asked 110 men about Tolstoy and Dostoiewski. Tolstoy proved much better known: twenty-seven men who heard this name could identify it, while only seven men had heard about Dostoiewski. Obviously international literature has little significance for working-class culture. One could say that this culture is much more national in character than that of other classes.

As the working man's culture is mainly absorbed from newspapers, radio, T.V. and cinemas, those names with news value are known much more than any others. Billy Graham was known to practically everybody whom I asked, but not Buddha, Mohammed or Confucius.

One can say also that the working man's culture is much more 'present-day minded' than that of other classes. The cultural heritage from the past is not absorbed to the same extent as present-day elements of culture. I could see this quite clearly in regard to literature. Bernard Shaw and H. G. Wells are much better known than Kipling, Byron, Shelley or Sir Walter Scott, though there are special reasons for the popularity of Bernard Shaw or H. G. Wells amongst the working classes. Out of ninety-three men in Vauxhall whom I asked about Bernard Shaw and H. G. Wells, only four did not know the name of Bernard Shaw and eight of H. G. Wells. From the past Dickens remains unsurpassed in popularity. Only seven out of ninety-three did not know his name.

What are the main questions arising from the tests and what conclusions can one draw from the results? Did performance in the test provide a clue to mental ability and intelligence? Would the test performance be related to I.Q.? Personally I believe it would—but how closely it is difficult to tell. Most men who ranked low in the test performance expressed themselves very poorly and their vocabulary was rather scanty. Names listed were frequently referred to as 'blokes'—a religious bloke, Eastern bloke, Russian bloke and so on. Sometimes, however, even among these men one could meet a wit and intelligence which was rather surprising. They had native reserves of intelligence which had not been tapped and which might perhaps have been developed by stimulation from outside.

However, those who scored zero in most cases showed a blank mind. Altogether there were twelve men out of 210 in Dunlop and Mullard who scored zero (nine in Dunlop, three in Mullard, and none of these were among skilled men or supervisors). In addition, four women operatives out of sixty-seven scored zero. So about 5 per cent scored zero and in fact they were in most cases dullards. They were often poor readers in the sense that they could hardly read or they were not used to reading.

The test performances also show (if such proof is necessary) that a man's mind is an extremely selective instrument. If a person is not interested in ideas, or they are beyond his reach, names like Marx, Darwin, Buddha or Rembrandt can be repeated to him a hundred times and they will not penetrate the wall of his indifference. One may argue that television could and should aim at higher cultural standards, but the fact is that programmes which are beyond the reach or interest of certain layers of society cannot penetrate these walls, which are so well protected from the intrusion of anything outside the interest of the recipient.

How is it possible, we may wonder, that 60 per cent of the men did not recognize the name with which the greatest conflict of our time is linked? Some people might take the view that it is a very good thing if the majority of workers do not know the name of Karl Marx, if they prefer Groucho Marx to Karl Marx, and Marks and Spencer to Karl Marx and Herbert Spencer. But can this view be accepted at a time when the world finds itself at a crossroads where one way bears the name of Marx?

The prevailing image of Marx amongst the men I met is that of the 'Russian', or the 'Communist' (the two concepts tend to merge into one), or 'The man of the Russian revolution', or 'the Russian Dictatorship'. It has a derogatory undertone. It is strange how certain ideas are concretized in simple images and phrases with an undertone of appreciation or disapproval. By the same token, Darwin was described as the 'Monkey Man', Einstein as 'the great mathematician', Buddha—'the Eastern Idol' and so on.

The results of these tests can give one a good deal to think about, and may also provide grounds for social action, if the public becomes aware of the fact that 'the two nations' may be a thing of the past in terms of economics but not in terms of education and culture. One cannot help feeling deeply disturbed at the apparent waste of human intelligence amongst manual workers. An enormous amount still remains to be done in the field of adult education.

The worker is now more prosperous than ever, and prosperity is often regarded as a prelude to art and learning. So we may hope that the rise in his cultural standards will come about in due course, provided that he is not deflected by vested interests into the marshlands of the candyfloss world. I believe all classes and all human beings have a right to participate in all the activities of culture up to their full capacity, as much as they have a right to participate in the wealth and income of the nation, up to the capacity of their productive powers.

17. PASTIMES, HOBBIES AND SIDELINES

WORKERS' HOBBIES, I thought, could throw an important light on the main theme of my enquiry, as they would indicate how leisure was used, and so I devoted a good deal of time to the exploration of this subject. The subject itself formed the easiest and most pleasant part of the interview and I often found it convenient to start the interview with a chat on hobbies. No one regarded this as a waste of time as the theme is interesting in itself and so much can be said about it. But although the obtaining of the material was the easiest, its presentation is the most difficult.

After all, what is a hobby? In a larger sense every pastime might be called a hobby, apart perhaps from drinking and gambling which have rather a negative connotation. The same activities were regarded by some as hobbies, by others not. For most men gardening was not regarded as a hobby. Some said: 'I have to', or 'It's a necessity but I don't like it'. Such men were perhaps living in a council house where keeping up the garden was obligatory, or were living in their own house and wanting to make it look respectable. Others kept a greenhouse and loved it, going in for shows and prizes, and a few developed gardening into a 'sideline', from which they could make extra money.

Many men were busy with what are called 'do-it-yourself' activities, but only a few recorded these as hobbies. Not all men with cars and motor cycles regarded motoring as a hobby; if they had had the vehicle for a long time, they took it for granted. It seems that the time factor plays an important part in deciding whether certain activities are classed as hobbies or not; some men had noticed this themselves. It was most clearly seen in the attitude to T.V., as some men who had recently acquired it, gave 'T.V.-watching' as their hobby. So a hobby is not a statistical unit. What one mentions as a hobby another takes for granted, saying that he has no hobby. One man gives his main hobby, others present you with a whole list of hobbies.

The data for hobbies are available for 114 men in Sheffield, 104 in Workington, 119 in Vauxhall, 115 in Dunlop and 101 in Mullard, both single and married men. In reviewing the data one has to keep in mind that one and the same man can appear under various headings, as he can be interested in gardening, house decoration, joinery, motoring, photography and so on.

The first question I asked myself was, how much of a man's leisure time is absorbed by his house and family? I asked specifically about gardening and 'Do it yourself' in four works and I give the results below, including also those who gave 'home' or 'family' as their main hobby.

	Gardening	'Do-it-yourself'	Home
Workington	37	40	6
Vauxhall	46	35	18
Dunlop	59	43	3
Mullard	47	30	9

Of course some men in this table appear under all three headings, others under two or one. But it is clear that most men are quite busy with their home and family.

The second question was this: Are the active sports, i.e., outdoor games, on the decline, or are they holding their own? Most of my informants contended that active participation in sports among working-class men is a declining affair, that most men from their early thirties content themselves with watching sports. The playing of games has a strong regional background: Rugby was mentioned only in Workington, and golf only in Birmingham. Very little tennis and hockey is played. Outdoor games, by which I mean football, cricket, Rugby, golf, tennis, hockey, were played by the following numbers:

Workington	9
Vauxhall	8
Dunlop	11 (including three golfers)
Mullard	7
Sheffield	10

But there were many other outdoor activities which also have a strong local background. Fishing, for instance, was conspicuous in Sheffield, where twenty-one men recorded it as their main hobby. This consisted of both pleasure and match fishing. (Match fishing is an organized excursion, involving 1,000 or more men, with prizes for the best angler and a great deal of betting. The cost of participation in such a trip is between 15s and £1 including the railway ticket.) In other places only a few men recorded angling as their hobby: seven in Dunlop, six in Vauxhall, five in Workington (sea-fishing) and two in Mullard. Climbing or walking, cycling or Youth Hostelling were mentioned mostly in Workington (nine men) and Sheffield (seven), both cities having an easy access to most beautiful scenery in Cumberland and Derbyshire. In other places it was only mentioned occasionally. Breeding and racing pigeons was also a speciality of Workington where five men mentioned this as their main hobby. Outside Workington pigeons were hardly mentioned. Breeding budgerigars was mentioned a number of times. Bowling was favoured by the older men and there was a whole list of indoor games—billiards, snooker (in Dunlop six men mentioned this), darts, dominoes (five men in Dunlop), cards, table tennis and so on. Dancing was mentioned only occasionally by younger men—four in Vauxhall, two in Workington, two in Mullard and three in Dunlop.

Now let us come to what may be termed constructive hobbies such as woodwork (joinery) and model-making (model railways, aeroplanes, boats, and so on):

	Woodwork	Model-making
Sheffield	4	3
Workington	5	4
Vauxhall	10	3
Dunlop	8	3
Mullard	6	7

The figures in this table do not seem to suggest that the interest in constructive hobbies is dying out. Besides those mentioned above, some were also engaged on repairs of all sorts such as car repairs, shoe repairs, watch repairs, upholstery repairs, sewing and making clothes. Radio and T.V. repairs were a speciality of Mullard men where four mentioned this as their main hobby while only two mentioned it in Sheffield, one in Dunlop and one in Vauxhall.

Arts and crafts are also fairly represented among the workers' hobbies as the following table shows:

	Drawing and painting	Photography	Instrument playing	Singing
Sheffield	2	4	2	2
Workington	2	3	4	2
Vauxhall	1	2	4	2
Dunlop	0	3	1	0
Mullard	1	6	2	2

The interest in music is very widespread, as can be seen from the number of radiograms and record players in the possession of men—quoted in another context.

The list of hobbies is practically inexhaustible and every imaginable occupation appears here, such as bar-tending in a club, hair-dressing, bricklaying for friends, shooting rats, shooting birds, bee-keeping, bird-watching, wine-making, sitting in the courts at the Assizes and listening to the cases, political canvassing, youth-club work, committee work of various kinds, church work (including preaching), and so on.

Now we come to 'sidelines', by which I mean subsidiary activities which produce earnings. We have seen that the most popular pastimes are those which can be classed as useful pursuits, such as gardening, house decoration, making or repairing things, or breeding animals. These are often turned into sidelines. I listed those who have a definite sideline, without counting doubtful or marginal cases, as follows:

Sheffield	6
Workington	8
Vauxhall	7
Dunlop	6
Mullard	6

The outstanding sidelines were: running a public house, running an agency, selling secondhand clothes on a barrow, keeping pigs (one man had forty to fifty animals), keeping poultry (one man had 500 birds), running and racing dogs (one man had eleven dogs in two acres of ground of his own), running a grocery shop, running a confectionery and tobacconist shop, caretakers' jobs, market gardening, upholstering, teaching music, teaching ballroom dancing, semi-professional entertainment (one man was making £6 a week for singing in clubs), radio and T.V. repairs, car repairs, clerical work for a bookmaker, debt collecting for a company and so on.

From this brief review we can see what an enormous variety of pastimes, hobbies and sidelines was cultivated. It was clear that most of them centred round the home and family or were useful pursuits. We see the working man as a very busy person with little time to spare. The pressure on his leisure time is considerable and comes from many quarters. Watching television takes time, motoring for those who have cars, gardening for those who have a garden, 'Do-it-yourself' for those who have a council house or a house of their own. So the time available for more constructive hobbies is restricted but, on the other hand, the worker now has more money for these hobbies if he wants to pursue them. Many working men are venturing into new fields of hobbies which were previously closed to them on account of their empty pockets.

The shadow of boredom foretold by many observers for the new leisured class has, up to now, not materialized. First, the worker is not so leisured as some observers might think, since he still works a good deal of overtime; second, he is kept pretty busy at home and he starts to learn his homecraft very early.

It is interesting to note that quite often the worker comes to work on Monday worn out from his weekend activities, especially from 'Do-it-yourself'. Quite a number said that the weekend is the most trying and exacting period of the whole week, and Monday work in the factory, in comparison, is relaxing.

As a result of the increase in 'Do-it-yourself' activities, the weekend seems to be fast losing its character as a period of rest, and is rather assuming the aspect of a second job, that of homecraft.

18. READING MATTER

'I'M NOT WHAT YOU COULD CALL A READER', or 'I haven't got time for reading—there's so much to do'—such were the typical comments heard on this subject. In fact, the worker nowadays is a very busy man with many claims on his attention.

However, no justice can be done to the reading habits of the working man by an over-all generalization. As a matter of fact, we have here an enormous variety of behaviour: on the one hand, we find almost complete non-readers, who never touch a book, and on the other hand, serious students. There are those for whom the 'Telly' has crowded out the last vestige of reading, and others whose reading has triumphed in spite of the Telly's allurements.

The figures for reading habits and reading matter are available for four works, namely for ninety-eight men in Workington, seventy-nine men in Vauxhall, 105 men in Dunlop and ninety-five men in Mullard.

I have divided the answers in five groups: (1) non-readers, i.e., those who do not read any books at all; (2) those who read only occasionally, very little, or very rarely; (3) those who read only Westerns, detective stories, crime, or mystery; (4) those who read non-fiction only; (5) those who read 'all sorts of books'.

	TOTAL	Non-R.	Occ. R.	Westerns	Non-Fic.	All sorts
Workington	98	35	7	23	12	21
Vauxhall	79	34	3	8	15	19
Dunlop	105	47	7	9	13	29
Mullard	95	36	8	8	18	25
TOTAL	377	152	25	48	58	94

We see that in the sample as a whole about 40 per cent were non-readers. In this group one heard comments such as: 'Not for many years'; 'Not since I got T.V.'; 'T.V. has killed my reading'; 'I haven't got the quiet at home' (from men with small children or large families); and 'I can't concentrate any more' (from men on mass production). Some, especially older men, referred to eyestrain: 'I have tired eyes', or 'I have trouble with my eyes'. One man of fifty-seven in Workington confessed: 'The only book I ever read in my life was a book my boy once brought home'.

Occasional readers would say they read 'Very little', or 'Very rarely', or 'Sometimes I do but I am not a reader, actually', or 'There is nothing for me in books'.

Those who were reading exclusively Westerns, mystery, thrillers, detectives, or 'Murder books' as they called them, formed a group of their own. Those who confined themselves to this sort of book made up 13 per cent of the sample as a whole. Of course, there were many more men reading these books, but not exclusively.

About 15 per cent of the sample was made up of those who were reading non-fiction only; as they said, 'Factual books only', or 'Technical books', or 'Hobby books', or 'Serious books only', or 'Books of knowledge', or 'Something genuine'. Among factual books, biography, history and war were favourite subjects. Among technical books, engineering, radio and television were frequently mentioned. Hobby books concerned the particular hobby men were interested in. I heard remarks such as: 'I read only on birds', or 'On angling', or 'On sports', or 'Motoring', or 'Gardening', or

'Photography', or 'On operas, as I belong to an operatic society'.

Those classed as readers of 'all sorts of books' were the largest category, making up about 25 per cent of the sample as a whole and about 40 per cent of the readers. It comprises those who read general fiction ('good books', as they say), not only thrillers, or those who read fiction and non-fiction or non-fiction and Westerns. Combinations often heard were: history and sea novels, sea and war books, biography and crime, war books and Westerns, science fiction and technical books, fiction and travel books.

There were a number of what we may call serious students or readers. In Workington, three men were studying engineering, one was taking a correspondence course in mathematics; one, a shop-steward, was studying Trade Union matters; one was systematically reading encyclopaedias; one was studying Shakespeare. Two men were seriously studying astronomy, and one of these, a yard labourer of thirty-seven with two children, was a Fellow of the Royal Astronomical Society, a member of the British Interplanetary Society and organizing secretary of the Workington and West Cumberland Astronomical Group. He was lecturing a great deal on astronomy, and making a seven-inch reflector at a cost of £20 to £30. Another yard labourer of forty-four with two children in grammar schools was building a telescope.

In Vauxhall, three were studying engineering, one was taking postal courses in English, another a course in mathematics, and one was a serious student of philosophy and theosophy, reading Ouspensky, Gurdjeff and others.

In Dunlop, six men were studying engineering, two were reading encyclopaedias and one belonged to a book club.

In Mullard, three were studying history, among them one who was studying ancient history, three were studying books on 'educational lines', two were systematically reading encyclopaedias, six were studying technical books on engineering, radio and electronics.

I was especially interested in a closer analysis of the group of non-readers, who formed such a big slice of the whole sample, to discover, first, whether they were closely related to those who had the lowest score in the test for cultural horizons, and second, whether there was a significant difference in this respect between age groups.

As the standard test for cultural horizons was given only in Dunlop and Mullard, we can compare the score of non-readers with that of the sample for these two works only. I compared the number of those who scored highest (10 plus) and of those who scored lowest (zero) among non-readers with those in the sample and here is the result:

	SAMPLE			NON-READERS		
	TOTAL	Scored 10 plus	Zero	TOTAL	Scored 10 plus	Zero
Dunlop	115	42	9	47	7	6
Mullard	101	52	3	36	16	2
TOTAL	215	94	12	83	23	8

In both works the non-readers made up two-thirds of those who could not identify any single name listed in the test paper. For the sample of the two works put together, those who scored 10 plus numbered 44 per cent, while only 28 per cent of non-readers scored 10 plus.

As to age differentials, I divided the non-readers into two groups, the under-forties and the over-forties, and compared the proportion with the age composition of the sample in a given works; I found that there was no significant difference between the groups in this respect.

The younger men, building up a home, raising a family and doing a great deal of overtime, are very busy, and they are also interested in cars and motor cycles and outings; the older ones are more home-bound and less active but they often suffer from eye-strain or lack of concentration and a certain decline of curiosity in general. A disturbing remark often heard was: 'I used to read, but I don't now' and 'I was a great reader, but that belongs to the past'.

Judging from the results of these tests for cultural horizons and reading habits, we can say that in our affluent society, though bodily needs are well taken care of, we cannot be confident that the same is true of the needs of the mind.

19. THE MOTOR CAR AS AN INSTRUMENT OF SOCIAL CHANGE

CAR OWNERSHIP is spreading rapidly among the working classes. I heard remarks such as: 'Next on my list is a car', 'I am exchanging a bike for a motor-bike', or 'a motor-bike for a car'. This is the usual gradation—with numerous other progressions from old pre-war cars to new Austins, Fords and Vauxhalls. New cars among the working classes were infrequent, although I came across several cases with an outlay of £700 to £800 for a new car, sometimes bought for cash, in other cases with two years to pay.

The percentage of men who owned a car varied considerably from place to place, the range being (motor cycles excluded) from 12 in Workington to 40 in Vauxhall. Sheffield with 18, Dunlop with 21 and Mullard with 32 per cent occupied the middle ranges. Vauxhall presents a special case, hardly to be taken as representative, as the firm provides special facilities for their employees to acquire cars, and the wage level was well above the national average.

A few types of car owners stand out in my casebook.

First came the single young man who dreamed about a car and whose life centred around it; and for whom taking a car for a continental holiday was the acme of achievement. 'I was courting, but instead I bought a car', I heard said.

Secondly came the man with a working wife and no children, who said: 'It's too much responsibility to have children: instead we bought a car'.

Thirdly came the shiftworker and keen overtimer. In many cases a car enables a man to do shiftwork, when he lives a long distance from his work, and even more so to work overtime at weekends when the buses are very irregular. As both shiftwork and overtime pay well, a car in such cases is a paying proposition. I often heard: 'I bought the car from overtime', or 'I bought the car for overtime and I count on it', or 'When I went on shifts I bought a car'.

Car-sharing in one way or another is a fairly wide-spread

practice. Typical comments were: 'I have half a car', or 'A quarter of a car', or 'Three other mates are paying for their passage'. If cars are owned they are often utilized for sidelines; a number of men had a van instead of a car, which they used for weekend work doing odd jobs.

The wife frequently pays for the car by going out to work and the car may enable her or make it easier for her to go out to work. One man said, 'I bring the wife with me to work and drop the kids at school. At weekends I use the car for shopping with the wife and that together with a fridge which keeps the food for a whole week enables her to go out to work.'

However, in many cases if not in most, a car is used more for pleasure, especially at holiday time, than for going to work. Many men do not use their cars for going to work. 'If you ask them how many miles they have done in their car, you would be surprised to hear that often it is 2,000 miles in three years,' said one of the Vauxhall managers, whose main topic of conversation with his men was cars. To test this I often asked men what was the mileage they did in a year, and I found that the manager was right in most cases. A married man of fifty-five with a girl of fifteen said: 'I come to work on a bike; it isn't far enough to use a car. I make 1,500 miles a year, of which 800 miles is on holiday.' Some lay up the car during the winter and keep it only for holiday times. Car-camping or day-outings from home in a car are very popular ways of spending holidays, and again a car can pay its way as holiday expenses are a big item in a worker's budget.

Is status a big factor in car acquisition? For both ends of the scale, supervisors at the top and labourers at the bottom, the answer is definitely, yes. In Vauxhall and Mullard the majority of supervisors had cars, and in Workington and Dunlop they showed the highest ratio of car ownership among all employees. In all these firms the figures for labourers were at the bottom of the scale.

As regards skilled and semi-skilled workers, the figures for car ownership followed differences in earnings rather than skill. The proportion of car owners was much higher for skilled men in Mullard, and also in Workington but to a smaller extent. In Dunlop skill made no difference, in Vauxhall the semi-skilled had pro rata more cars than the skilled. The later case can be explained by the fact that the total earnings of a semi-skilled man were often higher than those of a skilled man, and some skilled men turned to semi-skilled jobs on that account.

Is age a significant factor in car ownership? My figures for two age groups, the under-forties and forty-plus, suggest not. There is little doubt that the younger men are keener to go in for cars than the older ones, but they cannot always afford them. While single men and childless couples acquire cars, the young married men, when they build up their homes, often have too many commitments. In the older age brackets we come across a group of middle-aged men with grown-up children and wives working who have accumulated savings beyond what they think they will need. In Dunlop the affluent men owned the cars and practically every second car owner also had house property. 'Something to spend money on', was a comment I heard from these men. It seems a strange phrase to use, but if a man needs £10 for his living and earns double that sum, he really needs to have something to spend on. A car also provides an ideal outdoor hobby for the middle-aged man, not very exacting, but involving cleaning, polishing and fiddling with the car in addition to everything else. A young man will have a wider range of hobbies and pastimes. Those in their middle years who had a car, when asked about hobbies, invariably said: 'Motoring and fiddling with the car'.

As a pastime a car often squeezed out other pursuits. I often heard: 'Since I had a car I gave up drinking; drinking and driving don't go together', or 'Since I had a car I gave up gambling; gambling became a mug's game'.

Men often compared the car with T.V., an obvious comparison since together they are the most important playthings of modern times. Some said: 'A car goes against T.V., as T.V. keeps you in and a car keeps you out'. Others did not agree with this: 'They are not in opposition, T.V. is for the night and a car is for the afternoon', or 'T.V. is for the winter and a car is for the summer—but soon we will be able to have T.V. in the car'.

For most men a car is primarily a toy, a tool for pleasure. Some said almost apologetically: 'It is my main luxury; others spend £2 or more on beer, I spend it on a car and have something to show for my money'. The working-class car owner seems to have ambivalent feelings: in one way he is shy about having a car and when he doesn't come to work in it, it is often because he doesn't want to show off, or to show the management how well off he has become. Complaints about poor living conditions and low wages are still in many quarters the order of the day. But on the other hand the owner is proud of his car as the symbol of his status. He has not wasted his time, he has something to show for his work. The car gives him self-confidence, self-assurance. He moves with the times and understands the call of the times. He is no more at the bottom of the social ladder. He takes pride in having such a glittering smooth-looking and smooth-moving thing which gives him a sense of achievement. And he will treat it with affection, showering on it his love and care; he will spend half his weekend cleaning and polishing it.

In the matter of car ownership men seem to behave in a flock-like manner. Car ownership goes by department. In some departments most men had cars, in others none. Perhaps a man's 'conscience' about indulging in luxury is eased when all his mates have a car. Moreover cars provide a topic for conversation, where cars are popular.

Cars also have a deep social effect on the degree of integration of local communities and social life at large. Those who have a car move out of the reach of the 'local'. Previously they visited their own public house or club or other local centre of amusement where they could see their friends and neighbours. With a car they can visit more distant places of entertainment. There they are no more known as 'working class', there they come into contact with wider circles and layers of society.

Do they invite their friends in their car, and arrange outings with their mates? That rarely happens. Usually they take out their wives and children; a car outing is primarily a family affair. Typical comments I heard were: 'The car's for the kiddies', or 'For the wife', or 'The car's to take the family out', or in cases of ill-health, 'It allows them to get about'. Both T.V. and the car have a similar effect in this respect. The television keeps men at home with their families, and provides a family entertainment, while a car provides for a family outing, and once again keeps them with their families. Both innovations strengthen the family circle, while actually weakening the ties with mates.

We see how powerful an instrument of social change a car can be, and is going to be with time. It changes not only the land- and town-scape but also the compass of a man's mind, as he mixes with other classes and drops the insularity of his own class.

20. THE IMPACT OF T.V.

TELEVISION IS OBLIGATORY in nearly every working-class household. In Vauxhall, Dunlop and Mullard the percentage of married men who had television varied from 80 to 90 per cent. The lower percentage in Sheffield (62) and Workington (72) was partly due to the lack of electricity in old-type houses. In Workington, one in five without T.V. had no electricity in the house; a similar situation prevailed in Sheffield where one also heard that in some areas the reception was exceptionally poor. Apart from this, the reasons for not having T.V. were divided between 'I can't afford it', and 'I don't care', or 'I don't bother', with a preponderance of the first group. Those who could not afford it (for instance, those with long spells of illness or with over-large families) answered almost apologetically, in a low voice, 'No, only wireless'. A few very intelligent or very active men with a wide social life rejected T.V. as a time-waster.

However, the majority of those who had T.V. appreciated it very much, especially in winter time, but not without a few qualifications. 'It's a mixed blessing; good and bad', they would say.

What did they consider good? Those who had children regarded it as a fine medium of education: 'There is a lot you can learn from T.V.'; 'It helps your children'; 'We never had such a chance—the children learn a lot without realizing it'. But some were critical, saying: 'They learn but they waste more time', or 'They don't help their mother. Their mother has more work because of T.V.', or 'It helps the children in one way and harms them in another. Their head is full of rubbish, they view more rubbishy programmes than good ones.' They might have referred to the operation of Gresham's Law also in the field of entertainment: 'Bad coin drives out good'. 'It is not good for the children, believe me, I have found that with my children. It distorts their views on life, it's too artificial', said one man.

How does T.V. affect the husband–wife relationship? Again, positive and negative effects are intermingled. 'The T.V. is primarily for the wife' was the view of both shiftworkers and others. 'It keeps her out of mischief and gives her another interest.'

If the wife stays at home, it breaks the monotony of life within four walls. If she goes out to work, when she returns home she has little time to go out again to the pictures, but the T.V. brings pictures into the home. When she is ailing, the T.V. distracts her. My wife suffers from nerves but she is much better since I got T.V. for her.' Men who like a drink and want to go out by themselves use T.V. to keep the wife in good humour. 'I switch on T.V. and while she is watching, I slip out', confessed a steelworker in Sheffield; or as one woman in Mullard put it, 'Men, when they get a set for the wife, think that they have done all they should for their wife'.

However, T.V. restricts conversation between members of the family. When they have nothing to say to each other this may be all to the good. When a man comes home from work and the wife asks, 'Have you had a good day?', she may get a mere 'All right' for an answer, upon which they soon settle down to watch T.V. The wife may have found the answer unsatisfactory, but with T.V. she does not mind as watching-time is gained. Men said often: 'T.V. kills the conversation, nobody talks, we just listen'. T.V. may increase a man's range of verbalization, but it restricts the actual time when this verbalization can be made use of.

T.V. affects also hobbies and pastimes; many men referred to this: 'It makes you lazy. You just sit while there is so much to do at home'; 'It is the greatest hobby killer. Now you don't need to worry how you will spend your time'; 'It spreads the gospel of laziness. It's not a wholesome nourishment, it's like a drug. It feels good when you drug yourself but it leaves a nasty taste behind.' I wonder what Karl Marx, who described religion as 'the opium of the people', would have said about T.V.

How does T.V. affect social contacts with the extended family, friends and neighbours? 'It's anti-social', some said, meaning by it that the contacts are less frequent as people prefer watching T.V. to seeing their friends and neighbours. Others said that T.V. helps contacts because it is easier to entertain visitors by switching on T.V. Often when friends come, instead of conversing they all turn into a T.V. audience.

T.V. is a great instrument of social change, but T.V. behaviour itself is undergoing a change. The behaviour follows certain stages and phases. Whenever I heard strong criticism of T.V., I asked how long the critic had had a set, and in most cases it came out that he had been watching it for years. On the other hand, an enthusiast for T.V. had usually only acquired it recently. In the 'honeymoon phase' T.V. is fascinating. The wife suddenly discovers the means to keep her man and her whole family around the fireside. They are intrigued by this little silvery screen which lights the room in the darkness, and dances, sings and plays, simmering with fun and wit. But after a certain time it becomes flat and insipid. The pathos turns into bathos, and the killings, kidnappings and robberies of all the blackguards and gunslingers become fatiguing instead of relaxing. The time of watching becomes reduced and, in many cases, the man returns to his old ways. 'At first it was a grand entertainment but after many years of it I am fed up', I heard, and 'It's all the same. I don't enjoy it any more; it's boring.' One realizes the importance of novelty, surprise and freshness in any entertainment: one medium after another is born, wears out with age and is rejected. One wonders how much will remain of the medium after ten years. It is already struggling with sclerosis and high blood pressure. The tempo of life, especially in the entertainment world, is breath-taking. It has a fountain-like quality, with changing shapes and colours. The cry for 'something new', 'something fresh', 'something original' goes on all the time, and it taxes the strength of those responsible for keeping the masses amused and entertained.

To assess the impact of T.V. on the mentality of workers is an almost impossible task, and I am quite unqualified to do it; it would require deep penetration into the recesses of man's mind and his mental 'hinterland'. 'It breeds mediocrity'—one of the managers who had studied this problem said to me—'It is bad enough to be exposed to it for an intelligent man who can put up a conscious or unconscious resistance, but what can you say of an ordinary shop floor man on mass production? Imagine a man who spends eight or nine hours a day on mass production with its hustle and bustle and then comes home, settling to his T.V. Mass production in industry plus mass production in entertainment—what will be the joint effect on man's mind? We used to have much more colourful personalities among our working men.'

The working man used to be known for his great sense of reality and large fund of common sense. I believe that these qualities, although they are still there, are being somewhat weakened by his constant dwelling in the world of illusion and make-believe. He is too often exposed to the world of personal fantasies and the world of artificialities.

21. CONTACTS WITH FAMILY OF ORIGIN

CONTACTS WITH PARENTS are well maintained. The scale of answers for contacts with parents (living in the same district) included 'Every day', 'Two or three times a week', 'Once a week', 'Once a fortnight', and more rarely, 'Once a month'. When the mother died the contact with the father was less frequent. Only in odd cases, such as for instance when the mother left home or re-married, were contacts broken entirely. So I soon dropped the question of contacts with parents, as a common pattern of behaviour seemed to be established, and I concentrated on contacts with brothers and sisters.

The data for contacts with brothers and sisters are available for all five works, namely for 507 men. I have divided the answers into five groups: (1) Men with no siblings; (2) Men with siblings living in other districts; (3) Those who keep frequent contacts, at least with one of the siblings, or those who described themselves as 'clannish' or 'close' or 'very close'; (4) Those who keep up the family bonds, seeing one or more siblings from time to time, even if rarely; and (5) Those who have broken the family bonds, or drifted apart, and see each other very rarely or not at all.

	No sib.	Sib. in other dis.	Close	Keep up	Drifted	TOTAL
Sheffield	6	10	53	33	25	127
Workington	6	11	50	8	10	85
Vauxhall	9	32	37	8	7	93
Dunlop	5	19	28	37	17	106
Mullard	9	15	26	24	22	96
TOTAL	35	87	194	110	81	507

We see from the table above (which refers to married or once-married men), that the figures vary considerably from place to place. The population in Workington and Sheffield was more locally integrated than in Dunlop and Vauxhall, where a considerable element of outsiders from other districts was present (in

Mullard, siblings in Greater London were not classed as living in other districts although Mitcham is actually in Surrey). The intensity of contacts is also influenced by distance within the same district. In some localities the families live very close together, while in others, where new estates have sprung up, families are more widely dispersed. The labour market and the size of the firm have also a bearing on contacts. In Workington about 20 per cent of men worked with their brothers, and in Sheffield and Vauxhall also a number did the same.

In Vauxhall a very warm tone in attitudes to family contacts was noticeable: I ascribed this to the fact that the men often came from other districts with one or two siblings, while the rest of the family was left behind, so that a certain nostalgia was felt.

Men at both ends of the scale, those who kept close and those who drifted away, expressed themselves very definitely and often colourfully on the subject. From those with close contacts one could hear: 'Families should stick together', or 'Families are to help each other', or 'Don't let them stay away, always keep them together', or 'When in trouble turn to your family', or 'When in need we help each other'.

From those who drifted away one heard the following comments:

'A family's all right if it's kept apart.'
'I like to be free. The family hasn't done anything for me so far.'
'I've no family ties, I want to be independent.'
'I am on my own. I don't like connections.'
'I don't believe in family gatherings, only jealousies and quarrels result.'
'They don't bother me and I don't trouble them.'
'I don't bother with relatives. Last time I saw the family was at mother's funeral. That was ten years ago.'
'The family is only remembered when help is needed but best left alone. If you interfere or ask too many questions there is only trouble.'
'Relationship is the worst ship that ever sailed. Relations pull one another to pieces.'
'I got away from the family. They don't like my way of living.'
'The further away, the better friend you are.'
'There is no connection between us. That's best.'

We see from the above quotations that those who drifted away expressed themselves more forcibly and often with a touch of aggressiveness and resentment. Their dominant note is the quest for freedom as they understand it.

If we exclude those who have no siblings and those who have siblings (all of them) living in other districts, we find the following percentages of those who drifted away, as shown in the table below.

	Total with sib. in same district	Drifted away	Percentage
Sheffield . . .	111	25	22%
Workington . .	68	10	15%
Vauxhall . . .	52	7	14%
Dunlop . . .	82	17	17%
Mullard . . .	72	22	30%
TOTAL . . .	385	81	21%

We see that the percentages of those who drifted away are very close for Workington, Vauxhall and Dunlop, while higher for Sheffield and highest in Mullard (for the latter, long distances in London may have a bearing on this). For the sample as a whole, those who drifted away were, roughly speaking, one in five.

The intensity of contacts declines with age. As long as the mother lives she is the centre of attraction and the live wire of all family contacts. Young men still live close to their family of origin in more than one sense. Men grow apart, the fund of common memories and experience gradually evaporates. However, where the memories of youth and common upbringing are not so good, where childhood was bad or spent in frustration, the drifting apart starts earlier, though a certain reconciliation may take place later. Happy or unhappy childhood has a definite bearing on contacts with siblings and was often referred to by the men themselves. Men try to forget what they regard as stigma or black spots in their records. 'Nice people, worth keeping in touch with', or 'Happy family', or 'Respectable and helpful people', was the description of those with whom the contacts were well cultivated; and 'Not nice', or 'Mean', or 'Snobbish', or 'Quarrelsome', or 'Interfering, they like to control your life', was the description of those with whom the contacts were broken. If affection and warmth can be got from them, the contacts are well maintained, if prickles are expected they are shunned.

Where a family is in need, in cases of sickness, unemployment, distress, the family bonds reassert themselves if they were previously loosened ('When I was out of work, my sister brought me cigarettes and sweets for the kiddies'). Many men, even those who professed to keep apart from their families, said: 'Of course, if help were needed I would give it'. But when help is not given the family bonds are broken completely ('When my girl was ill no one cared—I don't bother with them any more').

A certain gradation of status or standards of living may be of help in cultivating contacts, but not if the gap is too large. The difference in status between labourers and semi-skilled, or semi-skilled and skilled, are disregarded, but the distance between a labourer and a senior foreman or between a semi-skilled man and a manager could be too trying. If the whole family has a tradition of clerical or staff jobs, a labourer will find himself out of place. 'I am the black sheep of the family, they don't approve of me', he would say. On the other hand where the level of prosperity is fairly high and more or less equal, the bonds are sustained by gifts or small courtesies, holiday visits, car-sharing and so on. In fact, car-sharing among close relatives was a very common occurrence.

The ideal family relationship was considered to be, in the phrase which I often heard, 'Close but not too close'—i.e., close enough to feel the warmth, but far enough away to avoid the prickles. Family squabbles were often referred to as resulting from living too close. 'Don't think that people who are close to their families make better characters than those who keep away; they often fight and bicker all the time'—I was warned by some whose experience of close family life was rather disappointing.

Whenever questions were asked about relative frequency of contacts with men's and wives' siblings, it came out that family life is kept up more with the wife's side than the man's side. The reason for this was given sometimes as: 'They live closer', but more frequently: 'They are nicer people'. Why should the wife's side be 'Nicer people'? A man is accepted into the wife's family as a newcomer, people are nice to him and try to oblige him. Should that not be the same on the man's side, in regard to the wife as a newcomer? Maybe not to the same extent. The wife's family are glad that the daughter or sister has got somebody to look after her. It seems as if they are more understanding and more obliging as a result.

The other reason given was: 'It's a new family. You know your own and you are not so curious about them. You want to make a better impression on your wife's people.' Maybe the new family is not associated with memories of bad childhood, where the childhood experiences were unsatisfactory. Whatever the reason, in all the places of my enquiry, where there were siblings on both sides in the same town and there was a difference in intensity of contacts, the wife's side was more favoured than the man's side.

The other characteristic feature was that when one side had no siblings, the contacts with the other side were very well maintained. The lack of siblings on one side seems to strengthen the need to keep in touch with the other side.

Now we come to a more general and most important question, that of social change. Are family contacts among the working classes increasing or decreasing? What is the general trend of behaviour? Unfortunately differential figures for behaviour of different age groups cannot provide a sufficient clue as to the trend of social change, since the age itself is an important factor in behaviour, as already explained.

However, from the qualitative material which I gathered in my enquiry I would have no hesitation in saying that social change favours family contacts. There are definite reasons for the more intense contacts with family of origin which are now maintained, such as happier childhood experiences in the working classes, less bitter memories of the past, better relationships with fathers who take an almost equal part with wives in bringing up their children, and more freedom in family relationships. With growing prosperity, the family may be expected to be a help instead of a burden. With the coming of greater affluence families are often visited during holidays and, for many, holiday-time is family-time, which means in this connection the extended family. As the members of the family disperse, the fear of family interference and family censorship becomes more remote.

22. CONTACTS WITH NEIGHBOURS

THE PATTERN of neighbourly relations was well established and nearly uniform in all places of enquiry. It can be summed up in two phrases which were often heard: 'Friendly but not too close', and 'Keep apart from neighbours, but be friendly'. The majority of men are on 'good-morning' terms and they are willing to help and oblige if the need for help arises. A cat or dog may be taken care of, garden plants may be exchanged, a hand may be given in repairing a fence, a bedridden woman may be visited, a schoolchild may be taken in while the mother is at work. But visiting is, in the main, discouraged. The proportion of those on visiting terms was about a fifth for Workington, Mullard and Dunlop. In Vauxhall it was about a third: this higher percentage may be explained by absence of family contacts of newcomers from other areas; besides many lived in small Bedford villages, where village life is very close.

The intensity of neighbourly contacts can be graded in this order: (1) villages; (2) old-established working-class areas; (3) new estates; (4) residential quarters with own house property. The sociability on new council estates is rather low, generally speaking. The community centres seem to lead rather a shadowy existence. A general rule can be laid down which holds good in most cases: the higher the level of prosperity, the higher the fences. With growing prosperity the need for mutual neighbourly help is not so pronounced and everyone can manage by and for himself, while the need for freedom comes to the fore.

From the qualitative material gathered in the enquiry I could see that the trend among the working classes was in the direction of decline in neighbourly contacts, for the following reasons.

Prosperity, as already explained, brings with it the erection of higher fences in more than one sense. The working of women is also a big factor in the decline of neighbourly contacts. The lowest percentage of neighbourly visits, namely 15 per cent, was recorded in the interviews with women operatives in Mullard. 'We have no time for gossiping', or 'We are out all day', or 'We are all working women', were the answers whenever neighbourly visits were in question. Small families are another factor. Children bring in neighbours; where fewer children are about, the contacts are likely to be less intense. The mixing of various social strata on new estates also has to be considered. Last but not least come the car and the television: 'They may disturb me when I am watching T.V.', or 'A neighbour's conversation is uninteresting compared with T.V.'—were not infrequent comments on neighbourly visits.

In all the pronouncements about neighbours there was a constant refrain that the intrusion of neighbours may restrict a man's freedom and his privacy: 'We won't be able to get rid of them if we are too friendly'. The fears and expectations in this regard can be summed up in a phrase which I heard in Mullard: 'Do a good turn if possible to show that you are friendly but if you are too friendly the place is never your own'. The warning was also heard: 'Don't spoil your neighbourhood by getting too close'. Again it is the right distance in a relationship which is aimed at. Not too far away for warmth but not too close in order to avoid inconveniences.

23. CONTACTS WITH WORKMATES OUTSIDE

THE CONTACTS WITH WORKMATES apart from work seemed to be sporadic. The majority of workers would subscribe to the saying which I often heard that 'mates are not pals', or as one man said in a curious language of his own, 'Mating is not palling'. Men do not choose their workmates but are assigned to do a job. 'We get on each other's nerves sometimes'—I heard. As one man put it, 'In the environment of work we are friends but outside we are more choosy'. Others were more cautious in phrasing the same attitude, putting it in this way: 'It happens but rarely that you work with a mate who is your personal friend'.

From figures in my sample I could see that between 60 and 70 per cent of men do not meet outside work; 69 per cent in Mullard, 67 per cent in Vauxhall, 61 per cent in Workington, 59 per cent in Dunlop. Of course mates who live close by cannot help seeing each other outside, they walk and travel home together and they often have arrangements for sharing a car, but seeing each other does not always imply social contact. Some contacts come about involuntarily through football or cricket or Rugby or a fishing match, or in social clubs or public houses. The Union plays a small part in meetings outside as most Union meetings are in the works and they are very badly attended if outside.

Visiting at home is rarely practised or encouraged. 'Work is left at work with all that is involved, including mates', was a comment I heard, and: 'My mates never visit me and I wouldn't like to see them'; 'We like to forget work as soon as we are outside the gates'; 'Don't we see enough of each other at work? We want new faces.' This may be regarded as the typical view. However, there are deviations from this rule.

Skilled men meet more frequently outside than semi-skilled or labourers. They have a real interest in the job and they do not mind discussing it sometimes outside. They also have common interests in cars and engines and similar things and they often help each other in 'fiddling' with these. Anyway, outside contacts between skilled men in my sample were more frequent than those of others.

Young single men congregate together, and young men in general, especially those who take part in the firm's sports, meet more frequently than the older men. Comments included: 'When I was younger I made more friends among mates', and 'I met them more frequently'. As far as married men are concerned the age of maximum sociability falls in their thirties and forties, the time when the children are growing up or leaving the home, when men are looking for new outside interests to refresh themselves in new relationships.

Working women fall in a special category, their outside contacts with each other being much more frequent than among men. They go out shopping together, to cinemas, dance clubs and so on. They find great pleasure in companionship at work and they do not mind keeping it up outside. In Mullard about 50 per cent of women had regular contacts with each other outside work. Summing up, we can say that a similar tendency as in other relationships can be discerned here: to be friendly with mates but not too friendly, not to get too much involved, not to mix work with home and leisure.

It is very difficult to evaluate the trend of social change from an enquiry of this kind, as the differential behaviour of age groups cannot be simply taken as a clue to social change; people change with age even within a constant system of behaviour. However, from the qualitative material I could gather that the trend in regard to social contacts with workmates leads rather downward than upward. There are several reasons for this trend, among them greater prosperity, tendency to spread out in living further away from work, greater home-centredness, stronger interest in family life and home, T.V., and all the comforts which keep men at home, and cars which bring the car owners within wider circles of society, making them mix with other classes.

PART FIVE

Savings and Property

24. ATTITUDES TO SAVING

THE DATA CONCERNING SAVINGS are incomplete and not very accurate, as must be the case with most data concerning money matters. These are regarded as the most private and intimate matters of life. So I often had to abstain from pressing the question about savings and content myself with a general answer. Besides, the enquiry into the problems of savings was intended rather to reveal the interviewee's mode of life and basic attitudes than to collect figures.

Some answers ran as follows: 'We both save'; 'A few shillings only'; 'A few pounds'; 'A lot'; 'A fair amount'; 'A fair figure in the bank'; 'Depends on overtime'; 'It depends on overtime and shifts'; 'I save in spasms'; 'I have a good nest egg'; 'I save for a target'; 'For holidays only'; 'For holidays and Christmas'; 'For a car'; 'For a deposit on a house'; and 'I have a life insurance of so and so'. These answers were difficult to classify and they are lumped together under 'other savers'.

Where figures for saving were given, I think they were usually an understatement. The figures were approximate, of course, as they often varied from week to week and were very often estimated without overtime or shift allowance. Men often added: 'More when on overtime or shifts'. The wife's savings were also usually not included. The savings were usually meant as gross savings on which they might draw in a short time. Savings through the firm were included, but not pension contributions in the firm. Payment of mortgages or hire-purchase payments were usually excluded but savings for a deposit or for buying durable consumer goods were included. Life insurances were usually mentioned separately.

The information concerning savings is available for four works,

Workington, Vauxhall, Dunlop and Mullard, and classified in three groups: (1) Savers who quoted a definite figure for their savings; (2) other savers; (3) non-savers.

	Workington	Vauxhall	Dunlop	Mullard
Total for whom the information is available	102	99	98	95
Savers giving a figure	58	56	64	49
Other savers	27	32	16	23
Non-savers	17	11	18	23

We see that the percentage of non-savers varied from 11 to about 24 per cent. However, not all of them abstained from saving altogether. In some cases the wives saved but not the men, especially those who gave the whole wage packet to the wife. Others were not saving at the time the enquiry was made, as they had on hand payments for cars, or for house decoration and repairs, or heavy repayment of mortgages. Only very few 'did not believe in saving' or 'did not care about saving' for various reasons, which were: 'I don't see any point in saving', or 'When you have nothing, nobody can rob you', or 'When you have less you can claim more', or 'I believe in living comfortably' or 'To-day the State looks after that'.

Those who gave an approximate figure for their savings week by week saved between a few shillings and £10 a week.

	Up to 10s	11s to 20s	21s to 40s	41s to 80s	81s plus	TOTAL
Workington	16	15	17	6	4	58
Vauxhall	1	12	26	7	10	56
Dunlop	1	21	24	12	6	64
Mullard	4	17	14	9	5	49
TOTAL	22	65	81	34	25	227

Those who saved up to £1 a week inclusive are not real savers as this amount is needed for holidays, Christmas and other occasions. Real savers can be regarded as those who save above £1 a week, and their total number varied from twenty-seven in Workington and twenty-eight in Mullard to forty-two in Dunlop and forty-three in Vauxhall. We see that the highest figures for savings are reached by Vauxhall and the lowest by Workington. This follows closely the average wages in those firms, which were at the time of the enquiry: £13 2s 1d in Workington, £12 8s 7d for semi-skilled and £16 11s 10d for skilled in Mullard, £15 13s 0d in Dunlop and £17 3s 8d in Vauxhall.

The order in which these firms appear with their savings in the above table follows also the figures of savings through the firm as ascertained from the wages departments of the firms concerned, and presented in the following table:

	Savers (approx.)	Average amount per saver
Workington	33%	15s
Vauxhall	40%	£2 10s
Dunlop	20%	£1 10s
Mullard	13%	£1

We see that the propensity to save is governed primarily by the ability to save. This comes out also very clearly when one analyses the situation of the best savers, i.e., those who saved above £4 a week. They were mostly either single men or young married couples (often without children) whose wives worked full-time.

THOSE WHO SAVED OVER £4 A WEEK

	TOTAL	Single men	Wives working full-time	Part-time
Workington	4	0	2	1
Vauxhall	10	4	4	1
Dunlop	6	3	3	0
Mullard	5	0	5	0

The figures for saving cannot be considered in isolation, but must be considered jointly with house and car ownership and home equipment. They must also be supplemented by figures for life insurances, pension schemes, sick clubs and so on. In Workington I recorded seventeen cases of life insurance, out of which three were for £1,000 or more, six for £400 to £600, two not specified and the rest for small sums.

Some men gave a figure of their total monetary savings which were usually termed the 'nest egg' and which in some cases were derived from compensations. In Workington, four had a nest egg of £1,000 or more and three one of between £200 and £500. In

Dunlop, five men stated their total savings; one man had £1,500, one £750, three between £300 and £400. In Vauxhall, three had £1,000 or more, three between £500 and £700, two between £100 and £300, and four said that they had a nest egg but did not give a definite figure. In Mullard, I recorded only two cases, one with £500, another with £200.

The ethos of saving is undergoing a very deep transformation. The phrase 'I don't believe in saving' or 'You may be dead tomorrow' is rarely heard; instead one can hear 'I look after the money all right', or 'I got so used to saving that it became second nature', or 'We both save and each of our children has a savings book'. An elderly man, asked whether he had a nest egg, referred to social change in such terms: 'Unfortunately not. The big money came only after the war. There was nothing worth-while saving previously. You might as well enjoy life.' Those who do not save use more frequently the phrase, 'Unfortunately I can't save anything'.

Savings conceived as deferred payment was previously the rule, now savings conceived as investment, or for old age, or for a rainy day are more frequently admitted. Life insurances are also more frequent and 'good nest eggs' are not such a great rarity as they used to be.

25. THE ETHOS OF HOUSE PROPERTY

PROPERTY OWNERSHIP by workers was, until recently, only a sporadic phenomenon; but it has been spreading considerably of late and I thought it worth while to devote special attention to questions of motivation behind the ownership of house property. Does house property affect the worker's way of life and ways of thinking? How does it affect his class consciousness? Does it whet his appetite for more possessions? Does he care a great deal for his property, and how does he treat it?

The tendency to consider house property as something worth having and struggling for, something which gives one strength and self-confidence and social standing, appears to be spreading among the working classes. I have no figures to offer here but I think that the working classes may be divided into three main groups, numerically not very far apart. One group tries to acquire property; the second does not think about house property at all, as it is beyond its possibilities and its ken; the third group rejects the acquisition of house property outright as undesirable and even pernicious for the working man.

People in this last group would often say: 'A house of your own is like a millstone round your neck', or 'I wouldn't touch it, it's only worry', or 'They want to catch you in this way', or 'Too expensive with all the rates and mortgages', or 'How do I know that I shall be able to keep it if a slump comes? I know a lot of fellows who had to give them up when bad times came upon them.' A number of men referred to the responsibility of which they were afraid. 'Own house?—too much responsibility', they would say. Others put it: 'I could have bought a house but I was afraid to speculate, it wasn't my line', or 'I was a bit cautious in my younger days'.

A very large number, maybe even the majority, would regard a council house as something to be preferred to one's own house. 'You have it for life, it's like your own, cheaper, nothing to worry about, when out of work you get consideration, no responsibility anyhow.' In some areas local councils are offering their houses for sale to sitting tenants for a small deposit and a slightly increased weekly payment, but many tenants do not avail themselves of this opportunity. For instance, the local council in Carshalton started this scheme four years ago and offered to sitting tenants of fully-occupied houses (each bedroom has to be occupied), on very convenient terms (£5 deposit and £2 11s per week instead of £2 6s rent for a three-bedroom house), but only 130 out of more than 800 tenants availed themselves of this opportunity, although not everyone could qualify under the full occupation rule. 'To some of them, even most of them, the idea is foreign'—I was told.

However, the general trend towards a desire for property is on the increase. The percentage of house owners among family men in my sample differed considerably from area to area. It was lowest for Sheffield, with 16 per cent, and highest in Luton, with 47 per cent. The three other places showed a near approximation to these figures in regard to frequency of house ownership, with 30 per cent in Mullard, 31 per cent in Dunlop and 37 per cent in Workington. The spread of house property among the work-people in a given firm would depend largely on the housing conditions and the policy of the local council, the composition of skill- and age-structure, standard of wages and opportunities for women's work. In Vauxhall for instance, with its very high standard of wages, young labour force, and large opportunities for women's work, the proportion of property owners was exceptionally high.

Status distinctions have a bearing on property holding but not to a very great extent and not everywhere. By and large one can say that the proportion of property-owners is higher among supervisors than among skilled men, higher among the skilled men than the semi-skilled and lowest among labourers. As far as my figures go, the majority of supervisors in Workington, Vauxhall and Dunlop had their own property, but that was not confirmed in Mullard where the proportion of property-owners among supervisors was more or less on the same average level as for the whole sample. The proportion of property-owners among skilled men was higher than that of semi-skilled in Workington and Mullard, but not in Vauxhall and Dunlop where skill made no difference. Labourers everywhere showed the lowest proportion. In both Vauxhall and Dunlop the premium on skill seemed to be either low or non-existent, and some skilled men had taken up semi-skilled jobs. However, it can be assumed that for the country as a whole there is a greater tendency among skilled men to acquire property than among unskilled, on several counts: the desire for property is greater; they settle earlier in the job and usually have a record of longer service; they put in longer hours; and their wages are a little higher (although not compared with shiftworkers and pieceworkers).

How does age affect property-holding? There is a tendency for younger men to acquire property, and one discerns also a greater desire for property among the young. Also necessity operates here as the waiting-time for a council house in many areas rarely falls below six to ten years. In my sample the lowest age of a council house tenant was very rarely below thirty. But on the other hand, younger men were often unable to save enough for a deposit. To return to the figures in my sample, if we divide the men into two age-groups, under-forty and forty-plus, and exclude the supervisors (who are mostly older men) we arrive at the following: the proportion of house-owners was higher in the younger age-group in Workington and Dunlop, but in Vauxhall and Mullard the reverse was true. The older employees in Vauxhall and Mullard had been in the habit of acquiring property for some time, their aggregate savings were higher, and one could say they had been exposed longer to the temptation of property.

Men with working wives emerged as owning property more frequently than others, the reason for this being that the wife often works to pay for the house. The payment for a house or a car was often referred to by working women and also by men whose wives were going out to work.

Property-owners often struck me as a brighter, more daring and enterprising breed than the rest. In the test papers they often fared better.

I often asked how people felt when they became house-owners. A very few dismissed this question by saying simply: 'In my case it was a necessity; I couldn't get married otherwise.' The overwhelming majority felt deeply about it. 'It means a lot to me', or 'It's a good feeling; it gives me more self-confidence', or 'Something to show for your labour', or 'Satisfaction—as I worked very hard to get it'. Freedom was often referred to when the topic was brought up. 'I am free to do as I like', or 'I am master in my own house, no one interfering', or 'Nobody can tell me what to do. I can please myself, I can knock any nails I like into the wall.'

Security was also mentioned as a valid reason. 'Something to fall back on, if you fall on bad times', or 'You feel more secure; it takes a bit of worry off your mind', or 'If you need money you can always get it on a house'. As one young man confided optimistically: 'I have a long life in front of me, the rents will go up and I have stabilised my cost of living as far as rents are concerned'. Many feel a sense of independence: 'I feel more independent since I got the house', or 'I'm not working for the landlord', or 'No one can take it from me', they said.

When talking with house-owners one gets the feeling that property, so to speak, is an extension of a man's personality. The property becomes a part of him and is shaped accordingly. It transforms his life in more than one way, giving him a part-time or spare-time job for life. Decorating and doing jobs around the house is a year-round occupation. I heard comments such as: 'My house is my hobby', or 'I am always improving or adding something in the house', or 'There is something you can improve all the time'. His house becomes a matter of pride ('I take pride in my house'), it becomes his baby which he nurses, and it testifies to his achievement. He is 'somebody', a rate-payer, and this enhances his standing in society, in his family, among his friends and in his own eyes. It gives him self-respect. As one man confided: 'I have done something I never thought would be possible for me, but I needed courage to go ahead. They warned me that it would be a millstone round my neck but it is nothing of the sort.'

There were a number of great enthusiasts for house property who exclaimed vividly: 'Everybody should have a house of his own, something to work for. The government should aim at that'; 'It's the best thing I have ever done in my life'; 'It's the best thing that ever happened to me'; 'It's like heaven to settle down in one's own house'.

The house is also a starting-point for many new acquisitions, it whets the appetite for more. Once the barrier of non-possessing has been crossed, a new wave sets in. By and large the house-owners have better equipped homes than others. As he has something worth-while to spend money on, a house-owner will be more careful about his spending. He knows that money can bring something more lasting than a few hours' enjoyment.

As property is often acquired in new residential areas, the property-owner tends to emerge from his old strongly-knit community, and meets people from other walks of life and other social strata. I can say that property-ownership has a definite bearing on class-consciousness, and many men referred to this when asked about it. A property-owner compares himself with his superiors and often finds himself in the same category. 'I have a house in the same neighbourhood as my manager'—said one such man.

House property also brings a man into contact with life insurance and banking. To start with, he often has to insure himself for life when engaging on a long-term mortgage. He usually gets a cheque-book, since he has to pay rates, mortgage charges, insurance and so on. He starts thinking about interest rates, local rates and local council affairs, he watches local developments in the movement of population in his neighbourhood. He wants respectable neighbours who keep their property in good order as that affects the value of his own. Often he is not satisfied with the neighbourhood, when his standard of prosperity goes up, so he moves out, in order to 'give his children a better chance'. He becomes 'respectability-minded', one could say even snobbish; he belongs to a class of his own among the working men, finding himself, as he often says, on the border of the middle classes.

Does the house strengthen the family bond? I should say yes. The men often referred to their house in such terms as: 'Something for the family', or 'Something to leave behind', or more specifically when they had a son or a daughter, 'Something for the lad', or 'Something for the lass', or 'My wife won't be destitute if I die'.

The children feel that they have something to expect from their parents and they are not afraid that the parents will fall back on them in case of need. Subconsciously it may affect their attitudes and behaviour, it may give them greater respect for their parents. When there are several children, they have a common stake in the affairs of the family.

A man who buys a house tends to settle earlier than others in his job. He will not buy the house if he is not convinced that he is already settled in his job, and also in his family ways. Settling in the job, settling in the family ways and settling in his own house—all these go together.

Is house property restricting the mobility of labour? To a certain extent, yes. But no more than council houses, and possibly even less. A house-owner can sell his property and buy one somewhere else, while a transfer from one council house to another elsewhere is a much more difficult proposition. On the other hand, the house-owner gets more attached to his house and, as already said, the house is bought mostly when the man feels firmly settled in the job.

It seems clear that possessing his own house can change a man's values and interests, way of life and way of thinking. House ownership is certainly an important element in the new 'gospel' of prosperity among the working classes.

26. THE REWARDS OF TEMPERANCE

THE DATA FOR DRINKING HABITS are available for four works, Workington, Vauxhall, Dunlop and Mullard, but are not as full as I would have wished. Actually, the total abstainers and occasional drinkers were more or less fully recorded. Only for Workington were drinking habits more fully recorded; the statistics here included weekend drinkers and those who drank fairly heavily.

The main interest of the enquiry centred round the following questions: (1) Is there a significant difference in temperance between younger and older generations? (2) Do those who are more temperate attain higher social status and are they better off as expressed, for instance, in the ratio of house and car ownership

A temperate man would class himself as 'A teetotaller', meaning a man who does not touch a drink on principle, or 'Practically a teetotaller', i.e., a man who has no such principle but in fact takes a drink very rarely, or 'Drinking only occasionally', meaning only on occasions or for company, in fact, only rarely. Now let us look at the table which records the number of men for whom the information is available and the number of temperate men in these three categories:

	Information available for	T.T.	Prac. T.T.	Occ. drinkers	TOTAL TEMP
Workington	102	20	2	16	38
Vauxhall	108	9	7	30	46
Dunlop	113	12	6	21	39
Mullard	98	11	8	23	42
TOTAL	421	52	23	90	165

The percentage figures for all four works are not far apart as they range from 38 to 43 per cent of temperate men in the sample. Anyway, more than one-third of the sample as a whole (to be exact, 39 per cent) were temperate men. The Temperance Movement as reflected in the number of total abstainers was most prominent in Workington, having a strong tradition in Cumberland.

Some men were teetotallers on religious and moral grounds believing that drinking is a vice difficult to control which can spell ruin for a man. Some were temperate because of disabilities such as stomach ulcer or diabetes. Others saw the disastrous consequences of heavy drinking in their fathers—'mugs' as they described them—and from early youth they had made up their minds to avoid following the same path. Car owners or those motoring or on transport were afraid of the effect of drinking on their driving ('I don't want to lose my licence' or 'Car and drink don't go together'). Some contended, 'I can't afford it', or 'I don't want to work for the publican', or 'I want something to show for my money'. Quite a few said: 'I knocked off drinking and smoking as well'.

I met only a few men in each place who indulged in drinking to any extent. I do not believe their number exceeded three or four in each place but my record in this respect is fragmentary. Only in Workington was the number higher, which is to be explained by the character of the steel industry where one often hears: 'No steel without beer'. There nine men who indulged in drinking were recorded, and made statements such as the following: 'I drink a lot'; 'I drink too much'; 'I drink every night'; 'Four times a week, eight pints each time'; 'eight pints but only on morning shifts'; 'Drinking is important for work'; and 'I couldn't carry on without my beer'.

In Workington the number of weekend drinkers was twenty-seven; this added to thirty-eight temperate men leaves thirty-seven who drank more or less regularly, not only at weekends.

The publicans with whom I conversed in the places of enquiry contended that the weekend business is gaining all the time at the expense of weekdays. Taking bottles home is also gaining ground and a few men reported this as their regular habit. The spreading of T.V. first affected public-house attendance very much, but after a certain time patrons came back, although not in the same numbers and not with the same frequency.

Taking a closer look at the age structure of the temperate men, I found that there was no statistically significant difference in my sample between the two age groups, the under-forties and the over-forties, though the figures show 43 per cent of younger men, as against 37 per cent of older men, as temperate.

As to the status distinctions among the temperate men, the proportion of temperance in the sample as a whole was higher for skilled men and supervisors taken together, than for non-skilled men (semi-skilled and labourers).

Our last question concerns the standard of wealth. Do those temperate men show the results of their discipline in acquisition of goods? After all, abstinence is a first-class saving device; it was often thus referred to by men on afternoon shifts, half jokingly: 'It's a saving shift'. In the table below we give the number of married temperate men, and those among them who own their houses.

	TEMPERATE MEN		HOUSE OWNERS			
			T.T.	Prac. T.T.	Occ. drinkers	TOTAL
Workington	.	36	8	1	6	15
Vauxhall	.	43	9	5	14	28
Dunlop	.	36	5	2	8	15
Mullard	.	41	6	2	7	15
TOTAL	.	156	28	10	35	73

The average proportion of home ownership among temperate men for the whole sample amounts to 47 per cent. This is above the percentage for all married men in the sample (see Chapter 25). The same phenomenon applies, though to a lesser degree, to car ownership. We see, therefore, that the temperate men gain their reward for their discipline and have something to show for their abstinence.

PART SIX

Class Consciousness and Religion

27. SELF-PLACEMENT AND CLASS CONSCIOUSNESS

THE BASIC QUESTION in this field was: 'How do you place yourself: working class or middle class or otherwise?' Comments were, however, invited and usually discussion followed. Most men placed themselves as working class, although a substantial minority classed themselves as middle class, or gave an indefinite answer such as working class/middle class, or refused to class themselves, saying they did not believe in classes or class differences—about which I shall say more later. Not all men who classed themselves as working class in fact believed that they were: but they would have regarded it as an act of snobbery to place themselves higher. As some said: 'It would be snobbish if I said otherwise', or 'I regard myself as working class, while others would take me for middle class' or 'Although I have a house and a car I am still working class'.

Some made a distinction between being working class and being poor. They did not feel that they belonged to the bottom layer of society. 'I am working class but comfortably off', or 'The middle-class people are worse off nowadays' were typical comments. Others did not like the term 'working class' at all: 'It's an old-fashioned term. It doesn't apply nowadays', or 'That's dying out', or 'I'm not happy about this division'. They would prefer, instead of working class: 'The ordinary run of people', or 'People who do not stand out', or 'People with lower income', or 'Respectable people'.

All agreed that class differences have narrowed down considerably. 'It's all levelled up—the army and the war were great levellers', they said, or 'Classes are coming nearer—the top grades of the working class are middle class really'; 'Working class and middle class are the same thing'; 'We are all middle class nowadays'; 'Actually I don't see any difference: I earn as much as a shopkeeper'; 'There are no differences: I live in the same neighbourhood as my manager, have the same kind of house and have a car'. Some referred to the public-house grouping: 'Most people go to the lounge; only the old element goes to the public bar'. One man expressed the narrowing down of class differences in historical terms: 'The working class has been brought to the level where the middle class was previously.'

The term 'class' was invariably linked with snobbishness but rarely, if at all, with class struggle. One could frequently hear remarks such as 'I am as good as anyone else', or 'I mix with anyone', or 'I can talk to anyone' and on the other hand: 'I'm not snobbish', or 'I hate snobbishness', or 'I don't look down on anyone'. Resentment on account of disparities in wealth and position was heard but rarely, although some referred to the middle class in disparaging terms such as: 'They are less friendly', or 'The nosey people', or 'Those who run you down', or 'Those who live beyond their means', or 'Those who starve themselves to keep up appearances' or 'Those who dodge the Income Tax'. But one could hear also frequently: 'I don't envy anyone his money or his position', or 'I am satisfied with what I am', or 'There must be classes, you can't get away from it', or 'You have to have rich people', or 'Some people are good at one thing, others at another', or 'I am working class but I haven't got a chip on my shoulder'.

When speaking about classes a man would seem to be thinking primarily about himself, about the individual aspect of the problem, and not about the social situation or the social structure. The other classes were of little interest to him. 'What are the other classes?' I often asked. A number of answers were given, such as: 'The boss class', or 'Business men and professional men', or 'Those who live on their money', or 'Those who are idle', or 'Those with fixed incomes and salaries' or 'Those with better jobs, more money and more education'. Education was very frequently referred to as a distinguishing mark of social classes: 'I call myself working class because I haven't got the education'; 'With my schooling I can't call myself otherwise'; 'My school pals snub me because I haven't got the education'. The myth of the redeeming qualities of the working classes as the *avant-garde* of progress, as the repository of all virtues, is for the majority practically discarded. Only occasionally one could hear: 'The working classes are those who provide all the wealth and get least of it'.

Were the men emotionally attached to their class, were they of and for the working class, did they assert their class identity as class allegiance? This appeared to be so only in a few cases, when a man would say: 'I am a socialist', or 'I am a shop-steward' or 'I am a party man'. The majority took a detached view: 'It doesn't bother me', they would say. Some expressed their wish to escape their class: 'I am now working class but in a few years' time I hope to be middle class', or 'I am trying to get above the working class', or 'I am still working class but on my way out', or 'I am working class but I don't like it' or 'I am, but I don't want to be working class'.

The intensity of both class consciousness and class subconsciousness seems to be on the decline. Class 'sub-consciousness' sometimes lingers in the dim recesses of man's mind, primarily fed by past unemployment, starvation wages, unfair treatment, class discrimination, by a common struggle against injustice, by all those bitter memories of the past which are now receding; it often comes to life when a man is confronted by some acts which forcibly bring home his status to him. One heard remarks such as: 'I never gave it a thought', or 'I'm working class but I'm not conscious of it', or 'I never thought about it'. A number of men really did not know how to place themselves: 'I don't know, really'; 'I'm not sure'; 'It must be working class if anything'; 'I suppose working class'; 'Rather working class'; 'We don't live beyond our means if that is what you mean'; 'I don't class myself and I don't class anybody else'.

It is interesting to note the distinction made by some between work and leisure time: 'I am working class only in the works but outside I am like anyone else'; 'The class distinctions are at work but not otherwise'; 'Here I am a worker but outside I am a human being'; 'Outside, I mix with all classes'. Class distinctions seem to be much stronger in the works than outside. The specific status of hourly-rated men, with the canteen divisions, forcibly remind the workers of their definite place in the social ladder. Outside, class divisions are now less pronounced. Those who made the distinction between their status in the works and outside often belonged to various clubs of a mixed character, such as the British Legion, ex-Service Men's Club, Catholic clubs, Conservative clubs, Buffaloes, Druids, various sports clubs, etc.

Now let us look at the data of self-placement available for four works, i.e., for forty men in Workington, ninety-eight in Vauxhall, 109 in Dunlop, ninety-nine in Mullard. I classed the answers in four categories: (1) those who placed themselves as working class; (2) those who placed themselves as middle class; (3) those who gave an indefinite answer; (4) those who refused to place themselves.

	Working class	*Middle class*	*Indefinite*	*Refused*	TOTAL
Workington	31	6	1	2	40
Vauxhall	54	21	6	17	98
Dunlop	70	17	8	14	109
Mullard	74	10	2	13	99
TOTAL	229	54	17	46	346

We see that about two-thirds of the whole sample placed themselves as working class. Those who gave an indefinite answer were nearer to middle class than to working class in their self-placement, as their remarks were more or less in this vein: 'I am working class as regards work, middle class as regards living'; 'I like to be middle class'; 'I am working class trying to get into middle class'; 'I call myself working class but my neighbours would call me middle class'; 'While I am here I am a working-class chap; outside I am middle class'; 'Nowadays the working class is actually the middle class'; 'I am on a boundary line between working class and middle class'; or 'I am trying to get above the working class socially'.

Those who refused to place themselves said: 'I don't care about classes', or 'I don't agree with classes', or 'I don't like to split people in this way', or 'We are all of the same blood'.

Status had a bearing on self-placement especially as far as supervisors were concerned. It was interesting to follow the self-placement of foremen; this can be seen from the following table which records the answers of the twenty-three foremen for whom the information is available.

Self-Placement and Class Consciousness

	Working class	Middle class	Indefinite	Refused	TOTAL
Workington .	3	1	0	0	4
Vauxhall .	3	0	1	0	4
Dunlop .	1	3	0	2	6
Mullard .	3	6	0	0	9
TOTAL .	10	10	1	2	23

We see that nearly half the foremen placed themselves as working class although the identification with working classes follows a different pattern in each works. It was interesting to note a remark from some of the shift foremen: 'It's working class while still on shifts'.

Skilled men have a stronger sense of working-class identification than semi-skilled men and labourers. Apart from Vauxhall they placed themselves, overwhelmingly, as working class, as can be seen from the following table:

	Working class	Middle class	Indefinite	Refused	TOTAL
Workington .	7	2	0	0	9
Vauxhall .	15	7	1	4	27
Dunlop .	21	1	0	5	27
Mullard .	25	2	2	2	31
TOTAL .	68	12	3	11	94

We saw that the strongest sense of working-class identification as expressed in self-placement of workers at large was in Workington and Mullard, the weakest in Vauxhall and Dunlop. This seems to be related especially to the strength of Trade Union membership. The highest measure of Union organization was in Workington (about 90 per cent) and Mullard (estimated at 85 to 90 per cent) while the lowest was in Dunlop (50 to 60 per cent) and Vauxhall (about 60 per cent). This may explain also the different degree of class consciousness between the skilled and semi-skilled workers, as skilled men are more highly organized than semi-skilled and labourers.

As to the matter of age: if we divide the sample into two age groups, the under-forties and over-forties, we find little difference in the pattern of self-placement, although older men in Workington and Vauxhall placed themselves more frequently in the working class.

Do possessions have a marked influence on class consciousness? In order to answer this question I examined the house- and car-ownership of those who did not place themselves as working class (those who placed themselves as middle class, or gave an indefinite answer, or refused to place themselves).

	TOTAL	House owners	Car owners
Workington	9	5	1
Vauxhall	44	20	22
Dunlop	35	22	8
Mullard	25	10	10
TOTAL	117	57	41

House property was often referred to in connection with self-placement, in the following ways: 'Your own house puts you up in class, doesn't it?'; 'I live in a middle-class neighbourhood where everyone has his own house'; 'My neighbours would call me middle class because I have my own house'; 'I am working class but have middle-class aspirations: I have my own house'; or 'I try to get into the middle class; having my own house, that was a start'.

Family connections were also a considerable factor in self-placement. Those who did not place themselves as working class often came from families of farmers, or small business men such as butchers, grocers, garage owners, builders, publicans, foremen or under-managers. They often said: 'I am not of a working-class family', or 'My parents are middle class' or 'My family are clerical people really'.

To sum up, I would say that working-class consciousness seems to be undergoing not only a process of deep transformation but also diversification. Instead of a more unified response, one gets a very large diversity of responses, some of a very curious and unexpected variety, with all sorts of combinations. The personal elements of class consciousness seem to be gaining the upper hand over the collective elements. One mould seems to break up into particles with more individualistic awareness.

28. INTER-GENERATION MOBILITY

A. SONS AND FATHERS

DO MEN WORK, I asked myself, in the same firm, in the same industry, or in the same job as their fathers? I found that this depends very much on the age of the firm, or its size compared with the volume of the labour market, and also on skills. Skilled men more often follow their fathers' trade, but the percentage of these men, generally speaking, is rather small. Only a few men like their jobs so much that they encourage their sons to follow in their footsteps, and the sons, often in opposition to the paternal authority, try to get away from the trade of their fathers. Curiously enough, men often take up their grandfather's trade or their uncle's trade.

The highest percentage of men working in the same firm as their fathers before them had done, was in Workington (53 per cent), where it happens that the firm represents a very considerable slice of the total labour market; also in Dunlop the percentage was relatively high (about 15 per cent).

The number of men who were working in the same firm as their fathers had done is shown below:

	Total in the sample	Men working in the same firm as father
Workington	104	55
Vauxhall	120	4
Dunlop	114	17
Mullard	101	1

A number of men were working in the same or a similar industry or trade (in addition to those who worked in the same firm as their fathers): in Workington ten, in Vauxhall twenty-six, in Dunlop ten and in Mullard ten. So, in Workington, two-thirds of the sample were recruited from families of steelworkers and engineers, in Vauxhall a quarter from engineers or fathers working in the metallurgical industries and in Dunlop again one-fourth from rubber or engineering workers.

The remainder came from families in a host of industries, from railway and other transport work, building work, mining, docking, and a number of non-industrial occupations, such as clerical work, retail trade, service trade, etc.

Miners' sons were most frequent in Workington (nine) and in Vauxhall (eleven, mostly Welshmen); in Dunlop and Mullard there were only a few (three and two respectively).

The sons of railway and other transport workers, dockers, and seamen, were well represented in all firms (eight in Workington, ten in Vauxhall, ten in Dunlop, and nine in Mullard), and also sons of men engaged in building trades (seven in Workington, eleven in Vauxhall, six in Dunlop, ten in Mullard).

A few men, about twenty-three altogether, came from families in farming, forestry or gardening; nearly half of these were in Vauxhall, coming from Bedfordshire homes; a few men, mostly in Vauxhall and Mullard, came from retail and service trade.

The percentage of clerical fathers was, apart from in Mullard, consistently very small, amounting for the four works to about 4 per cent (seventeen altogether, out of whom seven were in Mullard). The highest percentage of clerical fathers was, characteristically, in electrical engineering.

Now we come to the subject of inter-generation mobility in terms of status and skill; here let us deal with the problem by distinguishing four grades—supervisors, skilled men, non-skilled (comprising both semi-skilled and labourers), and finally those who had had a skilled trade but had discarded their skill for one reason or another. As to fathers, for the purpose of comparison we will class coal-miners, dockers, private soldiers, sailors, shop assistants and farming hands as non-skilled labour, though I am fully aware that such people could, in fact, have a considerable skill of their own. Clerical workers, business men, independent farmers, salesmen and all self-employed are classed together under the heading 'clerical and business'.

Let us take first the supervisors:

STATUS AND SKILL OF SUPERVISORS' FATHERS

	TOTAL	Clerical and business, etc.	Supervisors	Skilled	Non-skilled
Workington	8	0	3	3	2
Vauxhall	7	2	0	1	4
Dunlop	8	1	3	2	2
Mullard	9	1	3	3	2
TOTAL	32	4	9	9	10

Inter-Generation Mobility

We see that less than one in three supervisors had non-skilled fathers, and the ratio of supervisors', clerical and business men's sons to the rest is very high, amounting to more than one in three.

The skilled men showed the following distribution of their fathers' status and skill (one was an invalid without occupation):

STATUS AND SKILL OF SKILLED MEN'S FATHERS

	TOTAL	Clerical and business, etc.	Supervisors	Skilled	Non-skilled	Invalid
Workington	21	0	2	8	11	0
Vauxhall	36	7	6	13	10	0
Dunlop	19	5	4	6	3	1
Mullard	31	9	1	12	9	0
TOTAL	107	21	13	39	33	1

As with the supervisors, only about one in three of skilled men had non-skilled fathers, but unlike the supervisors the supervisors' sons form a relatively small percentage.

Now we come to non-skilled men (excluding those who had a skilled trade of their own but were on non-skilled operations). The distribution of skill and status of the fathers presents the following pattern (a number of them had not known their fathers or their fathers had died very early and their trade was not known):

NON-SKILLED MEN'S FATHERS

	TOTAL	Clerical and business, etc.	Supervisors	Skilled	Non-skilled	Un-known
Workington	75	2	6	16	51	0
Vauxhall	65	13	3	11	38	0
Dunlop	77	11	10	21	31	4
Mullard	55	15	5	9	24	2
TOTAL	272	41	24	57	144	6

More than half of the non-skilled men had non-skilled fathers. The proportion of supervisors' sons is the lowest in this group. We can say that at least one-third had failed to maintain the status of their fathers.

Those who had skills but were not using them formed a group

of their own, amounting to about 9 per cent of non-skilled labour in the four works (twenty-six men altogether). Their fathers showed the following pattern of status and skill:

	TOTAL	Supervisors	Skilled	Non-skilled
Workington	3	1	1	1
Vauxhall	10	1	3	6
Dunlop	8	1	5	2
Mullard	5	0	2	3
TOTAL	26	3	11	12

The percentage of non-skilled fathers is higher here than for other skilled men but lower than for the non-skilled.

We see that there was a significant difference in pattern of skill and status of families between different grades: the higher the grade the higher also the percentage of men descending from families of such a grade. A supervisor's son had a better chance of becoming a supervisor than the son of a skilled man, a skilled man's son a better chance to become a skilled man than the son of a non-skilled man. However, there was a considerable movement up and down in all grades. Even among the non-skilled about 8 per cent of men had descended from supervisors and about 20 per cent from skilled men.

However, not all men think in terms of grades and status, as a considerable number are discarding their skilled trades, turning to more profitable operations. Men nowadays seem to be concerned more with money than with status. They are not status-seekers but seekers of home comforts and pleasures which they can get for money. When I asked one man how his wife felt about his giving up the status of a tradesman, he answered: 'She doesn't mind; she married a man not a tradesman, and she enjoys a fatter wage packet'. The discarding of skills may be regarded as wastage of skills on a national scale; on the other hand, it is also a corrective for faulty expectations, imposed by the changing industrial structure.

As might be expected, the pattern of occupational and status distribution of fathers varies considerably from place to place, according to the conditions of the labour market and the changing occupational structure.

B. FATHERS AND SONS

We now consider the third generation, i.e., the sons of men who appear in the sample: we wanted to know whether they were faring better or worse than their fathers. In order to answer this question I concentrated on older sons, aged eighteen or more, as at this age status and skill are already in the process of formation; younger sons, even if apprenticed, are left out in this count. In the four works for which the full information is available there were ninety-four fathers with 135 sons of eighteen-plus, as follows:

	Fathers	Sons
Workington	25	35
Vauxhall	20	33
Dunlop	27	34
Mullard	22	33
TOTAL	94	135

Some sons were working in the same firm as their fathers, namely, nine in Workington, four in Vauxhall, three in Dunlop and four in Mullard. For the sample as a whole about 22 per cent of sons (eighteen-plus) worked in the same firm as their fathers, but apart from Workington where nearly one in three sons worked with their fathers the average ratio in the three remaining firms comes down to about one in seven.

Now let us compare the status of fathers and sons. Fathers with personal skill, although on semi-skilled operations, were counted as skilled. Sons in apprenticeships were classed as skilled, as they were so potentially, and those in college or university, or in clerical, supervisory, professional, or business occupations were classed as 'Staff' (I shall say more about this category later).

SKILL AND STATUS OF FATHERS

	Non-skilled	Skilled	Supervisory	TOTAL
Workington	16	6	3	25
Vauxhall	13	6	1	20
Dunlop	19	7	1	27
Mullard	15	6	1	22
TOTAL	63	25	6	94

STATUS AND SKILL OF SONS OF EIGHTEEN-PLUS

	Non-skilled	Skilled	'Staff'	TOTAL
Workington . . .	12	14	9	35
Vauxhall . . .	13	13	7	33
Dunlop . . .	16	11	7	34
Mullard . . .	11	10	12	33
TOTAL . . .	52	48	35	135

We see that the total number of skilled men in the next generation was nearly doubled and the total number of 'Staff' increased more than five-fold. Of course, not all those men who were apprenticed would necessarily finish their apprenticeship, or subsequently take up a skilled job, but the overall figures show in which direction the sons seemed to be moving.

Now, let us see more specifically what were the occupations which were classed under the heading of 'Staff'.

Workington
    One studying mining engineering at Durham University
    One studying mechanical engineering at Glasgow University
    One Research Chemist
    One Sanitary Inspector
    One Commercial Traveller
    One Supervisor
    One Police Officer
    One Clerk
    One Professional Army Sergeant

Vauxhall
    One Teacher (B.Sc.)
    One Student at Agricultural College
    One R.A.F. Officer
    One Police Officer
    Three Salesmen

Dunlop
    One College Lecturer on Electronics
    One Sales Manager
    One Farmer-Owner in Cornwall
    One Supervisor
    Two Insurance Clerks
    One Time-and-Motion-Study man

Mullard
    Two Factory Managers, one in Canada, one in New Zealand
    Two Civil Servants, one in New Zealand
    Two Accountants
    One Commercial Artist
    One Designer
    One studying science at Manchester University
    Two Supervisors
    One Clerk

We see that about one in four (26 per cent) boys are in the process of what may be called social advancement, joining the ranks of the middle class or lower-middle class.

Now let us see who were the fathers of these men classed here as 'Staff'.

'STAFF' BOYS DESCENDING FROM FATHERS WHO WERE:

	Non-skilled	Skilled	Supervisors	TOTAL
Workington	6	3	0	9
Vauxhall	5	2	0	7
Dunlop	4	3	0	7
Mullard	7	4	1	12
TOTAL	22	12	1	35

Now let us see who were the fathers of the skilled men:

SKILLED BOYS DESCENDING FROM FATHERS WHO WERE:

	Non-skilled	Skilled	Supervisors	TOTAL
Workington	7	2	5	14
Vauxhall	8	4	1	13
Dunlop	7	3	1	11
Mullard	7	3	0	10
TOTAL	29	12	7	48

If we add together skilled and 'staff' boys, we arrive at the following over-all pattern:
    Six supervisors brought up eight skilled and staff sons;
    Twenty-five skilled brought up twenty-three skilled and staff sons;

Sixty-three non-skilled brought up fifty-one skilled and staff.

The supervisors show the best performance in this field, while the difference between the skilled and semi-skilled fathers is not very striking. In some places where high wages are paid, such as in Vauxhall, the performance of semi-skilled fathers equals that of the skilled (thirteen non-skilled fathers 'produced' thirteen skilled and staff, six skilled fathers, six skilled and staff).

The gap between the chances of boys coming from skilled families and non-skilled families has been considerably narrowed down. Only the supervisors' sons still show a definite advantage over non-supervisory grades. A skilled man's son has still some advantage over a non-skilled man's son but the advantage now is very small and it is diminishing with the higher levels of prosperity. A quarter of the boys coming from factory workers' families are reaching middle-class level.

29. RELIGIOUS CONSCIOUSNESS

RELIGION is not regarded as a suitable subject for conversation. Some said: 'I never converse about religion, it's really silly to talk about it'. Still, to my main question: 'Do you believe in God or a Supreme Being, or something in a religious way?' no one refused an answer. However, some answered more fully than others, with comments and views. Roman Catholics invariably stated their denomination, also most Nonconformists; those who were firm believers or regular churchgoers invariably volunteered this information. I also often asked whether, in their view, religion is or can be of help to a working man, and whether they had had any personal experience in this field.

The overwhelming majority were believers in one way or another; only a small minority were non-believers or agnostics. However, the nature of their beliefs was, in many cases, very vague and groping. Some said: 'I believe in something but what it is it is very difficult to say', or 'There must be something', or 'There is something there', or 'There must be some governing factor'. Some believed in a Supreme Being or Supreme Power or Controlling Power, as they described it, others in God or Jesus Christ. But, in fact, there were far more men who stated their belief in theistic or in cosmic terms than in biblical or denominational terms. The ethical and practical side was very frequently stressed as the true nature of religion in such terms as: 'My conscience is my religion', or 'My religion is to be a clean-living man', or 'To be straight and honest, that is religion', or 'To be helpful to everybody, that is religion', or 'I believe in doing good; even if you are not rewarded you feel happy'.

Often, what may be called secularization of religious beliefs was attempted by translating dogma into a social code, as for instance: 'Jesus was a very clever man who distinguished right from wrong', or 'Jesus Christ was the only Communist the world has ever known', or 'Jesus was a wonderful man and what he meant was that we should help one another and not be at each other's throats'.

The will to believe is very strong and nearly universal, often acknowledged by non-believers. One heard: 'Everybody must believe in something', or 'Men are born to believe', or 'It helps you if you can believe', or 'I want to believe, but no one can prove religion', or 'If you have faith it helps you, but you can't make yourself believe'.

The belief in prayer was also widespread. Even non-believers or agnostics referred to the psychological need for prayer. 'To whom do you pray?' I asked the non-believers or agnostics, and the answers came: 'Oh, I don't know to whom', or 'To myself probably', or 'It doesn't matter, it's psychological', or 'I must believe to a certain extent if I'm praying'.

When churchgoing was mentioned the most frequent remark one heard was about hypocrisy: 'I hate hypocrisy', or 'I am not taken in by hypocrites', or 'I am a believer but not a hypocrite', or 'There are schools of hypocrisy', or 'While in the Army I saw a lot of hypocrites among churchgoers'. Some described their relationship to their church as: 'It's a wedding and funeral affair', or 'Wedding and christening affair'.

Some referred to the value of religion as a help to family life: 'It helps to keep the family together'; 'It keeps you in check'; 'It enables you to give a proper answer to the kiddies when they start asking questions'. The belief in the value of religion as an instrument of education for the children was accepted practically by everyone. The non-believers and agnostics subscribed to this view also, and most of them were sending their children to Sunday schools. 'It's part of their education; they have to know the Bible', they said, or 'It's good for the lad', or 'It's part of the training for the young', or 'A child should be able to say: 'God doesn't like me to do this or that', or 'Since my daughter was born I realized that I need to have a religion', or 'The trouble with those Teddy Boys is that they haven't had a religious training'.

Now let us look at the sample data relevant to this problem. The information about religious beliefs is available for four works, namely for eighty-five men in Workington, ninety-eight in Vauxhall, 115 in Dunlop and ninety-nine in Mullard. I divided the answers into five groups: (1) Non-believers; (2) Agnostics, or those who never thought about religion; (3) Firm believers; (4) Other believers—who may be called lukewarm believers; (5) Roman Catholics, who form a group of their own which I treat separately, as they show distinct characteristics.

	(1)	(2)	Religious Beliefs (3)	(4)	(5)	TOTAL
Workington	9	7	15	44	10	85
Vauxhall	7	7	9	67	8	98
Dunlop	18	7	25	47	18	115
Mullard	14	12	16	50	7	99
TOTAL	48	33	65	208	43	397

We see that about 80 per cent were either 'firm believers' or 'believers' or Roman Catholics, who, in the overwhelming majority, were believers; about 12 per cent were non-believers and about 8 per cent were agnostics. Now, let us look more closely at those categories.

Non-believers

Not all non-believers were of one mould. Some called themselves atheists or atheist-materialists, using a strong and determined language of defiance, presenting it in a reasoned way; others did not believe, but did not have much thought behind their attitude. The last category were in the majority in this group.

From atheists one could hear the following comments: 'The Universe is too big a place to be created by one Being called God'; 'If God created the world, who created God?'; 'With all those wars, cruelty and violence how can you believe in God or in His goodness?'; 'If there was a God He wouldn't allow so much violence and murder'; 'God would be a monster if He existed with all this which is going on in the world'; 'I can't accept a Supreme Being with all the incurable diseases'; 'Religion in the past did more harm than good and divides people more than it unites'; 'I can't soak it up. It doesn't seem reasonable with all that's been revealed by science.'

Others were less defiant or less thoughtful. They said: 'Religion means nothing to me', or 'It's all invented by man', or 'It's business really', or 'They believed in Heaven, now they are sending rockets there', or 'To be frank, I have no time for religion, a man can get by without religion', or 'It's all blarney', or 'You can't question the Ten Commandments, but for the rest it's opium for the masses'. It is notable that the non-believers often started apologetically with 'To be frank . . .'

There is one category of non-believers worth mentioning in this context: those who had lost faith because of a personal shock—so to say, out of a grudge against the Maker. 'Since I lost my child I lost my faith', such men would say, or 'How can God allow an innocent child to suffer for years?', or 'Since I lost my young wife I do not believe in anything'. The death of near relatives often revives religious interest, but only if death seems natural, or a relief, not if it is felt as a tragedy or grievous loss.

The non-believers often produced a kind of substitute for their lack of religion. They would say: 'I believe in luck', or 'I believe in fate. What has to be, will be.' Others said, 'I believe in human beings', or 'I believe in kindness', or 'In being helpful to each other'.

Agnostics

Those who were classed as agnostics consisted of two distinct groups: (1) those who were agnostics in the true sense and who often used this term, i.e., who had reached this conclusion after some thought, often deprecating the parochial views of believers, and (2) those who never gave it a thought, who regarded religion as immaterial, not worth thinking about.

From the agnostics came the following: 'You can't really know the Infinite'; 'It's preposterous to pretend to know'; 'It is all surmise only'; 'No one can really prove that'; 'It's all what somebody told you'; 'No one came back to tell us'.

Some had only 'strong doubts', but doubts which were strong enough to prevent them describing themselves as believers: 'I am unwilling and unable to decide', they would say, or 'I am mystified; I am not clear in my mind', or 'I can't say that I believe but I am not a disbeliever'.

Those who had never given the matter a thought spoke in the following way: 'It doesn't interest me; I never gave it a thought', or 'It doesn't concern me', or 'I can't tell you truly; it's beyond me', or 'I never had anything to do with religion. I think a strong-minded person does not need a religion.'

The Firm Believers

These were nearly as numerous as the atheists and the agnostics put together, even without the Roman Catholics whom I have grouped separately, though they too belong mostly to the category of firm believers. Not all of them were churchgoing, some were deeply religious but not in terms of an organized religion. Many of them were Nonconformists, Methodists, Baptists, Jehovah's Witnesses, Plymouth Brethren, Spiritualists, Pentecostalists, etc. Some had had personal religious experience. Many spoke highly of the help religion can offer: 'It's very helpful'; 'It gives you self-confidence'; 'It gives comfort and peace of mind'; 'It helps you to think better'; 'It helps you to plod along'.

They were also strong believers in the efficacy of prayers: 'It relieves tension', they said, or 'If nothing else, it gives you peace of mind', or 'It is uplifting', or 'If you have faith in God He will give you the strength you ask for', or 'When you come to a critical moment in life it is the only help you can get', or 'God is the only Being you can always rely upon', or 'If you pray it does seem to help'. Some described their ways of praying: 'It's mental praying which counts'; 'Every morning I pray with my wife as we get up'; 'Every night I say a little prayer'; 'When I say a prayer at night I am confident. I thank God for the love of my wife and my children and for the happiness which I get from my married life'; 'We would all be better if we knelt by our bedside and said our prayers'.

Some related their experiences: 'When in a Gas Company I

was finding it very hard and I prayed to get another job and it came—like that'; 'When my wife was seriously ill in hospital I prayed, and when I came to the hospital I knew that my prayer was answered'; 'There were many occasions when I felt someone was looking after me'; 'During the war it helped me a lot'; 'When I lost my parents it helped me to relieve my pain and sorrow'.

Some were active in their respective churches and chapels as lay preachers, Sunday-school teachers, youth leaders, caretakers or canvassers. They would all have subscribed to the view expressed by one of them: 'If you miss religion, you miss something valuable and important in life'.

Believers

This was the largest group, comprising more than half of the sample. They 'believed' but had no real religious interest; they believed, but had their doubts. They would say: 'I believe to a certain extent', or 'I believe sometimes', or 'I seem to go through stages, there is a stage when I believe, then for a long time I lose my belief', or 'When I face great problems it comes back', or 'When I do something wrong I come back to it' (here we have again a case of the homeo-static principle, tending towards balance), or 'When in a tight spot I would pray, but not otherwise'.

Many referred to their upbringing. 'You're brought up in it, it's part of you whether you like it or not', they said, or 'I still believe what my father taught me', or 'What you learn as a child you can't forget', or 'I don't believe it really, but it's there. Once it's there, you can't get it out.'

Some referred to the need for religious revival in such terms as: 'We need religion, but it has failed us', or 'The Chapels are more friendly and practical, not so highbrow', or 'Religion could do more if they came out to meet people', or 'What is needed is simplicity in putting it over to the working man'.

Age Composition of Non-Believers and Firm Believers

I wondered whether there was a significant difference in age composition of those who believed firmly on one hand and non-believers on the other. I divided these categories into two age-groups, the under-forties (1), and the over-forties (2), which are shown in the following table:

	Non-believers (1)	(2)	Firm believers (1)	(2)
Workington	6	3	3	12
Vauxhall	5	2	6	3
Dunlop	9	9	11	14
Mullard	10	4	6	10
TOTAL	30	18	26	39

These figures may suggest that there is some difference between the two age-groups in the matter of belief, though the sample is too small to establish this with any certainty.

Roman Catholics

This group, as we saw, consisted of forty-three men, representing about 11 per cent of the whole sample (I did not count here men who only had Catholic wives and children or who wanted to become Catholics). Out of these forty-three only eight were out of touch with their religion: three described themselves as bad Catholics; one was divorced and married again, one lived 'in sin' (concubinage, in fact), and one had married into the Church of England ('I don't keep my religion as I married a girl of the Church of England. My marriage is not valid in the eyes of my Church'). One was Catholic only in name ('I became a Catholic because of my wife to have peace and avoid arguments'). One was a nonbeliever and three others did not go to church, or only occasionally. All the others were more or less regular churchgoers. In the majority they were firm believers, and they would say: 'You can't live without religion'; 'A man without religion is like a ship without a rudder'; 'Religion gives you something to live for'; 'Life is empty and meaningless without faith'; 'If you don't believe you are not human'; 'Religion is good for you: my wife is always a better wife after confession'.

Is there a tendency towards larger families among Catholic workers? Excluding single men, there were thirty-seven married Catholic workers in my sample, and I compared those with families of four or more children with the total number of families of this size in four works, and here are the results:

Men with Four or more Children

	TOTAL	Catholic
Workington	11	3
Vauxhall	8	1
Dunlop	20	8
Mullard	11	0
TOTAL	50	12

A higher percentage of Catholic men had large families than was the case in the total sample. But it must be noticed that the higher proportion of Catholics with large families in the total sample is almost entirely due to the exceptionally high percentage in the Dunlop contingent.

We have seen that there seems to be a great variety of religious ideas, with clashing currents of thought, among working men. Far more men have strong religious beliefs and experiences than may be generally supposed. If Roman Catholics are added, about one in four are firm believers and have deep religious interests. For the rest, there is a will to believe in a vague and groping way; there is a strong latent layer of religious consciousness or subconsciousness which, at present, comes to the fore only in exceptional circumstances.

PART SEVEN

Groups of Workers

30. SINGLE YOUNG MEN

THE YOUNG MEN I met were not angry, but rather placid and quiet. The great issue confronting them was whether to get married or stay single. Would life slip by if they stayed put, or would they be able to enjoy life to the full if they got married? What is better, a car or a wife? 'I was courting', confided one, 'and should have been married by now, but instead I bought a car'. At first I treated it as a joke, but afterwards I heard it so many times in different versions ('I can't afford both a car and a wife, so I drifted away from my girl') that I had to regard it as a main issue for youth at present.

The other important choice is presented by expensive holidays. Some simply lived all the year round for their holidays, concentrating all their hopes and dreams on them. Would they be able to indulge in this luxury when married? 'Last year I went to Spain, this year I am going to Austria with my car', confided a man of twenty-four with pride. Another said: 'This year I am going on my motor bike to France, Germany and Italy. My girl wants to get married—but if I marry will I be able to afford such holidays?'

It is not only whether to get married but also when. Some would say 'I am too young', setting themselves an age limit. Others set themselves targets in the form of savings, house purchase, paying for a car, getting a settled job and so on.

However, the majority of young single men whom I interviewed were contemplating marriage sooner or later. Even those for whom married life had no special attraction were forced to do so, because their friends got married early and they lost their company. Those who stayed single 'Knocked about with mates and pals' and were 'Very pally', as the expression went.

I recorded interviews with fifty-three single men, as follows: eleven in Sheffield, fifteen in Workington, thirteen in Vauxhall, nine in Dunlop and five in Mullard. I have divided them into two main groups: young men in their twenties (twenty to twenty-nine inclusive), mainly courting or 'going steady', altogether thirty-one in number, and older men, twenty-two in number, already hardening or hardened bachelors. Here I deal only with the first group.

The group of single men gradually thinned out. There were seventeen men in the age bracket twenty to twenty-four, fourteen in the age bracket twenty-five to twenty-nine, seven in the age bracket thirty to thirty-four, and so on. A high proportion of men in their twenties were courting, i.e., twelve out of thirty-one, while among older men only three out of twenty-two.

Those who were courting formed a group of their own. They would say, if asked whether they wanted to settle in the job: 'I intend to stay on. I am courting now.' They were keen overtimers in spite of the income tax, and they took on nightshifts, often permanent nights which suited them for two reasons: they could see their girls in the evening (what they disliked most was the afternoon shift) and they could make more money, which was very important. 'I need £700 right away', said a skilled young man in Vauxhall, 'as I am getting married in six months, and I think I will make it. I get £16 net but at times £20.' Some of them were saving prodigiously, as much as £5 or £6 a week.

For these young men, this is the most go-ahead period in their lives, when they day-dream of what they will achieve when they get married and have a home of their own. They are on the look-out for the best-paid jobs with the greatest measure of security.

The second group of young men, who were not courting (nineteen out of thirty-one) can be best described as 'happy-go-lucky fellows'. 'I like to enjoy myself', or 'I like to please myself', they would say. A few who were already hardening as bachelors would confess: 'Marriage is too big a gamble for me', or 'I see how unhappy my pals are who married'. They were not interested in overtime or shiftwork. Asked about overtime they would simply answer: 'I am a single man', implying not only that tax was heavier but also that he did not need it. A few among them were drinking heavily, gambling, or making 'a big splash'.

Those who were courting came, in their behaviour in the works, near to the ordinary run of married men; but those who were not, were not very popular with the supervisors. They were not regarded as the most reliable, industrious or go-ahead workers. They often over-slept, lost shifts, did not pull their weight in the same way as young married men. 'Give me a young married man every time' was the verdict of one foreman. 'They are the best workers we have.'

The other great issue confronting young single men is whether to stay in the job and 'carry on', in order to get the benefit of long service and a certain degree of security, or to go round experimenting, seeing different places and perhaps finding a more rewarding job. Those who were skilled mostly stayed put. It so happened that out of thirty-one men, only five were skilled, which was much below the average for married men. Does this suggest that skilled men marry earlier because they settle in a job earlier? Anyway, out of these five skilled men, four had had only one job in their working life, staying in the same firm where they had started their apprenticeship.

There was only one real labourer, doing a cleaning job, apart from six labourers in the steelworks who occupied the first rung on the promotion ladder to more skilled jobs. These labourers in the steelworks had also kept their jobs tenaciously, as four had had no other previous jobs and two had long service behind them, exceeding five years.

The remainder, i.e., nineteen, were semi-skilled men, mostly machine operators. They had changed their jobs more readily, and some even drastically, from such jobs as gardening, building, milk delivery, grocery, bakery or shoe repairing, to jobs in steelworks, engineering and motor works. Three among them were former apprentices in brick-laying, joinery, or tool-making who had given up their apprenticeship, but this had often been conditioned by the demands of the labour market ('I couldn't find a job in my trade', they said, or 'I became redundant'). However, courting was also responsible for giving up apprenticeship, if quick money was needed.

Were they interested in their jobs? The majority, apart from those who had a skilled trade, were not very interested, or not at all. They regarded it 'just as a job' and what they liked most about it was 'money', and often also the 'good sort of fellows around'.

'When I finish work I am happy', answered a young man when asked if he felt happy. And that was confirmed by another man who said that he felt happy for half an hour after he finished work. 'Nobody likes his work really', confided another man, 'but I wouldn't throw it away just because I don't like it'. 'Carry on' was their motto. 'It's good, easy money'; 'I take the rough with the smooth'; 'Not really interesting'; these were the most common attitudes of the young men. It was obvious that they expected something better, more exciting, more satisfying than this. One could say that they were not yet broken in to the job.

Only very few had real ambitions to go higher, outside the automatic promotion ladder. Only a few were interested in becoming foremen, and these were usually the men who were courting, spurred by ambition to show their mettle to their girls.

The majority of young men still lived with their parents or with a sister, i.e., twenty-two out of thirty-one; eight lived in furnished accommodation and one had a house of his own. They paid their parents on the average between £3 and £3 10s for their keep, but some between £2 and £2 10s and others as much as £5; only one gave his whole wage packet to his widowed mother. If the mother is widowed the son often keeps her, and that may prevent him from getting married. Mother-attachment figured frequently as the cause of remaining single.

There is a fairly large proportion of the mobile population in this group, as nine men out of thirty-one came from other districts; these men were mainly Irish, Scottish or Welsh. I looked up the records of leavers in the firm I visited and I could see that the percentage of young single men among those who left of their own accord, or who were dismissed, was much higher than that of married men.

The savings effort of this group was fairly high. In four works, Workington, Vauxhall, Dunlop and Mullard, out of twenty-six men in their twenties, eleven saved between £3 and £6 a week, and others saved smaller amounts; there were only three who did not believe in saving.

As to hobbies and pastimes, their main interest lay in sports and motoring. One in three took an active interest in such sports as football, cricket, or swimming, and for those who had a car motoring was the main hobby. Music, singing and dancing were also favourite pastimes. Out of twenty-six men in four works, nine had record players or radiograms, two had tape-recorders and one who wanted to become a professional singer had a piano of his own.

When asked about drinking habits, eight men out of twenty-six in four works classed themselves as teetotallers, near-teetotallers, or occasional drinkers, but four were drinking heavily.

There were only three men who stood out from the ordinary run: an Australian globe-trotter who was working his passage on his tour of the world, a singer in a men's club who wanted to become a professional singer, and a man breeding and racing eleven greyhounds, with two acres of land, his own house, a van, radiogram, piano, washing machine, with ambition to own a racehorse and with savings in cash of more than £600.

I would say that a young married man is a more interesting man than a single one, with a more fully developed personality. He has many more roles to play, not only as workmate, son and brother, but also as husband, father, son-in-law, brother-in-law, as tenant or house-owner and so on. He comes into closer contact with another family, maybe of a different kind, which is often by its novelty attractive to him, giving him a new range of experience and widening his interests. His life is richer and he must model himself on a much larger and more complex pattern. His emotional life and his motivation have also a much broader sweep of love, fear, anxiety, hope and expectation.

A young single man may think that he is better off financially than his married friend, but in fact, more often than not, he is not. There are many reasons responsible for this, such as the previous savings of his wife, her wage for a number of years, income tax allowances and more careful spending, but most important of all is his own work, which becomes with marriage more steady and effective.

31. CONFIRMED BACHELORS

THE BACHELOR TYPE becomes 'confirmed' sometime in his thirties. He comes to the conclusion that he has 'missed the bus', he is already set in his habits and too old to learn new ways. However, there is a whole panorama of characters and temperaments which appear in this type.

Altogether, twenty-two single older men, of thirty and over, appear in my casebook, derived from five firms. The crowd of single men continues to thin out considerably with age; there were ten in the age bracket thirty to thirty-nine, eight in the next age bracket forty to forty-nine, and only four older. Only three men were courting, or courting again, all in their early thirties; apart from these, none contemplated marriage. With every year the bachelor seems to harden his heart still further. As one aged forty-eight confided: 'I am already in a rut, my ways are set; to get married would mean a constant clash of temperaments'.

The reasons which they proffered for staying single varied considerably, but a few themes recurred constantly. Three of them referred to their bad childhood. Is it that they were starved of love in their early childhood, and did not learn to expect, accept, or inspire love? 'I had bad luck, I was an adopted child. Mother ran away and left us while we were young', said one. Another said: 'We had a bad childhood. All my brothers and sisters remained single.' A third: 'I have seen in my own family the evil effect of a bad marriage and I was frightened'.

For three or four others mother attachment, especially when the mother was widowed, was the main reason for staying single. 'I couldn't do it to my mother, to leave her like that', they would say, or 'I was too comfortably off with my mother. I never thought that one day she might be gone and I would be left alone', or 'I am the only son and mother has nobody else'. One who was courting (or perhaps only pretending to be courting) said that although he intended to get married, 'the main snag is that the girl has to consent to live with the mother'.

Two men were not at all interested in sex, and had never had a girl friend. Two others gave as their reasons: 'I was in love' or 'I was courting and the girl let me down'.

One man 'missed the bus' while serving in the regular Army, another was a religious fanatic suffering from depression; another was a polio victim living with his mother, who didn't 'want pity', still another had a housekeeper and a flat of his own. All the others simply said: 'I don't like the responsibility' or 'I like to enjoy myself'. They often belonged to the selfish type, as could easily be gathered from their remarks about human nature: 'Men are a selfish lot. Everyone for himself.' On the whole, they were very self-conscious, self-centred and not very happy; a crop of diseases, accidents and handicaps had befallen them. Probably it is not just by chance that the majority (namely thirteen out of twenty-two) had a handicap or disease, or had had a serious accident; three had also had long bouts of unemployment at one time or another. Six had had serious accidents (one had lost an eye, another had lost hearing in one ear, one had a broken toe, three had a broken hand or fingers), three suffered from headaches, depression or general debility, one had had polio, one had had a rupture and pneumonia, still another had recently been laid up for a whole year with peritonitis. Was it that their poor health was responsible for their staying single, or was their status responsible for their not getting the care and comfort that the ordinary run of married men would enjoy? There would seem to be a vicious circle here.

But in fact the majority were not badly taken care of. Out of twenty-two, thirteen men, all in their thirties except one, still lived with their parents or parent, two lived with their sisters, one had his own house which he shared with his brother, one had an unfurnished flat with a housekeeper and only five lived in furnished rooms.

While staying with their parents most of them paid between £3 and £4 10s; only one paid as little as £2 5s and one as much as £6, but the last case was the son of a widow whom he had to keep. In furnished rooms they paid not much more for full board, on average between £3 10s and £4 10s.

They were closer to their families of origin than the married men. Only one man out of twenty-two did not 'bother with his family'; all of the others either lived with their families or were close to them, visiting their homes or being very 'clannish', as they described themselves. They felt the need to keep close links with their families of origin as they had no nuclear families of their own. It seems that somehow men need 'anchoring' somewhere. Those who had no brothers and sisters—there were three of these—felt very lonely and forlorn indeed.

The happy-go-lucky bachelor who makes good use of his freedom, gets around and enjoys himself, was not a very frequent occurrence in my casebook. However, one compensation stood out in their experience, and that was a regular and expensive holiday practically every year. Another compensation for these men may be the ability to indulge in gambling. Five of them were habitual gamblers, testing their luck in a big way on dogs and horses, and among them one was breeding and running his own greyhounds. Very few were drinking heavily. Only two could be classed in this category, many more were weekend drinkers or moderate pub-goers, and six described themselves as teetotallers. Strangely enough the unhappy combination of gambling and drinking did not occur: two of the heavy gamblers were in fact complete abstainers. A number had no hobby worth talking about and four said simply, 'no hobby really'. They were better readers than most of the married men as they had more time to spare and often had no T.V. at home.

There were only a few skilled men among them (four out of twenty-two), three were labourers and the remainder semi-skilled men. The majority were steady men who stayed on in their jobs and wanted to keep them. The skilled men were, with the exception of one, long-service men with ten or more years' service. But even the semi-skilled and labourers had, in the majority, not a bad record, as out of eighteen, nine had ten or more years' service. Only two had a record of ten or more jobs; one of these had thirty jobs to his credit.

On the whole, they were not very interested in their work. They felt monotony in their private lives and this monotony seemed to be transferred to the work itself. 'Monotonous', 'Dull', 'Uninteresting', 'Browned off', 'It's a strain', 'It's not a job I would pick for myself', 'Only money', 'I have to do a job, so I do it', were typical comments. The minority, notably the skilled men, viewed their job more favourably: 'Suits me', 'Reasonably good', 'I like it', they would say. There is a two-way traffic in attitudes between life and work: sometimes the attitude to work is transferred to life, more often the basic attitudes in life are transferred to work. It is not an interesting life which they lead, and this is reflected in their attitude to work.

As to possessions: only one had a house of his own, bought jointly with his brother, four had cars and two had motor cycles, and only two had radiograms or record players. There is little doubt that the standard of possessions of this group is much below that of married men.

They often wondered whether they had not wasted their lives living in isolation, but they had developed strong habits of living alone and leading a quiet life, and they enjoyed a great many compensations for the missing family life. Whenever they see a broken home or a home threatened with break-down, they console themselves, 'At least I am spared all that'. Whenever they see men grieving, they say to themselves, 'I have given fewer hostages to fortune'.

32. WIDOWERS

IN MY PORTRAIT GALLERY of widowers I found an array of most interesting characters, some invoking strong sympathy. Their basic problem was loneliness, and their main aim was to overcome this loneliness by building up new relationships, new ties, or new interests. However, some were nursing their bereavement, indulging in self-pity on the familiar line of 'Why should this happen to me?', looking backwards, and at the mercy of reveries about the past. 'No, I wouldn't put anybody in my wife's place', they would say, reiterating their resolution to devote their life to grief, and longing for things which lie beyond the compass of life.

The impact of widowerhood varied, first according to age (whether it caught the man in his prime or in middle age); second according to vitality (whether the man was able to start anew and rebuild his life); third according to experience (whether or not he had been happy in his marriage). Men with happy experience were eager to repeat it, provided they were not over-sentimental, or yearned for the exact replica of the old. The first marriage always has an impact on the second; most men either try to regain the image of the lost wife, or to gain someone entirely different with opposite traits.

According to the data of my enquiry most widowers marry again. Out of fifteen cases of widowers, eleven had married again, most of them happily, and in addition one was hoping to get married soon. However, two of them had had especially bad luck, and one had been widowed for the second time.

I grouped my cases into three classes.

First I had a group of nine widowers who had happily married again. The outstanding feature about them was that they had a full life with large and mixed families. As one of them said: 'It's a complete contrast to my previous life. In my first marriage with my ailing wife I had an empty house; now I have a full life with lots of children knocking about and knocking down everything and lots of problems, but I would rather have this than emptiness. The previous life is done for and although my first wife was good, I don't miss her. I have nothing to reproach myself with. I did everything I could for her.'

It was characteristic that this man suddenly started to excuse himself: a more or less unconscious feeling of guilt is frequently present where there has been a good and longstanding relationship. Most of the widowers were torn between the past and the present, between regret and satisfaction, between feeling guilty and feeling that they had done the right thing.

This man whose story is reported above had one boy by the first wife and another boy by his second wife, in addition to four step-children. Three sets of children are a common occurrence, and the resulting family circle is large, composite and almost patriarchal, with lots of problems and a great deal of movement, bustle and commotion. A big man, full of vitality, is needed to cope with all this. Out of nine cases of remarried widowers, one had nine children, three, six children, three, three children and only two had one or none.

It is not surprising that such men had a full share of upsets, accidents and illnesses. Two had stomach ulcers, one had been laid up with a heart attack for four months only recently, one had lost an eye, two had had pneumonia. But in the majority they stood up well to the challenge of life: they represented a more vital brand of men who did not shirk their duty and were willing to take on new responsibility.

They belonged to the more successful and prosperous class of workmen. That is probably the reason why they could afford to marry again, or why they were worth marrying. Five men out of nine owned their own houses and three had considerable nest-eggs, ranging from £300 to £2,000. They were hard-working men, very keen on overtime and piecework, and some had a 'sideline' or a profitable hobby. One man with nine children was a weekend salesman, selling second-hand clothes on a barrow; another with six children was a market gardener; another was a weekend carpenter.

They reported regretfully how their emotional upsets with their first wife's illnesses and death had affected their work, causing long spells of absenteeism or lack of concentration or neglect of work, inviting the cutting question of the foreman: 'What's the matter with you?'

They seemed to be good husbands, well trained and tested, and they wanted to carry on the same relationship with the second wife as with the first wife. Out of nine men, six passed over the whole wage packet to their wives, keeping only a small amount of pocket-money for themselves: this was, however, not surprising considering their large families and responsibilities. Four men provided washing machines for their wives and three radiograms, apart from T.V., of course, which is obligatory for nearly every workman, but none had a car. Only one of them had a wife going out to work—a full-time nurse.

The second group, five widowers who lived alone, presented a different picture altogether. They were mostly in their fifties and sixties, with one exception, a man in his thirties, who already looked for consolation in a new relationship. The tragedy had occurred when they were too old to start again and they wanted peace more than anything else. One had been unable to pick up the pieces of a ruined life and was simply waiting for death, but others had developed outside interests and hobbies. One was 'a big club man' (he was active in Working Men's Clubs), another was secretary of the local British Legion, one was a breeder of budgerigars, and yet another was a regular pub- and club-goer, playing darts, dominoes and snooker. They had their compensations, which consisted chiefly in shedding responsibility and leading a more peaceful (though restricted) life. 'I take life as it comes', they would say.

Only one had the help of a woman who did the washing for him, all the others were doing their own housework. 'I do everything for myself including shopping', they would say, but they would add: 'A working man needs his wife; I miss my wife very much. I was a better workman previously, there is nothing now to go home to.'

They did not care for overtime, not only because of lack of incentive, but also because they had housework and shopping to do. They were not very well off. Only one had his own house, a car and a considerable nest-egg; all the others had practically no possessions. They had also had a full share of illnesses and accidents; one had lost a finger, another had a stomach ulcer, the third had recently had phlebitis.

The job assumed for them an additional value as the home interest receded, and they needed companionship more than ever. A happily married man has two centres of interest; he walks, so to speak, on two legs, while a widower hops on one only. So they would say: 'It's better to be here than at home'.

Finally we come to a man who forms a class of his own, having had the double misfortune of widowhood and separation. A man of forty-five, after twenty-five years of happily married life he had lost his wife and married again. They had been courting for two years, and were both working in the same shop. She was a good workmate, co-operative and friendly; he thought he knew her well. She was a divorcee with a boy of her own. They were happy together only for a week. I know only his side of the story. She changed so much, he asserted, he couldn't recognize her, was moody, quarrelsome, suspicious, made up stories and followed him everywhere. She was strong and aggressive, she threw things at him whenever they had rows, she called the police, making up stories that he wanted to kill her. For a year they slept in different rooms in the same house. He couldn't get his sleep and rest, was permanently tired, suffered from hypertension and was finally laid up for seventeen weeks with legs almost paralysed from fear, resentment and worry. After long-drawn-out agonies he summoned up his courage and with the help of his brother-in-law threw his wife out of the house. He gradually got better and was living at the time of the enquiry with his married daughter and grandchildren, the wiser for this amazing and unfortunate experience. That was the end of his vain attempt to reconstruct the past. He was then devoting the remainder of his life to the memory of his first wife. The first wife triumphed, presumably, in this adventure and in his mind the experience assumed the form of a penance for what he regarded as unsteadfastness.

Speaking to widowers one could sense a note of melancholy in their attitude to love, life and death, a certain reflectiveness and depth of sentiment which are missing in the ordinary run of men who have been spared this experience. Those who had lost their wives suddenly, nearly overnight, had suffered a severe shock from which they were hardly able to recover. I often asked whether religion was of help, whether they turned to it in their days of sorrow. Most of them denied this. It looked as if religion was of help only to those who were prepared for death and where death was looked upon as a release.

33. MEN NEARING RETIRING AGE

THOSE who were nearing retiring age form a group of their own, with specific problems and handicaps. They look now with benevolent eyes on those who still hustle and bustle about. They know that all this will soon come to a standstill for them. They are treated with special tolerance by the foremen who are willing to exempt them from all arduous tasks (in some firms they are exempt from shiftwork and overtime) but not from dirty jobs. 'I have to do all the dirty jobs because the young ones won't have it', said one man. Many men at this age are put on cleaning.

They never argue, they do as they are told. As one man put it, 'The secret of good work is just to do as you are told'. They are afraid of losing their job as they couldn't get another one. 'Age is against me everywhere', said another. One man in Mullard pretended to be ten years younger: 'I am fit and I didn't want to be permanently on the Labour Exchange. I didn't risk much; the worst, if they found me out, would be the sack.'

They find the work far easier than in the old days: 'Everything has improved so much; the young would never know what we have been through'. They like working with young people, although they are not very popular with them. One young man described them blatantly as 'Miserable old devils'.

None of those firms which I visited practised compulsory retirement at the age of sixty-five. In Mullard one could carry on subject to medical examination every two years; in Dunlop manual workers could carry on up to seventy; in Workington they were granted extension if they were fit; in Sheffield they could carry on indefinitely if they were fit and one of the men I interviewed there was eighty-one. All the firms had a contributary or non-contributary pension scheme which provided for a small pension according to the length of service.

Altogether I had, in my sample, thirty-eight married men of sixty years and over (actually thirty-seven men in their sixties and one man of eighty-one). Apart from at Mullard they had a record of long service in the firm, as shown in the following table:

	YEARS OF SERVICE					
	Up to 10	11–20	21–30	31–40	40 and over	TOTAL
Sheffield	3	3	1	1	2	10
Workington	1	1	0	0	7	9
Vauxhall	0	0	2	0	1	3
Dunlop	0	2	0	3	1	6
Mullard	8	1	1	0	0	10
TOTAL	12	7	4	4	11	38

Mullard and Workington present the greatest contrast in this respect. This was caused by the character of the labour market on one hand and the length of operation of the firms on the other.

Men nearing retiring age were on the whole well off, although the standard of wealth and welfare differed from place to place. In three firms, Vauxhall, Workington and Mullard, every man without exception lived in his own house or a council house. (Out of twenty-two men eleven had their own houses and eleven lived in council houses.) In Dunlop only four had a council house and none had his own house. The data for Sheffield are incomplete, but out of four for whom the data are available, two had a council house and one had his own house.

The majority were good savers. In Workington five men had a nest-egg of £1,000 or more and one had two houses and savings of £300. In Vauxhall two had savings of £1,000. In Dunlop one had £1,500 to his credit, and two £700 to £750. In Mullard two men saved £2 or more a week, two £1 a week and the rest less. No nest-egg was recorded there; only one man had savings of £200 from lump-sum pension rights—he had been an engine driver on the railways for thirty-five years.

The nest-eggs of some were connected with compensation money. In Workington, for instance, one man had received £1,500 for a fractured spine, in Dunlop one man received £700 for a broken shoulder, another £5 a week for a broken hand.

One of the striking features of this group, especially in the heavier type of industry, was the high incidence of disability. In Workington there were four cases of serious injury: one had a fractured spine, one had lost an eye, one had a broken leg and one had lost two fingers. In Dunlop there were three compensation cases, one with a broken shoulder, one with a broken leg and one with a broken hand; in Sheffield three had had serious accidents.

These men were also losing shifts through frequent illnesses. In Mullard, for instance, three had had recent operations, and one suffered from spine trouble.

In Mullard one could study the process of demotion which goes with advanced age. There, six out of ten men had been demoted: a man who had been a works manager in India was only doing a skilled job in Mullard; a civil servant was doing a semi-skilled job; a skilled engine driver was doing a labouring job; a charge-hand was demoted with the reorganization of the department; a salesman was doing a semi-skilled job; and a semi-skilled operator had been demoted to labouring after he had come back from hospital. In Workington there were only two cases of demotion, one a previous foreman, the other a semi-skilled operator who had been demoted to a labourer after an accident; in Dunlop there was only one case of demotion.

Were the men looking forward to their retirement, or did they prefer to carry on working? That depended on many interconnected factors. In light industry such as at Mullard many more men wanted to carry on than in heavy industry such as at Workington or Dunlop. Or where the majority of men had a long-service record as, for instance, in Workington, they could look forward to getting a pension which would be an addition to the Old Age Pension.

The information concerning the will to retire or to carry on is available for twenty-seven men, as follows:

	THOSE WHO WANTED:		
	To retire	*To carry on*	TOTAL
Sheffield	0	4	4
Workington	4	3	7
Vauxhall	2	0	2
Dunlop	3	3	6
Mullard	2	6	8
TOTAL	11	16	27

Those who wanted to carry on expressed their view very forcibly:

'When they carry you out that is the best time to retire. We live to work and work to live'; 'As long as a man is fit to work it is good for him to go on working. When he stops working he starts going'; 'Work as long as you can'; 'I want to carry on as long as I am fit' or 'As long as I am able'.

Two men wanted to retire at sixty-five but they said that unfortunately they couldn't afford it. As one man said, 'A man, after fifty years of hard work, should be able to live in comfort. I believe in retiring, but retiring on something. Unfortunately I have nothing to retire on.' Those who want to carry on often showed a special interest and zeal in the job in order to justify their claims for keeping the job.

Those who wanted to retire argued: 'I am looking forward to retirement', or 'I am no longer active as I used to be, my health is failing', or 'I won't be like one of those who sit on a bench in the park with nothing to do; I will be able to afford a drink'.

However, four men out of eleven who wanted to retire said they would be looking for an easy job or for 'a little job' or part-time job ('Two days a week will do for me', said one, and another, 'Four hours a day would suit me').

A part-time job would be the answer for many, and this answer could be forthcoming if imagination and care were applied for the benefit of those concerned as well as for the national economy. Half-shifts, in the case of female labour, if properly organized as in Mullard, can be a great success. Two pensioners could easily do one full-time job between them and be treated as one unit. Most men are afraid of the prospect of sudden displacement, emptiness and void, and half-shifts for them would soften the transition to full retirement.

PART EIGHT

Women Operatives in Mullard

34. THE ENQUIRY IN MULLARD

MY SAMPLE CONSISTED of sixty-seven married women, chosen at random from all departments. Single girls were excluded, while widows, separated or divorced women were included. Three girls were foreign-born, one German, one Italian and one Russian, but as they were married to Englishmen and settled here they were retained in the sample. All the women were willing to co-operate and talk freely about their problems. The great majority were semi-skilled; only two were supervisors and two others part-time cleaners.

Most of them were full-timers; only nineteen worked part-time. The sample in this respect does not represent the true distribution of the labour force in Mullard, which is almost equally divided between full-timers and part-timers. I chose to concentrate attention on the full-time 'family' women because it is among this group that one would expect to encounter the maximum adjustment problems between home and work responsibilities.

Married Women at Work

I use the term 'married women' here to include women who were or had been married. It might be expected that there would be a higher percentage of widows, separated and divorced women among married women at work than among married women in the population at large. Out of sixty-seven women interviewed six were widows, of whom three had married again, and four were separated or divorced, of whom one had married again. Two others were separated *de facto*, one of them having a husband certified as mentally defective, another a regular soldier serving in Germany.

As to the age composition, the majority of married women in my sample were in their thirties (twenty-seven) and forties (twenty-three); only eight were in their twenties and nine in their fifties; none was older.

As to family size, out of sixty-seven married women seventeen had no children, thirty-six had one or two children, five had three children and nine, four or five children.

Attitudes to Work

The firm is very much appreciated by the majority of women operatives. 'It is a good firm to work for'; 'Fair conditions'; 'They treat you well'; 'They give you every consideration', they said.

Forty-eight out of sixty-seven enjoyed their work, according to their answers to my question, 'Do you enjoy, tolerate, or endure your work?' They were very interested in their jobs and they spoke highly of them in such terms as: 'A very nice job'; 'The best job I ever had'; 'Enjoyable and easy going'; 'I'm happy in my job'; 'I enjoy it, otherwise I wouldn't be here'. A woman who had been in the firm only one and a half years said: 'If I had known that it was so nice I would have come here sooner'.

Another four women enjoyed their work, but only 'up to a point' or 'sometimes': 'It depends how you feel', they would say.

Only nine women said that they 'tolerated' the job rather than enjoyed it; five others spoke of boredom and monotony. Characteristically enough the latter were mostly those who had been transferred to another department recently. ('I enjoyed it up to recently but they spoilt the job for me by transferring me to another department.') Women dislike being moved from jobs even more than men, and they develop strong bonds of companionship with their fellow workers. Only one woman felt that she 'endured' the work.

Preference for Housework or Factory Work

Would these married women have preferred to stay at home rather than go out to work? The big majority, that is, forty-two out of sixty-seven, answered this question in the negative. They were very outspoken on this point, saying: 'I would rather be here—the mind is occupied'; 'I am not keen on housework, housework does not satisfy me'; 'I incline to fidget at home when by myself—I've got to do something, I can't sit idle'; 'Keeps you young'; 'I dread the four walls'; 'Fed up at home'; 'Nothing to do at home'; 'Sooner go out to work'; 'Factory work's better than housework'; 'Would worry me more to be at home'; 'It is good to be with the young'; 'There are domesticated women, I am not one of them'; 'I don't like housework although I like cooking.'

Companionship was again and again referred to and stressed as the great incentive. 'You can have a laugh here. It gives you a break,' said one widow. 'It is good to be with others.'

Some stressed the point that they were too active to stay at home. 'I've got to do something; I am too active.'

On the other hand, fifteen preferred housework and they expressed their preference in such terms as: 'If it weren't for the money I would rather stay at home', or 'Housework is better, your time is your own, nobody watches you', or 'There is plenty to do at home'. It was interesting to note that among those fifteen only two had school-children, seven had no children and the remainder had grown-up children. So apparently for the majority of domesticated women the care of children was not the decisive factor.

Domesticity is actually an attitude of mind fostered or atrophied by the conditions at home and husband–wife relationship. I believe that this relationship plays a big part in domesticity. If the relationship is very good, the wife becomes domesticated; if, on the other hand, the relationship is not very satisfactory, she seeks companionship outside in order to find relief from her isolation and loneliness. Surprisingly enough, all mothers of large families (four to five children) declared that they enjoyed coming out to work, and preferred factory to housework. Perhaps drudgery at home endured for a long time made the change seem enjoyable by contrast. Those who preferred to go out to work often added that they were not 'very fussy' about the home being 'spick-and-span'. 'I am not houseproud', they would say, or 'The polish is not the most important thing in life', or 'The house is for us, not we for the house', or 'Anyway, we are not living in Buckingham Palace'.

Those with a more introvert frame of mind, it seems, are happy at home, and find enough interest to occupy their minds, while the extroverts need stimulation from outside and wider interests. However, those inclined to brooding, worry, anxiety and fears, or to morbid introspection, are better off at work. 'You have no time to worry when you come out', they say.

Another batch of ten women were not very definite about their preference. 'A bit of each', they would say. For them there was not much to choose between factory and housework. 'At times I prefer here, at times I prefer home.'

Working Mothers and Care of Children

Do working mothers neglect their children? What are the provisions made for young children when they are at work?

Let us review in detail the age groups of working mothers in my sample, and the size of their families. None of the eight women in their twenties had any children. Out of twenty-seven women in their thirties, seven were without children, fourteen with one or two children, six with three or four and none with larger families. However, there was none with a baby. There was only one with a toddler of three, who was taken care of by his grandmother; the remainder were with school-children or grown-up children.

Out of twenty-three women in their forties, three had no children, eighteen one to two children and two, three to five children. Again there was no baby, and only one woman had a toddler of three taken care of by the father, who was a shiftworker while she was on part-time. The remainder had school-children or grown-up children, some of whom had already left home.

Out of nine women in their fifties, only one had a school-child and two others had grown-up children at home.

So we see that among those interviewed none had a baby to look after, and there were only two toddlers. Now let us look closely at the position of the school-children. There were thirty-six school-children (up to the age of fifteen) altogether, out of whom fourteen were younger children up to the age of ten inclusive. What was the provision made for those younger children? Six were looked after by grandmothers, one by another relative, one by a lady neighbour, one by an older sister, and three were looked after by the mothers themselves, who were only on part-time. Only in the case of two children were no special arrangements made; one of these was a child of nine whose mother had to earn her own living and another was a foster-child of ten. Only two or three mothers (but neither of those who had made no arrangements) referred to their children as being 'a bit upset' by their going out to work; all others contended that the children were 'perfectly all right'.

Work as an Economic Necessity

To what extent is women's work an economic necessity? Out of sixty-seven married or once-married women six were widowed, divorced, or separated; two others lived apart from their husbands; three more had husbands ill or handicapped; five other women were not in receipt of sufficient housekeeping money, having either selfish husbands or wasters, as they described them, or husbands not yet settled in their jobs or earning very little. So, roughly speaking, one in four presented a case of economic necessity. However, that did not mean that they objected to their work; on the contrary, they often enjoyed it and felt all the better for the companionship which helped them to break the isolation in which they lived.

The other women worked for a great variety of reasons which were given as: 'Nothing to do at home'; 'Companionship'; 'Extras'; 'A better standard of living'; 'Help with the car'; 'Help with buying the house'; 'To keep the children at school as long as they can make it'; 'Until we get a family'; 'For holidays', etc. There was rarely a case with one motive only. The motives were blended in a tangle of complex situations. However, in one-third of the sample one motive predominated which came out in answer to my question: 'What is your reason for working?' Five women mentioned specifically: 'To help to buy the car', and three others 'To help to buy a house'. Eight other newly-married women wanted to keep on working until they started families, again thinking of helping towards a house or furniture. Four women wanted to keep the children longer at school and one woman wanted to help out a daughter in trouble with an illegitimate child.

Sometimes the economic necessity belonged to the past but the habit had grown. 'I started to work when my husband was ill', or 'had an accident', or 'was on the Labour Exchange', or 'when he was in the Navy', said some women. Once they had started they continued as they enjoyed the work and company.

Sometimes the economic motive was completely lacking: 'I work on doctor's advice'; 'I work in order to let my husband sleep during the day as he is on permanent nights'; 'I do it only for companionship'; but in the majority of cases the motives are complex and the economic motive crept in in one way or another. 'Of course the money comes in handy', or 'I enjoy the economic independence, not having to ask for every single penny', were typical comments.

Coping with Two Jobs

Can women cope with two jobs, home and work? Are they not over-reaching themselves? Can they expect help from their husbands? Out of sixty-seven married or once-married women only eight said that they felt the strain of coping with two jobs, or that sometimes they felt it was too much, or that they indulged in self-pity. Characteristically, of these eight women four were widowed or divorced or separated, and one of them said: 'It is one mad rush'. These women often felt lonely and dispirited, which might have sapped their strength—and they had no partner to help them.

Most women develop 'a method' or 'a routine' which consists of doing something every day but often concentrating most of the housework at the weekend, Saturday or Sunday often being their washing day. One woman described her routine as follows: Monday—lazy day, Tuesday—cleaning, Wednesday—washing, Thursday—out for a game of darts with a team of which she is the captain, Friday—ironing, Saturday—shopping and washing, Sunday—spit and polish.

'Without a routine', they would say, 'you would be lost.' They referred to the fact that they don't waste time in gossiping like women who stay at home; they organize their work, think about it and apply, so to say, their own time-and-motion study to it. Often they would say, 'I am quick', or 'I don't linger about'.

Every single member of the household is expected to give a hand in the housework. First of all the husband. Out of fifty-nine women who lived with their husbands, only seven stated that they didn't get any help from their husbands, saying: 'He wouldn't do it', or 'He is a waster—sailor's habits', or 'He used to help me, but not now', or 'Only helps me when I am ill', or 'He lost interest in the home'. Two out of those seven commented: 'I don't need any help' and 'I don't ask if I can manage by myself'.

The remainder of the women gave their husbands a good testimonial in such terms as: 'I don't ask but he volunteers'; 'He does anything in the house'; 'Anything dirty or heavy he does'; 'He cleans the windows, polishes the floors, and washes and irons'; 'He helps me out now since I came out'; 'He does all the shopping'; 'I wouldn't come out if we were not sharing the housework'; 'I help him out, so he helps me out, fifty-fifty'; 'He takes the children to school'; 'Things at home work out better since I came out'.

Many women added that the money frustrations are the worst of the lot; any other inconveniences involved in coping with two jobs are only half as bad. Money worries are the worst kind of worries; life runs so much smoother with money and whatever inconveniences factory work can bring they cannot be compared with the inconveniences and squabbles caused by shortages.

Appreciation of Women's Work by the Family

Are working women more appreciated by husbands and children? Does going out to work raise their self-respect and social standing?

Women who were asked whether they believed that working women are more appreciated by husband and children and feel more independent, answered without exception: 'Definitely more independent'; as far as appreciation of their work by their husbands was concerned the answers were divided.

The big majority, i.e., forty-four out of fifty-nine wives living with their husbands, answered this question in the affirmative, saying: 'He appreciates it all right', or 'I am buying the car for him', or 'He wouldn't be able to have a car', or 'He has less worry about money', or 'I often give him a treat'. They referred also to having wider interests, something to talk about, and to their good feeling that they 'justify their existence'.

The remainder of the women contended that their husbands take their work for granted or even resent it. Eight women declared: 'My husband takes it for granted', or 'He is not interested', or 'I do as I please', while seven others answered: 'My husband rather resents it'; 'Men like to feel that they are the breadwinners'; 'My husband doesn't like it'; 'My husband would prefer me to stay at home'; 'My husband likes the money all right but he doesn't like me out'; or 'A man is rather proud of his wife taking proper care of his home'.

Do the children appreciate their mothers working? Here also a big majority, let us say two in three, answered the question in the affirmative, saying: 'If you give them something extra, they appreciate it', or 'I am giving them pocket-money, they appreciate that', or 'They wouldn't have so much money in their pockets', or 'They know they benefit', or 'I am keeping my boy at school and he knows it'. However, a substantial minority, about one in three, stated that their children would rather have them at home: 'My children don't like me to go out'; 'My daughter misses me when she comes home'; 'My daughter tells me, "Mummy, I wish you would be home when I come from school" '; or 'The children ask me, "Must you go out to work every day?" '

Talking 'Shop' and Wider Interests

Do the women talk over their work problems with their husbands? Do they talk 'shop'?

Out of fifty-seven women who lived with their husbands and were asked this question, twenty-seven answered: 'Sometimes', or 'A bit', saying: 'Actually what we ask is, "Have you had a good day?" or "What sort of a day have you had?" '; or 'Only when we can have a laugh'; or 'Only if something interesting happens'; or 'Only when there is something on my mind'; or 'Only when I am a bit down'; or 'Only if I have small worries to confide'.

There were twelve other women who never talked shop, arguing 'We want to forget about work', or 'We think we shouldn't talk shop', or 'It isn't right'.

Only fourteen answered plainly, 'Yes', saying: 'I have something to talk about when I come home', or 'There is always something going on'.

There were three women who were in a peculiar situation as their husbands were foremen or shop-stewards. 'He talks about his problems, I don't', they said. There was also a shop-stewardess in the reverse position: 'I talk about my problems, he doesn't'.

On the whole, women talk about their work more frequently than men. I believe that the wife often wants to impress her husband that she has wider interests or a wider outlook acquired by her many contacts at work, that by virtue of her job, topics can come not only from him but also from her. However, the conversation is about people, not things, with the intention to lift up and to lighten the atmosphere at home ('We have a laugh'), not to dull it with reminiscences of work.

Financial Arrangements with Husbands

Out of fifty-nine women who lived with their husbands, sixteen had arrangements which they described as 'share and share alike', or 'Pool and share', or 'We put our money together'. Characteristically enough, most young women belonged to this category (six out of seven girls in their twenties described their arrangements with their husbands in these terms); two older women said: 'When we were younger we pooled and shared; not now'.

Four other women claimed that they received the whole wage packet from their husband. The remainder, i.e., thirty-nine, were receiving a housekeeping allowance, usually regular and satisfactory. Only five of these regarded the housekeeping allowance as insufficient, but only two of them complained about it; the other three stated that their husbands didn't earn enough or were not yet settled in their jobs.

Do the wives know how much their husbands earn, and vice versa? Only in thirteen cases the wives did not know, and in these cases the husband did not know how much the wife earned either. The standard phrase for this was: 'He doesn't ask and I don't'. Rarely I heard: 'He knows how much I make but I don't know how much he does'. In six other cases the wives knew roughly, or 'more or less'. In all other cases the situation was described as: 'No secrets'.

However, it would be wrong to class all those cases where the wife does not know her husband's earnings as unsatisfactory. In some cases it is simply lack of interest, or tact, or a measure of confidence, not to enquire. From men in the firms visited I often heard: 'Her money is her own; I never ask'.

Do women still budget their housekeeping money carefully? Is the custom of dividing the housekeeping money into little boxes, or separate compartments, still practised? All the women laughed when the question was asked, as if exposed in a secret or as if there was something funny in such a custom.

Out of sixty-three women for whom the information is available, forty-three were still keeping up this custom, although seven of them only used it for certain items such as rent, electricity, coal, or insurance. The women argued: 'I am afraid that I may be tempted', or 'To keep you out of debt', or 'To make sure it is there', or 'You know it is there', or 'You know you can spend the rest as you like', or 'We budget between ourselves', or 'We sort it out'.

Only twenty women did not budget and did not keep the money in separate compartments. They were amused by the thought of it. The idea that a social change is involved in discarding this practice is not borne out by comparison of age groups. Only one woman in her twenties belonged to the group of those who had discarded this practice; nine were in their thirties, seven in their forties, three in their fifties. Young wives follow this custom more than the older ones as they are more afraid of being out of pocket, having not yet acquired the necessary experience in spending.

Status within the Home

How does women's going out to work affect husbands' authority? Is the idea that the man is a sort of master in the house still valid? Out of fifty-nine women living with their husbands who were asked this question, thirty-three asserted that the idea of the man as the master of the house is 'Old-fashioned' or 'Victorian', that men are no more masters, and that wives are on completely equal footing with their husbands. Some even added that 'the children as they grow up have as much say in the house as we have'. It was interesting to hear their arguments on this point: 'It is stupid, the idea of a master'; 'I am doing as much as he does'; 'He doesn't keep me, so he is not in a position to order me about'; 'They haven't got a chance with women working'; 'We are equal—no bosses'; 'We share fifty-fifty'; 'We talk everything over'. Some women expressed this in a jocular way: 'There are no trousers worn by anybody'; 'I wear one leg of the trousers'; 'He has no chance with four women in the house, even the cats are females'. From these remarks it was clear that most of them were proud of the fact that they were wage earners, doing as much as if not more than the men.

There were three other women who also stressed their equal status but added that men like to think of themselves as masters in the house and, although they were not so in fact, the wives encouraged them to feel that way.

In addition, seven other women, although they acknowledged the principle of equality, implied that their husbands were 'one up' on them. One woman said: 'He has just a fraction more say as he takes more responsibility', and another, 'He knows more about things'. He is, so to speak, *primus inter pares*.

However, a substantial majority, fourteen out of fifty-nine, contended that the man is still 'the master of the house'. They seemed to think that this is, so to speak, a natural outcome of the inequality of the sexes, as if the male were naturally the stronger partner, with a leading and protective role. They said: 'He is the governor', or 'He is the head, I want him to be', or 'Naturally he is the head of the family', or 'He is the master, I know how far to go', or 'Even if I go out to work, he is still the head', or 'I had to give up my hobby in the Dramatic Society because he objected', or 'He should be a master of a kind, but not a bully', or 'I would like him to be master but he lost interest', or 'I would like him to be master but a good master', or 'If I have respect for the man, he is the master', or 'What he says goes', or 'He is the boss for me'. As one woman said: 'I encourage him to think that he is master; he needs this confidence, it is good for both of us'.

Lastly, there were two other women who contended that they 'wore the trousers'. 'I have the last word if anything', said one, and the other, 'I always get my way; with tact, of course, not to hurt his feelings'.

In fact, putting these groups in two classes, one could say that nearly two-thirds of women professed equality (thirty-six) or superiority (two) while one-third professed men's superiority (fourteen) or a degree of superiority (seven). It is interesting to note that, in addition, some of the separated or divorced women referred to the fact that their trouble was that the husband wanted to be master but he was a bad master or not equal to the task.

By and large, younger women asserted their equality more firmly than older women. Out of thirty women under forty who lived with their husbands only nine asserted men's superiority, while out of twenty-nine women above forty, twelve belonged to this category. But that is not the whole story. If the figures are broken down more closely they show that the difference may be not entirely due to social change, but rather to characteristics of relationship conditioned by the age of the partners or their relative age. Out of seven women in their twenties living with their husbands, four asserted men's superiority; out of twenty-three women in their thirties, five only; out of twenty-one women in their forties, ten; out of eight women in their fifties, two only.

Interpreting these figures (small though my numbers are), one may say that young girls starting their married life are a bit apprehensive and diffident, looking more frequently for the father image in their partners: the partners are lovers, the girls are inexperienced and easily grant the authority which their partners often claim. They acquire self-confidence and self-assurance with age and in their thirties they are at their best, feeling more secure and self-reliant, with growing-up children and well-established homes. In their forties they tend to lose their confidence, they pass through a difficult stage, they are in trouble, insecure and fearful, they expect help from their husbands. In their fifties the boot is on the other foot. They regain their self-confidence and reliance, while their partners often fall victim to breakdowns and illnesses, needing the nursing which is now given by their wives who thus regain their hold over them.

Sharing the Interest in the Children

Women living with their husbands and with children were asked whether both partners shared equally the interest in and care of their offspring. The big majority, i.e., thirty-six out of forty-two women, gave an answer in the affirmative, talking about their husbands in such terms as: 'He loves the children', or 'He is a very good father', or 'He worries more about the children than I do', or 'He helps a lot with the children', or 'We both go to school on open days', or 'He takes them out a lot', or 'The children tell him more than me', or 'He takes them to bed and reads them stories', or 'We brought them up between us'. Only six women stated that their husbands leave the children more to them, but some spoke in rather indefinite terms such as: 'He is not there', or 'He is on shifts', or 'The children cling to me; he is strict', or 'I am with the children'. There was little difference in this respect between the age groups as the majority of these women (thirty-four out of forty-two) were in their thirties and forties.

The Distribution of Wealth

The distribution of wealth and welfare shows a great contrast between those living alone (widowed, separated or divorced, or in fact not living with their husbands) and those living as a family unit. Out of eight women living alone, only one owned a house; another lived in a council house, three in furnished rooms, one with her mother and two others in a privately rented house or flat. From all the possessions listed in my questionnaire, only five T.V. sets were recorded.

When we come to women living with their husbands the position is radically changed. Out of fifty-nine women, seventeen owned their own houses, twenty-five lived in council houses, ten in privately rented houses, four with parents or in-laws and three in furnished rooms.

As regards possessions, twenty-four families had cars, nine motor cycles or scooters, twenty-four refrigerators, fifty-two T.V. sets, thirteen washing machines, forty-four radiograms or record players, two tape-recorders, four pianos. The standard of wealth and welfare as expressed in these figures ranks in some items such as cars and refrigerators above the standard of married men in my Mullard sample, which seems to suggest that women's work in the majority of cases presents an upgrading factor in the standard of wealth. Most women who go out to work make sure that their effort is not wasted; theirs are the acquisitive families, i.e., those who are preoccupied with the acquisition of wealth. In my interviews in the firms visited, men whose wives were staying at home frequently referred to this, arguing: 'I don't belong to those greedy men who are never satisfied with what they earn, I don't send my wife out to make more money'.

The strong contrast in standard of wealth and welfare between women who live in a married state and those who live alone is not confined to women: it also has its full counterpart in the situation of men. The married state, by which I mean living as a united family, is the state most conducive to the acquisition of wealth—for both men and women. The mathematics of married life show conclusively that 'M' plus 'F' exceeds the sum of both parts, following the Aristotelian rule that 'the whole is greater than its parts'.

Contacts Outside the Works

Contacts with fellow workers outside the works are much more frequent among girls than among men. They value companionship much more, they personalize all relationships to a much higher degree and they befriend their fellow workers much more than men do. Out of sixty-seven married women, thirty-two had more-or-less regular contacts with other girls outside the works;

two others had them only occasionally, while thirty-three had no contacts.

Those who had contacts referred to this in such terms as: 'We often go shopping together for such things as coats, dresses, or curtains', or 'We are going together to cinemas and theatres', or 'We go out foursome', or 'We have the same way of life and the same point of view', or 'When one is sick or a child is sick we visit her'.

Those who had no contacts gave their reasons: 'We live a long way out'; 'I am much older than the rest of the girls'; 'Not now since I married'.

The highest degree of sociability seems to occur in the middle years. Young girls, when they get married, are too engrossed in their own family and drop out of the social circle, and older women again fall back on their own homes, losing interest in the social life outside. Judging from my sample data I would say that the peak of sociability with women seems to be in the thirties, with a slow decline in the forties and a rapid decline in the fifties.

Contacts with Neighbours

The contacts of working women with their neighbours appear to be even less frequent and less close than the contacts of men with their neighbours, as revealed in the main sample for men. Out of sixty-seven married or once-married women, sixty-six were questioned about neighbours (one said that she had no neighbours as she lived over a shop). Of the sixty-five remaining, only nine were on visiting terms with their neighbours while fifty-three were only: 'On friendly terms', or 'On good-morning terms'; three others contended that they had no good neighbours, or at any rate had nothing to do with them. The proportion of those on visiting terms amounts to about 15 per cent, while in the men's surveys the proportion of these contacts never fell below 20 per cent. The main reasons given for not being on visiting terms with neighbours centred around the fact that they were going out to work, and their views were expressed in such terms as: 'I haven't got the time', or 'I am not there', or 'We are all working people', or 'I am working all day', or 'I am out all day', or 'There is no time for gossiping'.

These data seem to suggest that women's employment affects neighbourly relations, restricting the scope and opportunities for their cultivation, and perhaps also the need for them as they have had enough human contacts during the working day.

Contacts with Family of Origin

The contacts of women with their brothers and sisters showed more or less the same pattern as the contacts of men in the main sample. Out of sixty-seven women, thirteen had no siblings or no siblings living in the same district, thirty-five described their contacts as close or very close, nine were 'keeping up' or 'keeping in touch' with their families, while ten had drifted away from them.

Women who had regular contacts with families on both sides were asked whether family life was kept up more with one side than with the other. Out of fifty women, twenty stated that they kept up equally, in such terms as: 'Fifty-fifty', or 'No preference', or 'Fair, fair', or 'With both sides on pleasant terms'; twenty-one claimed that they kept up more with their own side than with that of their husband, while nine kept up more with their husband's side.

Although the information contained in these figures may be a little vague, as the terms of reference themselves are loose, it confirms the findings in the men's surveys that family life is kept up more with the wife's side than the husband's side, that the visits are more frequent and more social intercourse occurs with the wife's family. The wife's family is often regarded by the husband as the 'nicer' family, more friendly and helpful, while the wife is, generally speaking, more keen on cultivating the family bonds as 'the girls stick more to their families'.

Again when contacts had been cut or rarely kept up, the reason for this was often stated as: 'bad childhood' or 'nothing nice to remember'.

Keeping Oneself to Oneself

How far does this phenomenon, known as 'keeping oneself to oneself', apply to women workers? Women who lived with their husbands were asked whether they agreed with the statement that 'when we are married all the company we need is at home' and whether this applied in their own case.

Out of fifty-nine women, eighteen agreed, stating that 'We keep ourselves to ourselves', or 'We are complete in ourselves', or

'We are home birds', or 'There is no need to go out with T.V.', or 'I am happy at home with my husband and children', or 'I am very self-conscious with other people'. But actually the term 'keeping ourselves to ourselves' was used by only eight of these.

The remainder, i.e., forty-one women, did not agree with this statement, sometimes opposing it very strongly and saying: 'We need outside company', or 'It's bad to bury yourself at home', or 'You need your friends', or 'Go out and see what is going on', or 'You rot at home', or 'When we go on holiday we always arrange for another couple to go with us', or 'When we first married, that was true, but not now'.

The 'home birds' were mostly in their forties and fifties, namely thirteen out of eighteen; one was in her twenties, newly married, and four in their thirties. Again the age of the greatest sociability falls in the thirties.

Hobbies and Reading Matter

Have working women time for hobbies? Of sixty-six women for whom the information is available, seventeen had no time for hobbies. 'Too busy', or 'There is so much to do', or 'No time for such things', they said. Thirty others gave needlework, knitting, sewing, dressmaking, embroidery, or darning as their favourite occupation, 'if that can be regarded as a hobby' they added. Thirteen others mentioned physical activities such as darts, swimming, dancing, camping, tennis and gardening as their main hobby. However (often combining with knitting again), two others mentioned reading as their main hobby and two more, one of whom was a shop-stewardess, social work.

So actually the main generalization to be made on this subject is that women rarely develop a taste for hobbies or are too practical or too busy to have a hobby; the majority have no hobby or only a pastime such as is often part of their domestic duties, such as knitting and darning or dressmaking. Anyway, the impression one gains is that women do not need hobbies to the same extent as men; their energies are more fully spent in the two jobs they have to combine.

As for reading, out of sixty-three women for whom the information is available, thirty said that they had no time for reading and that they hardly read anything, ten others that they read only women's magazines, seventeen read only murder stories, detectives, thrillers and mystery books; only six were interested in more serious reading such as biographies, travel books and history. It is interesting to note that the percentage of non-readers among women operatives comes very close to that of the men in my main sample.

Self-placement and Class Consciousness

The sense of working-class identification of women in Mullard falls only a little behind the men's standards in Mullard, both in content and degree. Typical answers to my question on this point were: 'I suppose working class', or 'Never thought of it', or 'It is all snobbery'.

Out of sixty-four women for whom the information is available, forty-four placed themselves as working class but often added: 'Most people have to work for their living', or 'I have to work for what I want'. Eight women placed themselves as middle class, and twelve others refused to place themselves, saying: 'I don't care about classes', or 'I don't believe in classes', or they gave an indefinite answer such as: 'Working-middle-class', or 'At the moment working class but soon middle class', or 'Semi-working-class', or 'Ordinary class', or 'I belong to the class of people who work for their living but are no longer poor'.

Those few who gave the definite answer 'Working class', with a touch of assertiveness, were the women who added, 'My husband is a strong Union man'.

Women operatives in Mullard showed a high degree of Union organization, not falling behind that of the men, and that perhaps explains their relatively high sense of working-class identification.

Religious Consciousness

Sixty-five women were asked whether they believed in God or a Supreme Being or something in a religious way. In answer to this question, four declared themselves as Roman Catholics, and all except one were firm believers. Fifteen others were firm believers with strong religious convictions, some belonging to nonconformist denominations or sects, such as the Baptist or Spiritualist; others had had religious experiences of their own ('When I was ill I heard the most beautiful hymn', or 'I sent up a little prayer into the world', or 'Religion is a great comfort to me', or 'I am a very firm believer in prayer'). Five women were non-believers ('I lost my faith when the children were ill', or 'I lost too many of my family to keep my faith', or 'I suffered too much', they said). Six were classed by me as agnostics ('I am neither a believer nor unbeliever', or 'It puzzles me, I can't make it out', or 'Horrible things make me doubt', they said). The remainder, namely thirty-five, were believers to a certain extent or were believers 'but not interested really', or said: 'I don't bother', or 'Never gave it a thought'. The latter category, i.e., the majority, would subscribe to the saying that 'modern man is neither a believer nor disbeliever; he believes and has his doubts'. Frequently came the following remarks: 'I have doubts on a lot of things', or 'If I get a shock I start doubting', or 'Sometimes I believe and sometimes I have my doubts', or 'Some people have to bear more than others—why?', or 'I like to listen to the church services on the wireless but I don't go to church, my home is my church', or 'What I dislike is the talk about sinners; why are we being punished?'

The most interesting remark came from one woman who said 'The reason for the existence of the world, that is what I question'. Don't we all?

General Results

An interesting feature of the survey of women operatives in Mullard was that in many respects its data supported the findings in the main sample for men. The figures of self-placement, religious consciousness, contacts with family of origin and so on come very near to those in the standard sample for men.

This may be partly due to the fact that industrial work carries its own momentum and obliterates many individual differences by the pressure of conformity. In industry both men and women simply become operatives.

PART NINE

Generalizations and Conclusions

35. THE HOMEO-STATIC PRINCIPLE

THE ENQUIRY led me to believe that there is a certain self-regulating force operating in our minds, which tends to preserve our emotional balance and which is similar to many other self-regulating forces in our bodily economy. That is what I call the principle of homeo-stasis. I first came across it while investigating attitudes to nightshifts, where it was obvious that out of the inconveniences and discomforts of the nightshifts many relieving factors emerged, such as a warmer sense of comradeship, a sense of achievement, a certain satisfaction that handicaps endured for the sake of families can be overcome. The shifts were taken in good spirit and they were not felt to be as bad as an outsider might think. Most men who accepted the shifts were able to take the sting out of them, and there were a number of men who enjoyed them.

Also in attitudes to strenuous, heavy, dirty, or very uncomfortable jobs I could discern the same tendency. The attitude to these jobs was not infrequently better than the attitude to more comfortable jobs. A whole series of counterweights and offsets were put on the opposite side of the scale, consciously or subconsciously. I was astonished to hear some of the descriptions of such jobs: 'A first-class job', or 'Most interesting job'.

Talking to physically handicapped or disabled men I was struck again by the countervailing tendency apparent in their mind, which achieved the necessary balance. The answers to my question 'Do you feel happy?' often ran as follows: 'Why not? Nothing to worry about. I am still alive that is the main point', or 'Happy. We disabled are very well looked after', or 'No worry. It is more a handicap to other people than to me. It doesn't bother me at all. I do most of the things I want to', or 'Happy enough. I find people only too helpful. They want to do everything for me. They encourage me to be lazy.'

The question 'Do you feel happy?' was one of my standard questions in two works and I asked it frequently in other works as well. At least three hundred people were asked this question and out of this it was quite difficult to find a person who classed himself as unhappy. A pessimist might class this kind of optimism as shallow—and say that people repeat parrot-fashion the word 'happy' even without thinking; perhaps some do not even realize that they are unhappy. Then all I can say is that the realization of unhappiness is a very rare occurrence, though in some cases people were perhaps not prepared to admit to it. Even those who would be classed by an outside observer as very unfortunate cases refused to class themselves as unhappy. The scale of response varied from very optimistic phrases such as: 'Extremely happy', or 'Very happy', or 'Really happy', or 'Always happy', or 'Very much so, nice home and decent job', or 'Good life, nothing to grumble about', or 'I want to go on the same way', or 'I have an optimistic outlook. I don't worry for long. I look always on the bright side of everything', to more realistic statements such as: 'Reasonably happy', or 'Fairly happy. I like to make the best of my life', or '90 or 80 per cent happy', or 'I don't worry, what is to be will be', or 'I have only small worries of everyday life', or 'Quite content', or 'Content', or 'No worry at present', or 'I do my best, why worry', or 'Contented. I am achieving my main purpose in life, to rear my family and give them education', or 'No worry, no regrets', or 'Not exactly happy, but not unhappy', or 'Half and half happy'.

Some qualified their feelings of happiness in this way: 'I was fairly happy previously, not so much now'; 'I would be happy if I had a house of my own', or 'If I had a better job'; 'Happy apart from shifts', or 'Happy apart from wife's illness'; 'If I wanted to reach something which is above me I would be unhappy, but I am content to stay put'; 'Occasionally I don't feel happy, injustices may make me feel unhappy'; 'My only worry is about short-time'; 'Children's and wife's health are always in the back of my mind'.

Of course there were a number of men who at one time or another had been through a gruesome experience, but the wounds had healed and they had got over it. Those who were still suffering at the time of the enquiry were few and far between. All told they could have been 1 to 2 per cent of such cases. Of course, 1 or 2 per cent make, in a population of Britain's size, hundreds of thousands, but most of them will also get over it in due time, if they have normal reserves of strength.

The range of objective conditions which make for happiness or unhappiness seems very much larger than the range of responses or the range of self-evaluation. People in both bad and good conditions often find themselves making the same kind of responses as the result of the self-regulating, equilibrating force operating in their minds.

This tendency towards emotional equilibrium is at the very root of our feelings. It is implicit in the emotions themselves and acts as a sort of an automatic mechanism as the mainstay of our emotional health. It does not originate in our conceptions and ideas but it may be regarded as an extension of our instinctive equipment as it is basically automatic. Every pleasurable emotion produces its own negative, and vice versa. Or, to put it in more general terms, every mood, sensation and feeling creates its own counterweight in oppositely-coloured states of mind.

The principle of emotional homeo-stasis is part of the mechanism of behaviour which enables a man to carry out his life-tasks. A man who feels dissatisfied and uncomfortable in his job will try to change it, but if he decides for one reason or another to stay put, he will develop a compensatory mechanism by accepting the job and making the best of it, if he is a healthy-minded person, i.e., a person with full power of adjustment. He will try to build up all the 'pros' of his job and to focus his attention on all its bright sides. He will try to remember that the job keeps his family happy and well provided, that he has security in his job, that his mates are very friendly, that although the job is monotonous he doesn't need to strain his head, that he has nothing to worry about, that the hours are short and so on. In this way he will restore his balance and recover his spirit. The more he is able to do this, the more content and satisfied he will feel and the greater will be his strength for dealing with future strains and stresses.

The same process happens in reverse when we find ourselves in a position of overwhelmingly agreeable, joyful or pleasurable experiences, when we 'have it too good' or find our circumstances 'too good to be true'. We often feel bored, spoiled and over-privileged. We instinctively fear the 'jealousy of the gods', or the 'nemesis that follows too much happiness' to use William James's phrase, and we take upon ourselves to restore the emotional balance by focusing on elements in our situation which are adverse. Excess of pleasurable circumstances produces disgust, satiation or a sickening effect. This excess is thrown off mostly at the subconscious level by a counterbalance of emotional restoratives. The search for discomfort, sacrifice and self-denial, altruistic or philanthropic behaviour are emotional restoratives for excess of pleasurable circumstances.

This reversion of emotional forces is a generally-observed phenomenon, being part of the mental economy of man. It serves as a break on the intensity of emotional force, preventing us from going too far or reacting too violently in one direction. In this way every emotional state is split in two, and part of it is inverted, which has a damping effect on its intensity. The swing of our emotional responses is thus narrowed down. This inversion of feelings should not be regarded as perversion as it is a normal and healthy mechanism designed specially for the benefit of adaptation and adjustment. Only if the antidote produced is stronger than the dose required for balancing, can it lead to perversion. What is often called masochism follows from the principle of satiation or disgust, or feeling of uneasiness from 'having it too good'. It is well-known that over-privileged people, very successful businessmen, for instance, often fall victims to masochistic impulses.

Buddha was not the only one who, dissatisfied with a life of luxury, went off into the forest in rags. Many people have found a life of unbroken luxury and comfort too trying. Sigmund Freud quotes Goethe's dictum that 'Nothing is so hard to bear as a train of happy days'.[1] It is a common experience that luxuries make people recognize the vanities of life, miseries the grandeur and joy of life. The close links between pain and pleasure have been known since immemorial times as many proverbs and sayings bear witness ('Cry off thy joys and laugh off thy sorrows'). They are also part of the stock-in-trade of all religions with a doctrine of acceptance. 'Turn the other cheek' can be taken to mean 'Take the sting out of anything which offends or displeases you'.

[1] *Civilization and its Discontents*, p. 28.

The ancient philosophers knew all about this phenomenon. Socrates said that one of the gods tried to mix pain and pleasure in one mould, but unable to succeed he linked them at least by the tail. And Seneca said, 'Even felicity unless tempered overwhelms'.

So the principle of homeo-stasis refers to known facts, but it interprets them as part of the automatic mechanism of our minds, as a process of adjustment and adaptation to minimize both successes and failures, both luck and misfortune. It is of enormous assistance to man. Those who are deprived of this mechanism or of its full benefit are the maladjusted, or maladapted, who cannot stand either failure or success. They are unable to produce the antidote to any strong feeling, which, in consequence, unbalances them in one way or the other. However, I found in the process of my enquiries that in most men this mechanism works well though at different speeds. Some men adjust themselves to a new situation in a fortnight, others take a much longer time. But only very few are deprived to a large extent of the benefits of this mechanism.

36. HEDGEHOG BEHAVIOUR

SCHOPENHAUER'S SIMILE likening human beings to hedgehogs, clustering together for warmth in winter, uncomfortable and pricking each other when too closely packed and miserable when kept apart, struck me during my enquiry as containing a sober truth about human behaviour. Schopenhauer interpreted this as human predicament, as a tragic dilemma. But there is no need to interpret this in a pessimistic way. As hedgehogs try to find the right distance so as not to prick each other and still keep warm, so also we are concerned to keep the right proportion of human warmth and freedom. There is no need to go to extremes to expose ourselves to constant pricking by packing ourselves too close, or to grow cold, deprived of the vivifying experience of human companionship. There is a large range of middle zones where the need for freedom of action and the need for human warmth are met with the intensity required, not being sacrificed to each other. Admittedly, it is not easy to reach this point and the point itself moves all the time, like a most sensitive magnetic needle. The right point depends not only on cultural patterns and social environment, but also on age, temperament, past experience, marital status and social status.

When I submitted for comment the statement: 'We can say the least to those we love best', most agreed with me stating that they were afraid of upsetting their wives or being upset by them; obviously those whom we love have the greatest power to upset us. So all through the enquiry whenever the contacts with families of origin, neighbours or workmates were in question one could hear the same *leit-motiv*, 'close but not too close', in various versions.

The other outstanding principle in personal contacts is the principle of substitution. When, for instance, contact with family of origin is largely lacking, other relationships such as closer contacts with neighbours develop. Where social clubs are very highly developed this may also affect other contacts. Apart from the need for human warmth, the time factor also plays its part, of course.

When a man is very happy at home, this often results in his complete isolation from other contacts; this was often expressed in the phrase 'We keep ourselves to ourselves'. I rarely heard the term 'I keep myself to myself', it was mostly 'we'. A single man cannot keep himself to himself without the risk of becoming a recluse if not an outcast. In the places I visited between 15 and 20 per cent described themselves in these terms. The majority were older men but there were also young men among them, especially those who had just started their family life and were completely engrossed in it.

The question arises, what is general trend of behaviour in this respect: is the accent more on warmth or more on freedom? I would say that it is more on freedom, while the need for warmth is not so strongly felt as previously. Men suffering poverty and privation, men in a predicament, under strain and stress, need more sympathy and warmth, while men comfortably off, enjoying a good life, are more self-centred, desiring freedom more than anything else, freedom to enjoy life undisturbed. The warmth they need they can find in a small family circle, with their partners in the enjoyment of life. The wider circles of friends are to a large extent replaced by impersonal relationships, such as those developed around T.V. and other media of entertainment. A whole net of relationships which we may call 'uncommitted' has grown between the viewer and the T.V. personalities. It is a diluted, mute, and single-track friendship, uncommitted and anonymous, which develops between the viewer and the personality, who is built up by the T.V. into something approaching an idol. A gracious gesture, a smile, open arms, a sweet word, are received by the viewer as addressed to him personally, filling his heart with warmth, without effort or struggle, without commitment and without fear of frustration or upset. It is a counterfeit of the real thing, but the counterfeit is cheap, giving the viewer in essence what he needs and leaving him free. The quest for freedom has assumed an unexpected aspect: the freedom to watch T.V. and the freedom to drive a car.

37. 'AS IT IS'

'DO YOU LIKE a weekly change-about in shifts or a longer period?' I asked in firms where a weekly rota was an established practice, and to this the answer came from the majority: 'As it is'.

'Do you like shifts on a monthly rota or a shorter period?' I asked in work-places where a monthly rotation was practised, and to this the answer came again from the overwhelming majority: 'As it is'.

In other places I had the same experience. Whichever shift systems were in operation had the overwhelming consent of the work-people, and no change was sought after. Where the management felt that a change was necessary, and a switchover was introduced from one shift system to another as, for instance, in Dunlop in 1954 from a two- to three-shift system, the change met with a great deal of resistance, but was later on accepted, with a gradual swing-over in favour of the new system.

People can adapt themselves to practically anything if sufficient time is given and the conditions are not too exacting and do not demand an excessive outlay of energy or intelligence. Of course the process takes time, less time for younger, stronger, more resourceful and more intelligent men, with the same qualities in their wives, than for others; but once the process of adaptation is completed and all the changes are made, people want to stay put, and are afraid of new calls for another bout of changes.

Different piecework systems operated in the different works which I visited; for instance, the systems in the Workington Iron and Steel Company, Dunlop and Mullard were entirely different, but when people were asked whether they liked the system they knew or would prefer another, again from the overwhelming majority the same kind of answer came as before. Is it lack of imagination or inertia, or just a desire to come to terms 'with the devil they know' that is operating here?

Usually where piecework was a long-established practice, piecework was preferred to time rates, but where piecework had been replaced by time rates, as had happened in Vauxhall, the majority declared for flat wages. Perhaps people think that there is no sense in hankering after a practice that does not obtain and is not likely to. Or is it perhaps the superior prestige of an established practice which is asserting itself here? Sometimes maybe a sense of inferiority is expressed in this way: who are they, they ask, to dare to criticize an established practice which works and gives results—and after all, not bad results?

When people are asked to move from one job to another in the same factory, this is usually met by a great deal of resistance, even when the job is on the same level or a slightly higher level of payment. The first reaction to the request is the ejaculation 'Why, what have I done?' Is it the loss of friends already made in the department that they are afraid of, have they a lack of confidence that they will be able to master the new job in the same way, or is it that they have come to terms with the existing requirements so perfectly that any change appears distasteful?

Charles Fourier, the great Utopian socialist and visionary of nineteenth-century France, conceived his scheme of *phalanstères* (small working communities) on what he called 'the butterfly principle' (*papillonage*), assuming that men like frequent changes and variety in their jobs. In his communities men would switch over even on the same day from one kind of work to another to satisfy their craving for variety. No such scheme, it seems from my survey, would be acceptable or even conceivable to British workers. Once they are settled in a job and like it they prefer to stay put for their whole lifetime. True, they like 'variety', and this was frequently mentioned to me, whenever I asked what is it they liked mostly in the job, but they mean variety in the job in which they have settled, and not outside it. They like 'something new to learn' (this was also frequently mentioned), but it must be within their compass, in the framework of what they already know, not outside it.

Many men in strenuous or exacting jobs, in answering my question as to whether they liked their jobs, simply said, 'I am used to it'. This meant that they had done it for such a long time that the job had become part of them; they could not imagine themselves in any other job. Many men working long hours on permanent overtime, when asked whether they cared for overtime, answered again in the same vein. It meant not only that they had built their standard of living on overtime money and could not do without it, but also that they had come to terms with a way of life based on long hours of work, and so they would add 'Hard work hasn't killed anybody yet'.

A number of men and women in Mullard were asked whether they would like to move from their neighbourhood. Out of twenty-nine men only eight said that they were not specially attached to their neighbourhood, of whom two were Welshmen (one of these said: 'I am not especially attached, as a foreigner'). One was married to an Italian girl who imagined that she was snubbed by the neighbourhood, and a few lived in not very nice neighbourhoods. There were four others who qualified their willingness to move 'Not far away', or 'To less crowded area', or 'If it is an improvement', or 'Anyway not out of London'. The remainder declared themselves attached to their neighbourhood in such terms as: 'We have our relations here', or 'We were born and bred here', or 'Our roots are here', or 'We have nice neighbours; we wouldn't like to go', or 'We had two chances to move but we turned them down', or 'One makes a lot of friends over the years and we wouldn't like to leave them', or 'You are settled in a neighbourhood'.

Out of sixty-seven women who were asked the same question, twenty-one answered they were not specially attached, but out of this number, seven were actually attached to their previous neighbourhood, saying: 'I came from Putney; I would like to go back', or 'I would like to go back to Scotland', or 'I would like to go to Princes Road in Camden Town', or 'I am not attached to this neighbourhood, but to my previous neighbourhood'. So actually only fourteen women were not attached to their present or their previous neighbourhood. Of these fourteen, five or six had special reasons for not wanting to stay: 'Rough neighbourhood', 'Poor district', 'An overcrowded area', 'It isn't very nice where we live', 'We want a house of our own in a better district', 'We are too close to our parents who want to control our life', were their comments. All the others declared themselves firmly attached to their neighbourhood.

A number of men in the same firm were asked specifically about their attitudes to changes. Out of twenty-nine men asked, only four said that they liked changes, and all of these were fairly young. Nine others qualified their liking for changes in this way: 'Changes for the better, yes'; 'Not too much, not to be shovelled around'; 'Changes in the department but not from one department to another'; 'At home, yes, but not at work'; 'When I was younger, yes, but not now'; 'Little changes, but not drastic changes'; 'I don't like changes all that much'; 'Changes which I want, O.K., but not to be switched about'; 'You like changes of your own choosing but not by others'; 'I like changes now and again but not frequently'.

The remainder stated outright they did not care for changes in general, saying: 'Once I am settled, I don't like to be moved'; 'If you are contented you don't want to change, you can't help disliking changes'; 'If you keep moving you never make yourself contented, you are constantly disgruntled'; 'Once you get settled you don't want to move'; 'The way my life is now I wouldn't like to change anything'; 'I had to change recently, I got over it now but I didn't like it'; 'I like to settle down now, changes mean upheaval, I detest that'.

Now, what does all this evidence amount to? There is a strong streak of conservatism in the working man, not in a political sense, but in an everyday sense. Given a certain amount of contentment and satisfaction, he doesn't want to change, he wants to preserve and maintain things, to settle down, to 'stay put'. He is happy when he can stay put if the conditions are not too exacting, if they do not force him to move or demand changes.

There are, of course, two sides to every one of us, the will to move and the will to stay put; but in the working man's mind the will to move finds its expression more frequently in those who are restless and unsettled in themselves, or discontented with conditions, and both of these categories form only a small minority as conditions improve and restlessness can be expressed outside working hours. 'If you are satisfied why bother, let sleeping dogs lie'—as one man put it.

There is a certain weariness prevalent after the many upheavals of our present age. After nearly forty years of wars, upheavals and confusions, and rumours of atomic wars to come, and talk of automation (whose threat looms large in the working man's mind), men are weary of changes, and would rejoice in a period of peaceful freedom from change.

38. PROJECTIVE GENERALIZATIONS

I WAS ASTONISHED how many men were ready to make generalizations about the behaviour and attitudes of their fellow men. The generalizations came out, both asked for and unasked, very often in answer to a personal question; for instance, often when I asked 'Do you like your job?' a generalization was put forward such as 'No one really likes his job'; or to a question 'Do you work only for money; does the job give you something else apart from money?' the answer might be, 'We all work for money, there is nothing else in the job'.

It is with the greatest ease that a man passes from himself to his fellow men and to the world at large. The traffic actually goes in both directions. In answer to a general question, a personal answer may be put forward; for instance, to the question 'Is piecework popular here?' the answer may be given, 'I like it very much'. A man passes from himself to his fellow men, and from his fellow men to himself, without noticing the transition. The degree of generalization may vary considerably, from 'All men' to 'Most men' or 'Many men' and it may also be qualified by a series of adjectives, if a person is more cautious.

Not only managers, foremen and shop-stewards, whose job often requires a ready fund of stock phrases and generalizations about their men's behaviour, but also the men themselves indulged in generalizations about other people's behaviour, attitudes, frames of mind, modes of thinking, and interests. They obviously attempt to make the world more intelligible by summing up their fellow men, finding in this way a key to human understanding.

The generalizations may be true or untrue, or partly true. Personally I have found that more often than not they have little to do with reality even when coming from managers and foremen. Every generalization has to be verified and tested on its own merit.

The abundance of conflicting generalizations forthcoming was very confusing until I realized that the nature of the generalizations followed one consistent pattern. The stock generalizations about others were true only if they were regarded as pronouncements about the individual himself. In making generalizations about others a man thinks about himself. The process is a sort of projection of his personality into the world; his own personality is extended into a sort of universal law of behaviour. One could express it by paraphrasing the categorical imperative of Kant: 'Act as if the principle of your action were to become a universal law of nature'. Most men think of themselves as if the principle of their behaviour had a universal validity.

I shall now give a few examples of this constant projection of personality into stock generalizations. A man who felt badly about shifts would say: 'No one likes shifts really, they are unnatural', while a man who was happy on shifts would say: 'Most men don't worry about shifts'.

A man who was on visiting terms with his neighbours would say 'We are all in and out of each other's houses', while a man who kept away from his neighbours would say 'We are only friendly, on good morning terms'. A man who kept away from his family of origin would say 'Family is a dead loss, most men are glad to get away from it', while a man who kept close to his family would say 'Of course families always stick together'.

A man who talked over his work problems with his wife would say 'Of course everybody does it', while a man who never mentioned his work at home would say 'Work is always left at work'. A husband whose wife was happy at work and at home would say 'Most women are better wives for going out to work', while a man whose wife had given up work because she did not like it would make an opposite generalization. A man who was unhappy generally would project his unhappiness on to the whole human race, saying 'Who is happy anyway?'

Not only are rules of behaviour generalized, but personal character traits are promoted to basic characteristics of human nature. A strongly self-centred man would say 'All men are selfish really, everyone is only for himself', while a man who was helpful and friendly would say 'Most men are good at heart'. A man with a tendency to lie and cheat and keep everything secret would say 'Most men will cheat if they can get away with it'.

The interests of men are also projected. A gambler would say 'We all like a gamble'; a drinker: 'Beer is the sustenance of the working man; he would be finished without a drink'. As I pointed out in the chapter on cultural horizons, the men, while guessing at answers in my culture test, often answered that the famous names came from the field of their own main interests, whether they were sports, cinema, television or something else.

Once one has a clue to the nature of these generalizations one can use the method of provoking or exploring generalizations as a projective technique. One does not need to ask questions related to man's self-centredness or egotism but simply ask 'Do you believe that most men are selfish?'; one does not need to ask whether a man is happy with his wife, but instead: 'Do you believe that most marriages are happy?'; one does not need to probe into honesty or dishonesty, it is enough to ask 'Do you believe that most men are honest and straightforward?' If you want to explore man's emotional life you can learn much by presenting a few general sayings such as I presented to interviewees in my enquiry in Mullard. To my question 'Do you agree that love is the sweetest thing in life?' a man in love would say 'Most certainly', while a man who had already passed this stage would say 'It is far-fetched, too romantic; love is all right when you first marry, later on it is mere companionship'.

'Tender-mindedness', or 'tough-mindedness', friendliness or harshness, sociability or keeping oneself to oneself, extroversion or introversion, dominance or submissiveness, acceptance or rebellion, all those traits express themselves in the general pronouncements about human nature. Men rank others as they rank themselves, they think of others as they think of themselves. They do not know, perhaps, that their pessimistic view of human nature stems from their own low opinion of themselves. Those who believe that life is not worth living mean, in fact, nothing else than that their own life is not worth living. So, generalizations about others may be true or false, but they are generally true as indicators of what is going on in the author's mind; they reveal more about him than about others.

The saying 'Homo sum, humani nihil a me alienum puto' (I am a man, and nothing that relates to man is alien to me) can also be interpreted this way: 'I am a man, so what is in me I find in others'.

39. AMBIVALENCE

THERE IS ONE STRIKING FEATURE which repeats itself constantly in all basic attitudes of men, and that is ambivalence. Like and dislike, often love and hate, are finely intertwined and interwoven. There is a fine and constantly moving balance between the positive and negative in practically all men's attitudes, and more so in those of a more fundamental nature. The balance changes with every new experience or new situation, often with age, and it is also subject to secular change. Contradictions creep in all the time in a man's mind. The deeper he goes in his relationship to somebody or something, the more conflicting is his emotional attitude.

The ambivalence comes out most clearly in attitudes to work. In secular change the positive elements in a man's attitude to his work are on the ascendant but the negative elements are still there and they may flare up in specific situations of the group or the individual.

Men's attitudes towards their wives' employment are strongly ambivalent. The positive attitudes of men may be on the ascendant but the negative elements are still there and may take the upper hand in many situations. The attitude of married women to their employment is full of ambivalence. I believe the positive elements are being strengthened by social change but the negative elements are still strong, especially if the woman has young children at home.

A man's attitude to the management is strongly marked by ambivalence. He appreciates all the benefits of his job, including the social services and relatively good conditions such as are offered to him by the sample firms, but still there is an element of distrust, suspicion and antagonism. Again, the positive elements may be on the ascendant but the negative ones are still present and may become very virulent at times.

A man's attitude to his Trade Union is full of ambivalent feelings. He appreciates the good work of his Trade Union for him but often feels annoyed at having to follow too closely the dictates of his Union, and at the loss of his freedom of action in many fields. The negative elements may be gaining strength with the growing measure of his security and work satisfaction but the positive elements are still very strong and the balance is always moving with every change of situation.

Even man's attitude to security of employment has a measure of ambivalence. On the one hand he appreciates the security offered to him, with all the pension rights and 'fringe' benefits; on the other hand he is afraid that these may bind him excessively to the firm and turn his security into servitude. The positive elements in this attitude are being strengthened by social change but the negative elements may become more pronounced as the situation changes.

Man's attitude to religion cannot be understood without achnowledging his basic ambivalence. He wants to believe, he has great need to believe, it would give meaning to his life, a sense of security and peace of mind, but he has his strong doubts. Life is so inconclusive, the forces of hate and destruction are as strong as forces of love and harmony, and the great abyss waits for all. He often denounces Providence and defies Fate. Yet, he believes in a way and prays when the need arises. He loves his God, yet he hates Him. In the secular change the negative elements in his religious attitude may be on the upgrade but the positive elements are still very strong.

Even in a man's attitude towards home and family the swing of ambivalence is operating all the time. The positive elements here may be rising but the negative elements are still there. If I may venture into the field of individual psychology, I would say that the Oedipus complex is only a species in a large genus of ambivalence in nearly all the basic attitudes of men. I met a number of men who hated their fathers but I never met a man who at the same time did not also love his father.

The mixture of love and hate, of the positive and the negative, is a very basic social and psychological fact, and its realization is the beginning of understanding anything concerning human kind.

It explains many of the vagaries and irrationalities of men, the sudden outbursts and rages, the unexpected turns and twists in behaviour, the bitter disappointments and shocks.

I believe that a realization of this ambivalence can lead the way to better relations. Much harm is done through the belief that we can either love or hate but cannot do both. If a man discovers suddenly that he feels hate towards his wife, he may be shocked and condemn himself in his own eyes, or draw a false conclusion that he must separate from his wife. He may tear up his most intimate relationship and become unsettled, making himself and others unhappy, as he may discover later on. A man would be happier if he would realize openly that there is nothing unnatural in feeling love and hate at the same time, provided that love proves stronger, more frequent and lasting than hate.

I believe both the community and the individual are served better if this ambivalence is realized. The worker often feels resentment against his boss for various reasons and so he thinks that what he feels for his employer is only hate, and he develops or defends a social philosophy built on this premiss. But in fact, as I have already emphasized, what he feels for his employer is a mixture of love and resentment. Personally I believe it is useless to preach to the worker that he should love his employer because a social philosophy based on this would be as deceptive as a social philosophy based on hate; we should only make him realize that resentment does not exclude love, that elements of repulsion do not exclude elements of attraction, that both are part of the scheme, that any functioning system of energy is based on the tension between the positive and the negative.

I have always felt that those conceptions which deny the existence of a conflict between capital and labour are false to life. No amount of sermons on the theme of social solidarity will do away with the basic conflict between capital and labour. But the conflict is also not the whole truth. There is an area of conflict and an area of solidarity, and the point is only that the problems of conflict should be treated within the sphere of solidarity.

40. A NEW MODE OF LIFE AND A NEW ETHOS

THE PICTURE of the working man which emerges from this study presents tendencies which are characteristic of the fully employed welfare state, with all the gadgets of the new age.

These tendencies are still in progress, they mark the direction rather than the completion of the trend. They are battling against the older forces of the traditional code, ethos and mode of living, and against strong group resistance all round. The battle is very fierce but the ascendance of the new forces can hardly be disputed. However, its final outcome may depend on the future of the economy, whether it will continue in the new ways of full employment and prosperity.

Needless to say there are still large areas where the traditional code, ethos and mode of living hold sway, where the new forces are hardly discernible. I believe the new forces are likely to be stronger in the field covered by my study, namely that of the factory workers (in contra-distinction to other types of workers such as those in building, construction, mines, docks, farms, etc.) and even more so in large-scale, well-organized, well-conducted industrial establishments, and in progressive expanding industries. But the new forces are potentially at work in every domain of working-class existence.

Now let us summarize these new tendencies.

First we can witness a considerable rise in security-mindedness. The factory worker has a relatively high security of employment. The bitter memories of the past are fading away. If he is under forty he hardly knows what it is like to be unemployed. The worker has an established routine, both in working and living. His continuity of employment does not fall very much behind that of an office worker. He has a recognized niche and social position, he is attached to his work-place by many institutional arrangements such as pension rights or seniority rights and other fringe benefits which are constantly increasing. He stays put in his job if he can manage it. His greater measure of security makes him also conscious of security, as his stake is so much bigger and he has so much more to lose. Every threat to his standard of living, which has been raised so considerably, he views with great concern. The traditional type was reputed to have no concern for the morrow. 'I may be dead to-morrow', or 'To-morrow never comes', or 'To-morrow will take care of itself'—these were phrases commonly heard among the working classes. Now to-morrow seems to matter much more. This is also expressed in the worker's propensity to save, which is stronger than ever.

Next comes what is often called 'The revolution of rising expectations'. His appetite is whetted, he wants more. He has a good life but he wants more of it. He wants to better himself, not so much by promotion but by higher wages. He is prepared to work shifts and overtime to make more. He wants his own car, more gadgets, often his own house. When asked about his possessions, he would often use the term: 'Next on my list is . . .' The traditional standard of living is outmoded. There is no more of 'What was good for my father is good for me'; it is rather 'I have many things which would be unthinkable to my father', or 'I have achieved something which I thought would be impossible for me'.

Linked with this is the steep rise in acquisitive instincts. The traditionally-minded workman was known for his contempt for money, which went very well with his contempt for the moneyed class. This contempt is largely disappearing. The worker to-day doesn't want to waste his money. His pattern of consumption turns to more durable goods; he spends his money more wisely and more economically. He wants to show something for his labour, something tangible which can be seen by everybody and which speaks clearly the language of success. He wants to show that he has not wasted his life, but achieved something which does not fall behind the standard of others. In this way a large section of the working-class population becomes a property-owning class. For the time being it is mostly property for the worker's own consumption—a house, a car, T.V., a washing machine, refrigerator, post-office savings, savings bonds, insurance rights—but the overspill to capital assets is already on its way. I came across workers with considerable nest-eggs up to £3,000, well invested. In this way a new type of a bourgeois worker appears on the stage.

Closely linked with these traits is his family-mindedness and home-centredness, as security, acquisitiveness and family-mindedness go well together. He seeks his pleasures and comforts at home more than ever. 'I am a fairly domesticated animal,' was a typical remark which I heard. Family life assumes a romanticized image of happiness and joy. Family life stands, in his mind, for happiness, enjoyment and relaxation. As he sits by his fireside and watches T.V. he feels free and happy. The wife doesn't snap at him as she used to; the children are no longer seen crawling and messing about on the floor, shouting and screaming. The foul air, the vermin, the outside, smelling lavatory, the broken chairs have been removed as if by magic. Instead there is a nicely furnished house of his own, or a council house which is a near equivalent to his own property. His main hobby is decorating his home and he is busy with his brush all the year round: 'I never saw my father handling a brush, now it seems I have a use for my brush the whole year round'. These contrasts may be slightly over-drawn in relation both to the present and the past, but I believe they have validity in relation to the general trend.

Part of a worker's home and family-centredness is his intense interest in his offspring. If he has no ambition for himself, he has plenty for his children. 'In my days a man pushing a pram would have been a laughing-stock; now you see a great many men pushing their pram proudly', said an older man. He not only pushes the pram, he often washes the children and gives them baths, he reads them stories, follows their school records, calls at the school on parents' day, tries to fix them up with a good job or apprenticeship. 'It is the finest thing there is to give the children every advantage', or 'My boy has everything he wants', or 'I scrubbed and scraped to give my children every chance', he may say.

This has an enormous effect on the father-image among the working classes. The bullying father or the father whose authority was used as a bogey has largely disappeared, and instead an older brother relation comes to the fore. The father is there to assist and help, to give guidance; but he is no more the master with a big stick. In my previous enquiries I often found the father-image distorted among the working classes and strongly imbued with the shadow of the Oedipus complex. The working-class child often had only the care and affection of the mother, while the father was an aloof figure. Now the powerful figure of the working-class 'Mum' is receding, as in many workers' families the father steps into her place or occupies an equal place beside her, the more so as she often goes out to work. Anyway the balance of affection is nowadays more equitably distributed between the two parents. The changing father-image is an important factor in the changing ethos of the working classes. Whether a child suffers under arbitrary authority at home or enjoys a kindly and reasonable guidance has a great bearing on his character and outlook.

Somehow related to this is the process of softening in the worker, I would venture to call it his feminization. The workers' world was formerly known for its masculinity. The worker had little to do with children or womenfolk. He was a hard-working, hard-swearing and hard-playing man. His manners were often rugged and rough. His voice was often loud, his manner of speaking blunt and harsh. Now he has mellowed considerably. He smiles more frequently, his voice is softer, his manner of approach easier, freer, more obliging. The segregation of sexes, which used to be a marked feature in the worker's life, is on the decline. He marries earlier, he takes his wife or sweetheart out more frequently, he is more of a home-bird. The women around him imbue him with feminine values. He accepts his wife as his companion on more or less equal terms, especially when she goes out to work and earns her own living. The fear of being sponged on by women is not as prevalent as it used to be.

All this means that the worker is moving away from his mates. His home and family-centredness brings in its wake the tendency to keep aloof from his mates. Formerly he used to congregate with his mates, to 'knock about' with them, to scheme with them, and there was a great deal of mutual aid. Now he sees his mates outside the works only occasionally, mostly on the sports ground or in a club, or at matches. No help, no scheming is required. There are no campaigns to wage, as little mutual help and assistance are needed. The Unions are taken for granted, and do their work without his help.

Social contacts with neighbours suffer the same fate. 'Keeping oneself to oneself', either in the strictest sense or in a larger sense which includes seeing some friends occasionally, is on the ascendant. Is loneliness the outcome? No, the worker has no time for that. He is too busy decorating his house, 'doing it himself', or watching T.V. 'Nowadays there is no problem what to do with your spare time'—I heard.

In my enquiry I came across some Communist workers, not for the first time. What struck me about even the Communists was their lukewarm interest or lack of interest in the larger issues of the world or social problems at large; this showed a marked difference from the attitudes I had encountered previously. Their interest was primarily in their homes, their wives and children. They were also affected by the general mood and tendency towards domestication.

This moving away from his mates and strong home-centredness, with a romanticized idea of family life, fits well with another new characteristic, the 'personalization' of the worker's mind. He is intensely interested in persons, in personal life, personal stories, personal troubles and successes. He is not interested in ideas or general problems or objective situations, but in personal relations. Social relations are soon transfigured and translated into personal terms. Not 'what' but 'who' is the main question. The press, radio and T.V. have contributed largely to this process. This personalization, as the term suggests, is nothing but a process of identification, a projection of his own personality.

Home-centredness and personalization, together with the decline in gregariousness, involves also the process of greater individualization. The term may be misleading. The colourful or eccentric personalities of a kind once common among the working classes are fewer in number. Workers are more of a pattern, cast in one mould. They are more conformist than ever, but still the tendency is to break away from the mass, to think of oneself not as one of the mass but as an individual, a person. The home-centredness has brought about greater self-centredness as the home is only an extension of the 'I'.

The worker wants little things instead of big things, he wants them for himself rather than for society at large, he wants better and wider opportunities for getting along. Old slogans, old loyalties tend to leave him cold. The class struggle interests him less and less. The idea of the working class as an oppressed or an exploited class or the romanticized idea of the working class as foremost in the struggle for progress and social justice, is fading from his mind and is more and more replaced by the idea of the working class as a class well established and well-to-do in its own right. 'Working class but not poor' is his idea of himself. Class divisions are no longer marked out by hostility and segregation. They are still there, but class feelings are less active and less virulent. Also the ethos of class solidarity, of group movement, seems to be weakened, as a man thinks primarily of himself and his home.

His quest for respectability goes very well with the changes just described. His ideas and sentiments were previously often untrammelled by convention. Anyway the conventions of society did not mean very much to him as he often felt bitter about society at large. Now he has arrived; he is well-reconciled, willing to accept. He is more sensitive to praise and blame than ever. He approaches the 'other-directed type', to use David Riesman's term. He is more amenable to suggestions from others; he is trying to fall in with the demands and rules of the game.

He is more subtly influenced than ever by new inducements and incentives, by the social atmosphere of the works, by works routine, moving targets and time schedules, and general style of living—all without the whip which previously hung over him. He is manœuvred into the positions where he is required, often with his tacit or overt consent, though the consent is often more formal than real. The new forms of social discipline, the new human relations techniques of modern management, are the necessary counterpart of the new working man who is now emerging. The working man of old probably could not have been handled in such a subtle way as the working man of to-day. The new working man is a self-disciplined man, is much more thoroughly industrialized, more smoothly adjusted, and is part of the smoothly-working industrial machinery. He is no more bullied as it is no more necessary to drive him. He is a willing player of the game.

Is he happier than his father was? He is more contented, better pleased with himself, prouder of his achievements. Is he getting bored? Has he too much time on his hands? Has he already joined the leisured class? He is still very busy. The five-day week applies only in theory, as a great deal of overtime is worked at weekends. At home he is again kept very busy. The pressure on his leisure-time comes from many quarters. T.V.-watching for some programmes is almost obligatory. When he has a car or motor cycle, there are family outings to be undertaken. When he has a garden, as most working men have, he is kept busy gardening, whether he likes it or not. And when he has a house of his own or a council house, 'Do-it-yourself' absorbs a great deal of his time. In spite of this, a considerable number of men take up constructive hobbies such as woodwork, model-making, making and repairing all sorts of things, arts and crafts, not to mention remunerative sidelines. They may not have 'money to burn' but they often have enough to venture into new and exciting hobbies which were previously closed to them.

Have the worker's cultural horizons been enlarged, his cultural interests deepened? We can say that stomachs are being filled and bodily needs well taken care of in the affluent society, but whether minds and hearts are being filled is more doubtful. We saw, on the strength of the test paper for cultural horizons, that his cultural interests are still limited. The 'two nations' may be a thing of the past in terms of economics but not in terms of education and culture.

The worker is now more prosperous than ever, and if prosperity is a prelude to art and learning we may hope that a rise in his cultural standards will come about in due course, but it is doubtful whether it would be an automatic process, taking place without a determined effort of social action. It is also doubtful whether it can be accomplished without breaking down the resistance of vested interests in mass entertainment. A good case could be made for a movement whose standard programme would be the establishment of common ownership of means of education and culture.

The cleavages between classes in economic terms are fast breaking down, but new cleavages are being erected, stronger and more powerful than ever, namely cleavages of education and culture. As the heritage of science and culture increases, it seems that there is a widening gap between the creators or active participants in matters of culture and science, and those who are entirely ignorant or unreceptive. There is a parallel here with the gap between progressive nations and under-developed nations. The bridging of both gaps needs determined, protracted and lasting action.

It took the employer a long time to imbue the worker with his own values and to turn him into a full and willing partner in the acquisitive society, but he has finally succeeded, and the results seem to reinforce the working and the fabric of the society and to make it more secure from inside. The acquisitive society has succeeded in expanding its frontiers and converting its natural antagonists to its own creed. It seems as if the acquisitive society has only now come into maturity, reaching a uniformity and regularity which could hardly have been foreseen a generation ago.

As we see, social changes among the working classes in the last decade or two have been far-reaching and cannot be measured only in quantitative terms. There are deep changes not only in the mode of living but also in the code and ethos of the class as a whole. Large sections of the working classes are on the move, not only to higher standards of living, but also to new standards of values and conduct and new social consciousness. The impact of these changes on social, political and economic life can hardly be foreseen. They are the augury of a new age, a new social horizon which is unfolding before our very eyes.

APPENDICES

Local Background of the Five Firms

I. RIVER DON WORKS IN SHEFFIELD
May and June 1958

Local Background

The workshop city by the Sheaf, which rose to fame and wealth by means of the quality of its products, still holds its own against the competition of new steel-making centres. Its unique place as a workshop can be illustrated by the fact that, according to figures of output in 1952, it produced one-sixteenth of the steel output in the country, but this one-sixteenth was equal in value to all the rest. About 130 separate companies were engaged (in 1954) in steel-making and steel-processing, employing about 40 per cent of the insured population of the city.

The tool industry ranks as the second most important in the city. The famous cutlery trade still holds its own. Next in importance come silverware and electro-plated goods, machine knives, surgical instruments, cranes and mechanical shovels and miscellaneous industries such as canned food, refractory industries and so on.

The River Don Works, together with Grimesthorpe and Stevenson Road Works, belonging to the English Steel Corporation Ltd., a holding company for seven principal manufacturing companies, has a history dating back to 1805. At the time of the enquiry it employed about 10,000 people of whom 7,930 were hourly-rated men on the books. The actual clock numbers, i.e., men at work, were 7,550, of whom 650 were youths up to the age of twenty-one and 600 were women. So actually the firm employed about 10-11 per cent of the steel-making and steel-processing population in Sheffield (about 93,000 altogether). The works is one of the most vertically integrated steel-works, combining melting furnaces, rolling mills, forges, spring-making, foundry and engineering departments.

The steelworker in Sheffield is renowned as a solid, industrious, reliable and skilful worker, and the enquiry fully substantiated this reputation. Although technical progress has eased his lot, toil, sweat and dirt are still very much in the picture. But there is some sort of fascination about the work, especially in watching the conversion of iron into steel, or the pouring of molten steel into ladle and ingot moulds.

Technical progress has somewhat reduced the range of occupations, but still there is an enormous variety of jobs and skills with a very complex wage-structure. Although the percentage of skilled men in the works was between a quarter and a third of the total, many so-called semi-skilled men had a skill of their own based on long and varied experience.

The working population was strongly local in character; only a small percentage came from outside areas, of which 1 per cent was foreign (there were 107 foreign workers, of whom forty-eight were coloured); these were found more frequently in the foundry and the fettling shop than on the engineering side. A number of men had family attachments to the firm. A third of the men in my sample had fathers and/or grandfathers, and even great-grandfathers, who had worked in the same works; a number also had brothers or in-laws and sons working there.

About 25 per cent of all work-people in the firm lived close by, within a radius of half a mile from the works, 50 per cent within a radius of two miles, and the remainder within a radius of five miles or more. Those who lived further out, mostly skilled and better-paid workers, enjoyed better-class houses, often on housing estates, while those who lived in close proximity to the works in Brightside occupied old-type houses mostly privately rented. From a test sample of 137 names taken haphazardly from the firm's card index, about 42 per cent lived in Brightside or near by, while 58 per cent lived on estates further out. Those on Brightside or near by often lived in sub-standard houses without inside conveniences and sometimes without electricity.

The housing conditions in Sheffield have improved of late but they are still far from satisfactory. The waiting list for houses comprises 21,000 couples, and the average waiting time for a council house is about ten years. About 50 per cent of the houses are built to replace slums.

The company also has its own houses, 2,500 in number, acquired primarily for further development of the works. However, only one-fifth of the houses are occupied by people who work in the firm, and on a normal tenancy, not a service tenancy. About 250 men are on the waiting list and the average waiting time is two and a half years, although in some cases the houses are used to attract particular grades of labour.

Length of Service and Turnover of Labour

The manpower in the firm can be divided into three concentric rings or layers. The nucleus is formed by men strongly attached to the firm who stay put practically their whole lifetime. About 25 per cent of men in the firm had given more than twenty years' service. Skilled men, or those who had acquired through seniority jobs requiring greater skill often came into this category.

The second layer is formed by stable men who move from time to time, but very infrequently. About 20 per cent of men in the firm had between ten and twenty years' service, and 15 per cent five to ten years' service.

The third layer is made up by the so-called 'floaters', men who come and go: these form the greater part of the labour turnover, which operates only on a small percentage of the total labour force.

The ratio between these layers varies from department to department but the greatest gulf exists between the foundry and the fettling shop on one hand and the engineering side on the other. The foundry and the fettling shop show the highest turnover of labour; next come mills and forges, while melting and light engineering have the lowest turnover. The reason for leaving given by most of the short-service employees was either 'job not suitable' or 'got another job'.

However, taking the works as a whole the turnover of labour was moderate and below the national average. Based on figures for the fifteen weeks 1957–58 the turnover of labour from all causes amounted to 29 per cent, but if unavoidable causes such as retiring, death, accidents, call-up, transfer to staff, are excluded, the total is 18 per cent per annum. Dismissals for misconduct or unsatisfactory work were very rare, amounting to about ½ per cent of the turnover.

Working Conditions and Interest in the Job

Men on steel-making, manipulating, rolling and forging were on what is called the Sheffield shift system, mostly working three shifts, each of 8 hours without a fixed break for a meal; they took their meals as their work permitted. The premium for shifts amounted to one-fifth of a normal wage, as, for five shifts, worked in a week, they received six shifts' pay. In January 1958 about 1,840 men were on this system.

Men on the engineering side were on the '44 hours [1] engineering code'; some worked in two shifts, others regular days, and some nights. The hours were from 7.30 a.m. to 4.48 p.m. and 10.12 p.m. to 7.30 a.m. with a half-hour break for a meal. About 4,800 men were on this code.

A small group of about 350 were working continuously long hours, about 12 hours per shift, including overtime. Another small group of about ninety were on a three-shift engineering code with $7\frac{1}{2}$ hours per shift and half an hour's break for a meal. The remainder of the work-people (about 470) were labourers, cleaners, canteen workers and so on with various arrangements, but basically on 44 hours.[2]

[1] It was reduced to 42 hours in March 1960.
[2] Now 42 hours.

Working conditions vary from department to department; some, such as melting shops, mills, forges, foundries, etc., are regarded as heavy, hot, sometimes noisy, and even dangerous. In other departments, i.e., machine shops, the pattern shop, and some maintenance departments, the work is of a much lighter character and done in much more congenial conditions. Each of them had, however, its own peculiar conditions, its own atmosphere, its own code of comradeship, its own strains and stresses. The strains and stresses in the job expressed themselves not only in the turnover of labour but also in the figures of absenteeism. While the over-all figures of absenteeism (lost shifts from all causes) for the works as a whole was fairly low, amounting to about $3\frac{1}{2}$ per cent, in some departments, as for instance in the spring shop, it amounted to 5 to 6 per cent, in the foundry 9·6 per cent, reaching, in the fettling shop, 10·5 per cent (the highest absenteeism falls usually on Monday morning and Monday night; it is lower before holidays and higher after holidays).

The interest in the job differs from department to department, not only according to the nature of the job and working conditions but also to the atmosphere, comradeship and leadership. Men in the same departments tend to form similar attitudes to the job and opinions about the value of the job. The value of comradeship, even in jobs regarded as inferior, is often expressed in such a phrase: 'I am stuck here, you get good pals, you don't like to leave them'.

There was a marked difference in attitudes to jobs among skilled men for whom the job is 'very interesting', or 'interesting', or 'comes natural', as compared with semi-skilled men. The semi-skilled men who had moved up the ladder of seniority to more skilled jobs often appreciated them, as they said, for 'variety' and the opportunities they gave for learning. Length of service was also a big factor in attitudes to the job, as the process of adaptation takes time. On strenuous jobs such as in fettling or in the foundry or in heavy engineering, the newcomer is very basically handicapped.

However, the most important single factor in attitudes to work among semi-skilled men seemed to be money, and most semi-skilled men when being engaged asked mainly about wages and the prospects of working overtime, not so much about the nature of the job and working conditions. Among the leavers, twice as many men stated their reason for leaving as 'Dissatisfied with the wages' than 'Dissatisfied with working conditions'. When overtime is reduced there is a tendency for young, vigorous men to leave. Most grievances and complaints are about money. The inconveniences of heavy work, or long hours, or shift-work are brushed aside in the quest for more money. One-third of fettlers whom I interviewed suffered from perforated ear-drums or were becoming hard of hearing or had other complaints but none contemplated leaving. One man had lungs affected, as shown by X-rays, but he was hoping that the management would disregard it. A few had thrown away their skilled trades to make more money on fettling or in the foundry.

Altogether I had, in my sample of 161 men interviewed, sixteen skilled men who had turned to semi-skilled operations, some because of money, others because of age, accidents and redundancy. In addition ten men had started their apprenticeships and had not completed them, some because of money, others because of redundancy.

Nightshift

'Nobody actually likes nightshifts but we have to do them—and of course the money comes in handy'—one heard frequently when one started talking about shifts.

The realistic mind of the worker does not for a moment separate the issue of nightshifts from monetary incentives. They are one. Some men were, at the time of the enquiry, concerned about the falling off of nightshifts as a threat to their standards of living. When nightshifts are falling off some men leave and look for a better-paid job; others, when applying for a job, ask specifically whether they will have the chance of nightshifts. The difference in weekly wages may be anything from three to five pounds.

Nightshifts vary considerably from department to department and job to job in length of hours as well as in frequency and periodicity. Some men were on two or three weeks' rotation, others on one week in four or five, but the prevailing pattern was a weekly basis for shift rotation.

From seventy-nine men who were on shifts there were nineteen men who stated that they were upset by shiftwork as it affected their health or sleep, and there were nine men who were disturbed by shifts, being also affected in their health, but to a smaller degree. Let us hear what these men have to say about their problems:

A trumpet runner on three shifts: 'On Monday I can sleep only up to 11.30 a.m., on Tuesday up to 12.30 p.m., on Wednesday up to 3 p.m., Thursday up to 4 p.m. and Friday up to 5 p.m. Only gradually I work my way back to sleep.'

A borer, forty-five, on two shifts: 'I live in a busy and noisy street and I sleep very lightly so I can't sleep during the day very much. Still, stomach upsets are a greater trouble than loss of sleep. I have a cup of tea when I finish nights, then have dinner at 4 p.m. after my rest.'

A turner, fifty-two, on two shifts: 'I used to sleep well when on nights, now I can't and I have stomach upsets also, starting usually on Tuesday or Wednesday. From that time on I eat very little, only drink, but not beer.'

A turner, thirty-six, on two shifts: 'Nights upset you one way or the other. Lots of wear on your nerves, you become short-tempered and snappy.'

A fitter, twenty-nine, one week on nights and four weeks on days: 'I don't feel the same on nights, I am a different man. I don't eat or sleep properly. The worse days are the first two; gradually I feel better.'

A labourer in the foundry, forty-two: 'I suffer from bronchitis, so the nights are very difficult for me especially in the winter time'.

However, the majority of men, namely forty-five, took shifts for granted, and a small minority, namely six, consisting mostly of young men (five out of six were under forty), preferred shifts apart from the money factor.

A rough turner of thirty-six: 'I prefer nights; somehow I sleep better during the day than usually'.

A crane driver of twenty-five: 'When we married we decided I should go on nights to make more money. So I worked for a whole year on nights, 13 hours per shift, earning about £21 a week. From this we bought a car. I prefer nights, not only for money, somehow the nights go quicker.'

A steel miller of forty-three: 'Actually I prefer nights. Somehow the work comes easier.'

As we see, there is a large range of adjustment to the challenge of nightshifts.

Wages

The average adult wage in spring 1958, at full-time working, was about £15 per week: in June 1958 about £14. However, there was a considerable difference in wage-earning over the whole range of skills and jobs, depending also on shifts, overtime and output on piecework.

The highest-paid jobs were those of first and second hand melters (in May 1958 £24 16s 0d for 48 hours), welders (£23 2s 9d for 44 hours), moulders (£20 6s 1d for 44 hours), coremakers (£18 15s 11d for 44 hours).

The lowest-paid jobs were those of labourers on days (£8 16s 5d for 45 hours), slingers (£10 19s 5d for 44 hours).

There was also a considerable variation of wages for the same man from one week to another. To quote two examples for May 1958: (1) A labourer in a foundry earned £9 19s 7d for 44 hours, and the same labourer earned £13 19s 3d for 62 hours; on nights for 57½ hours he earned £14 2s 9d; (2) A fitter earned £13 5s 10d for 44 hours on days, and £21 17s 11d for 59 hours on nights. During the time of the enquiry the highest wage was paid out in the foundry (£30 0s 0d for 70 hours).

As most men are on piecework there is also a large range of earnings on the same job; one dresser, for instance, earned £14 5s 2d while another dresser for the same 44 hours earned £9 1s 11d.

About one-third of men operatives were saving through the firm amounts which varied from 10s to £5, the usual amount being £1 per week. However, the savings through the firm did not always represent a real saving effort as a number of men were taking out their savings at the end of the month—they had recently been warned by the bank that the arrangements would be discontinued.

Labour Relations

Labour relations were regarded as satisfactory and hardly any complaints were heard from either side; however, they depended on full wage earnings and as soon as the firm cut down overtime they tended to become somewhat strained. The Unions were co-operative and had a very realistic attitude, working with very little friction. There were twenty Unions operating in the firm, the main Unions being the Bisakta (The British Iron and Steel Confederation) and the A.E.U. (I was fortunate to obtain the blessings of both Unions on this enquiry). There were 130 to 170 shop-stewards and other committee men recognized by the firm, but the office of convener of shop-stewards was not recognized by the management at the time of the enquiry because six or seven years before the convener had been held responsible by the firm for leading an unconstitutional strike.

The reputation of the firm among its work-people was high. 'This is a very good firm to work for', some men stated, and others, 'Although the Company doesn't pay the highest wages in the district, they care for you and deal with you fair'.

Accidents and Industrial Health

In spite of improvements in industrial safety, accidents are still a serious problem. The frequency rate (number of accidents per 100,000 hours) amounted in 1957 to 2·53. The total number of serious accidents in 1957, with a loss of one month's work, was 426. But there were no fatal accidents in 1957 and no one was permanently disabled.

The works doctor reported a marked improvement in industrial health compared with before the war, as the impact of industrial diseases was so much smaller. The main industrial diseases are dermatitis, burns, hernia, tenosyrivitis (inflammation of the tendon caused by the vibration of the pneumatic drills) and silicosis. A number of men suffered from stomach ulcers, nervous breakdowns and rashes which the doctor attributed to home worries more than anything else. 'They develop all sorts of symptoms which don't boil down to any diagnosis. When the cause of trouble disappears the symptoms also disappear.' The doctor attended three afternoons a week, two nurses were in constant attendance, and twenty-three first-aid men were trained for seven ambulance rooms.

Welfare Services

The social and welfare services of the firm were expanding all the time and they bound the operatives more closely to the firm, being very much appreciated by them.

There was a non-contributory pension scheme known as 'Old Age Gratuities', providing a small pension for anyone with ten years' service or over. (A man of sixty-five with thirty years' service would receive £20 0s 0d gratuity and £34 0s 0d a year pension; a man with twenty years' service, £10 0s 0d gratuity and £22 0s 0d a year pension.) There was no fixed retiring age and the workmen could work as long as they liked and were able to. One man interviewed by me and pointed out as the oldest employee was eighty-one.

There was a voluntary convalescent fund with a 2d per week contribution and 90 per cent membership—apart from sickness and distress clubs organized on a departmental basis.

An interesting scheme had been introduced in 1945, called Home Help, basically free of charge, although the men who made use of it were expected to contribute something towards its upkeep. It was meant as a temporary help in emergencies for about a maximum of two to three weeks, until the man could make proper arrangements. The idea was that the men affected do not need to lose shifts. Characteristically enough the staff people make greater use of the scheme than the work-people, as half of the fifty-six cases attended to in the last year were those of staff. The typical cases are maternity, nervous breakdowns, wife's illness, death, desertion, or after-hospital care. At the time of the enquiry six women were fully engaged on this scheme, working in homes between 8 a.m. and 5 p.m. When I asked a workman who was just in need of such a help, why he didn't make use of the scheme, the answer came: 'I am too proud for that and I don't like strangers in the home'.

Every second year an Open Week is arranged for the families of the employees and in 1958 about 1,200 wives of workmen and 500 wives of staff visited the place.

All hot departments have warm showers and heated lockers, but only 50 per cent of men in these departments were using them as some men are most eager to get away from the works as soon as the whistle blows. Clean overalls with a drawer are provided on demand for 2s 2d a week by the Works Facilities Committee.

The Social Life in the Firm

Social life in the firm centres around the Sports Club, Licensed Club and the canteens. The social life is more developed in the departments than for the works as a whole. Tea-mashing units are more important than the canteen itself with its nine eating places. Only 4 per cent of hourly-rated men made use of the canteen for their main meals but many more made use of the canteen for tea and snacks. The Licensed Club provided beer a little cheaper than public houses; some of those living close by made use of it as their 'local'. Dancing took place every Saturday night. Trips to the seaside and other places of interest were arranged on a departmental basis.

An Old Servants' Club for the retired comprised about 1,000 members, arranging trips, matches for bowls, snooker, darts and fishing; all facilities were provided without contribution.

The Sports Club with about 9,300 members had eighteen acres of sports ground, two soccer pitches and so on. The older men were active mostly in the angling section, gardening and bowling. Actually the most popular single section was angling, with 1,850 members, which arranged an annual fishing match and three sweepstakes. The gardening section arranged two shows annually in which about 120 men exhibited their produce. There were about four bowling teams.

The younger men had their football, rugby, cricket, tennis, swimming and archery. There were five main football teams, apart from thirty-six departmental teams; rugby had five teams but it was played mostly by staff people; cricket had six teams, apart from thirty-six departmental teams, but two-fifths of members belonged to the staff. Tennis had 150 members, with the same proportion of staff. Swimming, for which a Corporation swimming pool was hired every Monday, arranged an Annual Gala for which, the last time, 172 men had entered. Altogether 2,000 people, both workers and staff, took part in competitive games for trophies during 1957.

The interest in gambling was made use of for the benefit of the Sports Club. There was a weekly 6d sweepstake with 23,000 tickets issued every Wednesday and twenty-five prizes up to £200.

Diary of a Steelworker

One of the steelworkers interviewed by me in Sheffield had kept a diary for me for five work days which I include here for the interest of the reader.

A DIARY OF A STEELWORKER

MONDAY, MAY 5th

4.45 a.m. Up for work, enjoy double shift. A little mad at 9.15 p.m. having missed 9.15 p.m. bus, have to wait till 9.45 p.m. through crane driver not starting work sooner, get home at 10.20, wife cooks supper, have words with the wife about daughter leaving school at midsummer, daughter wants to be tailoress, headteacher says she would do well in office. Bed 11.20. P.S. Wife has been busy washing, we have a washing machine.

TUESDAY, MAY 6th

I awoke 7.50, daughter crying Mam, Mam! I nudged the wife told her it was 7.50, she got up to get the children's breakfast, called the boy who was very tired, told him he would have to go to bed at 8.0 tomorrow. Got up myself at 8.30, sawn some wood then chop it. Had a shave, fetched the Express to read, daughter said she had fallen and hurt her shoulder playing rounders. She had fainted with the pain getting out of bed. Put some hardboard round the door to keep the draught out. Wife said she was fed up and browned off with the house, had an argument about her nerves, told her she should get out, said if she could go out she would go to work, but fear stopped her from going out, felt a bit down after that argument, had dinner of 2 eggs then work, after which at work not very happy when foreman did not ask me if I wanted overtime, knowing we already had Sunday nights knocked off the working week, finished work very down in the dumps having worked very late and missed the 9.15 bus again. Arrived home 10.20 took the watering can out as soon as I got in to water the lawn, washed, had my supper wrote this and then to bed. The wife says the boy ran in at 8.55 asked if his father had come home then washed and went straight to bed, the wife went to bed 10 minutes before me but she has just come down again sobbing saying she has been ill all day with her head.

WEDNESDAY, MAY 7th

Had a good nights sleep, awoke at 7.0. Wife got up at 7.25. I dozed on and off till 8 thinking of the wife been at home ill yesterday with no one in the house no overtime and a poor wage to draw in a fortnights time. The boy asked his mother when he got up if his father had said anythink about him coming in late but the wife said no then told him I had said he was a good boy so he came to me and asked if I would buy him a pellet gun but I had to say no so off to school he went. I fetched the Express to read whilst the wife did some ironing, daughters shoulder a little better, a lot of wood to saw, off to work and feeling a lot better after the promise of some overtime, the day went very well at work, I also caught the 9.15 bus home.
P.S. Wife and son have been in the garden from 6.0 to 9.30 and enjoyed it.

THURSDAY, MAY 8th

Did not sleep too well, up at 4.45. Wife up at 6.50 messing about all day swopping and changing and cleaning carpets upstairs and downstairs, son out helping the polling officers, the wife says she cannot explain how her nerves affect her, she has to go to the hospital tomorrow. Daughter says her shoulder has been hurting her today. I have had $3\frac{1}{2}$ pints of beer today and enjoyed them. Missed the 9.15 bus as usual had to wait till 9.45, the boy has asked his mother to ask me if he can stay up tomorrow night because he has not got to go to school on the Saturday morning and so to bed 11.45.

FRIDAY, MAY 9th

Had a good nights sleep got up 8.5. Wife asked me what I was doing getting up at that time. Had a bit of breakfast wished the children good morning has they were going to school. Had a little chat with the wife, then helped her to shake a big carpet we both had a good 2 hours in the garden, it was now time for me to go to work, I bought a bottle of good sherry for the wife I had been told that with an egg in it it will help her nerves and also make her sleep better at night. At work I tried to get monday Morning or afternoon has an extra shift for next week but there was no chance because the furnaces were shut down through lack of power and the 3 men detailed to stay double shift Friday night were told to go home instead. It looks has if we are going to get a poor output and poor wages for this week. I had a pass to go out of the firm for 2 pints of beer which I enjoyed. I caught the 9.15 bus home. I told the wife I was going to have a bath the first thing but when I went up the bath was dirty so I had a few words with the wife about it because it was she who had left it liked that so I had my supper in rather a gloomy manner. Today the wife went to the hospital the doctor asked her if she thought if she went to work in the company of other people if it would help her to get better the wife said she would be alright there but it is the travelling there and back that she is afraid of, the doctor has left it up to my wife to decide what she is going to do. So to bed 11.30.

I am sorry about the ungrammatical and non punctuation of the writing, but I have been in a hurry doing this. I hope you can make sense out of it.

II. THE WORKINGTON IRON & STEEL COMPANY IN WORKINGTON

November and December 1958

Local Background

Workington, the industrial centre of West Cumberland, its seaport and market town, was in the inter-war period a very depressed area. In 1932 about 44 per cent of the persons insured under the Unemployment Insurance Act was at one time out of work. The memory of that time is deeply ingrained in men's minds. The upshot of those days can still be seen in the hard core on the Labour Exchange which comprises some 120 men who have had little employment during the past ten years.

To-day, Workington is a prosperous area, but still with a rate of unemployment slightly above the national average and a level of wages slightly below, and even more so for female labour. By and large the labour market is restricted to a few heavy industries such as coal, steel and heavy engineering which account for nearly half of the working population. There are three coal mines which employ, roughly speaking,

3,000 men, two firms belonging to the United Steel Companies, namely Workington Iron & Steel Company and Distington Engineering, with about 5,000 men jointly, and 'High Duty Alloys' with, roughly speaking, 800 men. This means that about 9,000 men are employed in heavy industries out of a total labour market comprising 18,000 insured population. The remainder of the labour market is taken up by two textile mills, a few factories, transport, retail trade and so on.

Labour Force Recruitment

The Workington Iron & Steel Company itself employs about 20 per cent of the working population—a higher percentage if only the male labour force is considered. In October 1958 it employed 3,736 personnel, of whom 3,075 were clock numbers of hourly-rated men, and 661 staff. The general trend of staff expansion can be seen also in this firm which in the last six years has increased the percentage of staff from 13·2 per cent to 17·7 per cent.

One can describe the labour force as very steady and solid. The men are hard-working, reliable and very loyal to the firm. The firm has a high reputation among the work-people in terms of level of wages compared with other firms, as well as in working conditions, labour and human relations. Although the firm, for the six months preceding the enquiry, had suffered from recession, no workmen had been declared redundant (altogether only eighteen men were discharged during twelve months, i.e., 0·6 per cent); only recruitment had been suspended, overtime cancelled and some departments had been on short time. Most men regarded it as a privilege to work for the firm and they joined for life. About 50 per cent of men in my sample had never worked for any other firm. The firm was regarded by the men as a family affair, as many worked there with their fathers and brothers. More than 50 per cent of men in my sample had had fathers working in the firm at one time or another. Accordingly, the firm can pick and choose their labour force, getting in fact the cream of the labour market. Altogether, for the previous twelve months, only seventy-nine men had left on their own request, which amounts to 2·4 per cent; among these, ten men were leaving the district, others left because of domestic troubles, and so on.

However, the over-all men's leaving rate from all causes, including death, retirement and incapacity, amounted to about 7 per cent in 1957–58 and had dropped considerably and steadily over the previous eight years, from 12·7 per cent in 1950–51. It was very low compared with other firms of this character. However, this reflected partly the restricted nature of the labour market.

The employment office of the firm knew practically every steelman in the district as almost everyone had, at one time or another, served in the firm. In such an area, as I was told: 'A man cannot make a fool of himself and get away with it because soon everyone knows his real value'. The appreciation of the firm by men was expressed in such terms as: 'I want to die here' or 'I hope I never leave here'. After forty years of service the firm presents a gift in kind to be chosen by the employee to the tune of £40. In fact, during my stay there was a presentation ceremony of this kind, with seventy-three awards: the choice made by the men has a bearing on the theme of my enquiry. Thirteen men asked for a T.V. set, eight for washing machines, five for radiograms, thirty-one for pieces of furniture such as bedroom suites, five for gold watches, including ladies' watches, one for a coloured slide projector. This indicated that most men were home-minded and asked for pieces of home equipment.

The firm has also a retirement scheme on a contributory basis. The original contribution had been 1s 6d per week but at the time of the enquiry it was 3s 0d per week. The pension earned was three times that earned by the original 1s 6d per week. A man starting with the firm now would, after forty years' service, expect a pension of 60s 0d per week. Men now working with the firm will get a pension varying from about 25s 0d per week to 60s 0d per week, the amount depending upon their contributions. The retiring age is sixty-five but the firm grants an extension for six months to those who apply.

In addition to the pension there was a life assurance benefit for men who died while they were working for the Company. This benefit was covered by the Company's contribution. It was a graduated benefit varying from £250 to £400; the latter figure was for people who had had fifteen years' service or more with the Company.

The age composition of the labour force, as based on the figures given to me by the management, was slightly older than average—55·2 per cent were over forty and of these, 31·5 per cent were over fifty and 8·7 per cent over sixty.

The firm runs a good training school for youth with a five-years' training period for trade apprentices. No sacrifice in wages is required; it is rather the other way round as the rates are slightly higher than for blind alley jobs in other firms and the firm selects applicants carefully. The demand for places in the training school is very high and outstrips the vacancies in a ratio of four to one, so the school can select the best youth, mostly from grammar and technical schools and only very few from secondary modern schools. The policy, however, is in future to recruit more from the secondary modern schools, particularly from those which are running end-on courses in craftsmanship.

Through better schooling and training, better-educated craftsmen are joining the firm, although some foremen are prejudiced against them: 'Boys with big ideas', they are called. The parents are very interested in the training school and try to place their sons there.

The recruitment area for the whole labour force is wide, stretching to Whitehaven and St Bees in the south, Maryport in the north, and Cockermouth, even Keswick, in the east. The majority, however (about 83 per cent), lived within three-miles' radius of the firm. Housing conditions were improving although 20 per cent of the population in Workington was estimated not to have a bath. The waiting time for a council house was twelve years. The firm had a few company houses, about sixty altogether. In my sample about four-fifths lived in a council house or in their own property.

Labour Relations

Labour relations were considered by both sides as satisfactory. There had been no major strike since 1926. There were fourteen Unions operating in the firm. Union allegiance was very strong and the Unions had the men well in hand. The strong Union allegiance may be partly due to the characteristic structure of the labour market where the firm exercises (because of its importance) a virtual monopoly of demand: this is being counterbalanced by the virtual monopoly of supply exercised by the Unions. The Unions were, on the whole, co-operative and reasonable in their demands, but they had to be consulted about every change contemplated by the firm. The worker did his job in a traditional way, which meant that he carried it out according to an established practice: the management had full control over him to make him carry out his job in this way, but as soon as a certain deviation, a change, a switch-over to a new process, new methods, new ways of working, or something extra or out of the ordinary was required, the worker would not move unless told to by his Union representative. The resistance to change by the worker has been a frequent topic of study but the truth is that it is partly the outcome of his Union allegiance. Every change and everything extra, anything new or unexpected, must have the Union's blessing. My investigation had a general blessing from two main Unions in Sheffield and also from the Joint Works Council in this firm, but in nearly every department I still had to see the Union representative first to obtain his blessing. Until the word went round that it was 'O.K. from the Union side', no man would budge. It was not that he was resistant or unwilling; he simply did not know whether the new thing had the blessing of the Union or whether he was transgressing the code of comradely behaviour.

Promotion Scheme

As in other steelworks, there was a very strict promotion scheme based on seniority, but only on the production side, not for the maintenance men. As labourers, men joined one of the two main gangs. They were the spare men who could be used anywhere where necessity arose. They represented the flexible part of the labour force as all the others were tied down to specific jobs and could not be used anywhere else outside the department. The Company ensured that every man in the department could do either one or two jobs other than his own, so that absenteeism caused by sickness or holidays was catered for.

Seniority goes with ability, but as not much ability is required for most jobs, the management rarely dispute the ability of any man, so that in fact very strict seniority prevails. Men on the same jobs move up on the numerical scale and when the next job becomes vacant, take over. However, not all jobs are worth jumping at to the same degree. Usually the jobs in the line of seniority are regarded as more interesting but some require greater responsibility or greater exertion, while the wage differential in proportion is low. All the better-paid jobs are also shift jobs worked on a three-shifts' basis. Wage differentials have been considerably narrowed down by the operation of the cost-of-living bonus and national wage increases and the management were concerned about this, as some men in a few departments did not care to take the next step in promotion.

However, not all production jobs have an unbroken line of seniority leading to the top. There are jobs with a more restricted range of seniority leading towards what are often called dead-end jobs. For instance, a crane driver who was thirty-six, with fourteen years' service, had made four moves up the ladder of promotion and had a key job on the cranes but he could not go any higher; or a driller with twenty years' service, who made two moves up, had come to a dead end. Only a very few jobs lead to the top of the ladder. If a man refuses to take the next immediate step, which may not be worth having in itself, he is barred from further promotion. When, for instance, a good job which requires working shifts comes to a man in his middle years and he is not used to shiftwork, he may decline to take the next step—but that bars him from further promotion.

The seniority rules go by departments and once a man moves out of his department he has to start again from the bottom. The same applies if a man interrupts his service in the firm, perhaps only for a week or two. There was such a case during my stay in the firm, when a man somewhere in the middle of the ladder of promotion was lured away by another firm: after two weeks of disappointment he came back but he could not be re-instated in his former position and he had to start as a labourer in a new department. The seniority rules thus have their drawbacks in lack of flexibility. In this way some jobs may be under heavy pressure, while other men may be looking for a piece of work to do.

The great majority of men on the production side are 'promotion-minded' in the sense that they care for the next step and try to go as high as possible. However, on the maintenance side the opposite is true, as there is no promotion scheme at all. The general principle, which, I believe, can serve as a clue to the understanding of the problem of promotion-mindedness, is very simple and can be stated in these terms: where there is a good promotion scheme and the next jobs are worth having, men are 'promotion-minded', but where these conditions are absent the promotion-mindedness disappears. In the latter case, men would say: 'It would never occur to me to think of promotion'. In the maintenance section, which employed more than 1,000 men, men could be promoted by the management at will, but the chance was no more than one in twenty or one in thirty; such a chance might never occur in their lifetime or in their younger days. Besides, a foreman would earn very little more than a craftsman, with very much more responsibility and worry. So it was not surprising that men on the maintenance side, when asked whether they cared for promotion, often answered: 'I never thought about it. Besides, too much worry and too little money.' The percentage of men on the maintenance side who cared for promotion varied (according to the statement of supervisors) from 4 to 6 or 7 per cent.

The Wage Structure

The wage level of hourly-paid men at full-time working in July 1958 was £13 2s 1d. At the time of the enquiry it had dropped by 18s, as overtime was cancelled and some departments had gone on short time. In a normal week (July 1958) the difference in average wage between departments could be as high as £2 14s 0d. In General Services, for instance, where most labourers were engaged, the average wage was £11 19s 6d while in Coke Ovens it was £14 13s 5d.

The range of wages for different grades for 44 hours can be seen from the following figures: a labourer—£9 to £10, a semi-skilled driller—£11 15s 7d, a fitter—£13 10s 9d. Some jobs reached £20 per week or over.

The wage structure is often distorted by overtime working as lower grades often work more overtime to make up total earnings. In full production with overtime in July 1958, a labourer could earn £13 and more, a semi-skilled man £15, a craftsman £18 and so on.

It is interesting to note that the average wages of hourly-rated men were higher than those of weekly-paid clerical staff. A clerical man, at the age of twenty-one, would receive £9 13s 2d and at the age of twenty-five £11 6s 2d—and after that he could be promoted by merit at the yearly review of salaries by increases of from 5s to £2. The foremen were getting £800 to £1,000. Members of the clerical staff were recruited mostly from grammar and technical schools, very few (about four or five in the last few years) from men on the clock.

The wage rates of hourly-rated men were made up of a base rate, cost-of-living allowance, a bonus which varied from department to department and odd premiums for additional responsibility or bad conditions, like, for instance, 'dirt money' (when I asked a man whether he minded the exceptional muck on his job, he answered: 'Why should I, it's good dirt, I get paid 17s for it!').

There were various systems of wage determination differing from department to department. For instance, men on Bessemer furnaces and in rolling mills had straight tonnage money for a team with a guaranteed minimum plus cost-of-living allowance; men on blast furnaces, on the rail bank and in the cinder plant, had datal rates plus tonnage money per team or department plus cost-of-living bonus and so on. There were dozens of grades in each department and the tonnage money earned by a team was shared out in varying ratios according to seniority. On the other hand, in the maintenance department there were only three grades, labourers, semi-skilled and skilled, with no merit money or length-of-service money.

On the production side the distinction between labourers, semi-skilled and skilled was more arbitrary and vague. Some jobs were regarded as skilled, others as semi-skilled and still others as labouring jobs. For instance, in Bessemer, with fifty-four men, six jobs were regarded as skilled, that of the first mixer, the first vessel man, box man, the first ladleman, the first pitman and, of course, the blower; eight other jobs, of crane drivers, cupola keeper, second mixer, electric loco driver and slag mill charge-hand were regarded as semi-skilled, and the rest were regarded as unskilled. The management reckoned that in the production department about 130 men were skilled and 700 semi-skilled, while the rest were unskilled: these distinctions were also accepted by me in the sample. It is interesting to note that the term 'labourer' is reserved mostly for spare men; where a job is definite a new term is invented to give a certain status to the man, as most men do not like to be called labourers. 'We give a proper name to each labouring job and although no outsider knows what it is, it's all right as long as it sounds important'—a departmental manager said to me.

Working Hours and Shifts

The production men who were on shifts divided themselves into two main groups. One group, comprising 540 men, was on continuous production, working twenty-one shifts a week with 42 hours per week on average. This group included coke ovens and blast furnaces. The second group, the Bessemer and the rolling mills, comprised about 640 men who worked theoretically seventeen shifts, making on the average 45 hours a week. The remainder in other departments worked regular days, 44 hours a week. Some men were on two shifts, mornings and afternoons. Odd men worked 48 hours on days only.

Now let us see how the two main shift systems worked in practice, and what it means for a worker to be on shifts.

In Bessemer the shifts ran in a three-weeks' cycle as follows: On mornings, men worked six shifts, from Monday to Friday from 6 a.m. to 2 p.m. and Saturdays from 6 a.m. to 1 p.m., making altogether 47 hours a week. There was no official break for meals; the men took their meals as they could while at work. On afternoons, which are often called backshifts, the men worked five shifts, Monday to Friday from 2 p.m. to 10 p.m., making altogether 40 hours. The nightshift, from 10 p.m. to 6 a.m., comprised six shifts from Sunday night to Friday night, making 48 hours.

Steelmaking was stopped between Saturday 1 p.m. and Sunday 10 p.m. for repairs, and one weekend in three what may be called 'productive overtime' was worked regularly, on average 12 hours, but sometimes more, up to 24 hours. Usually overtime was worked from 10 p.m. Saturday until 10 a.m. Sunday. So some men in Bessemer who theoretically worked 45 hours, in fact worked on average 49 hours a week (i.e., 47, 40, 48, plus 12 which makes 147 hours in a three-weeks' cycle).

Where there was a continuous process, as in the blast furnaces, where the furnaces were never stopped, there were four teams and the shift rotation was more complex, varying from week to week. For instance, a squad No. 1 starts working on mornings from 6 a.m. to 2 p.m., six shifts a week, and is off from Friday 2 p.m. to Monday 10 p.m. The following week it works nights from 10 p.m. to Saturday 6 a.m., again six shifts, and has two days off, Saturday and Sunday. The third week it starts Tuesday afternoon 2 p.m. to 10 p.m. for six consecutive shifts and has two days off, Monday and Tuesday. The times off changed from week to week but there were always two clear days. The working week was shorter, comprising only 42 hours with no overtime.

There are obvious advantages and disadvantages in both schemes, though both require good health and vigour, adaptability and flexibility from the shiftworker.

The attitude of men to the shift system was complex. Among the reasons given for liking shiftwork were the following: shiftwork jobs are better jobs all round and they are allocated by strict seniority—very few men like to be bypassed. The difference between daywork and shiftwork in wages may be something in the region of £4 to £5. Daywork leaves only one day free while shiftwork usually leaves two clear days. A great deal of overtime is worked on days, while occasional overtime is excluded on shifts. Some men liked the constant variety that goes with changing shifts. 'It isn't so monotonous, time seems to go quicker.' Those who cared for shifts expressed it in this way: 'More money, more time, more variety'.

Listening to the problems of shiftworkers, one realized that shiftwork presents a specific way of life. There are actually two different ways of life, that of shiftworkers and that of dayworkers. Both can be enjoyed but they don't mix easily. As most good jobs in Workington, in coal, steel and heavy engineering, are shift jobs, shiftwork is well tolerated, in Workington perhaps more than anywhere else. In my sample, out of sixty-eight men who had been on shifts or were recently on shifts, nineteen said that they liked and preferred shifts, apart from the money factor.

Attitude to Work

This was very ambivalent and full of complexities. Again many attracting and repelling forces are in operation in men's minds. The mind of the worker is very realistic, thinking in terms of alternatives. Actually he has very little understanding for abstract questions and does not see any point in asking them. There is no point in asking, in abstract terms, whether he likes shifts or not. 'Do you mean'—he would say—'would I prefer the same job with two days off with the same money on days? To this I would say, yes. Or would I prefer an inferior job for less money and with less free time? To this I would say, no.' The same applies to the question whether he likes his job or not. He has to like it. This question, in fact, was answered by the overwhelming majority in the affirmative. The scale of answers ran as follows: 'It is as good a job as any', or 'It is all right', or 'Nothing to grumble about', or 'It is a good job', or 'I like it', or 'I like it very much'. The difference was only in emphasis or in tone of voice. But asked if they would carry on in the job if they won big money on the pools, the big majority, about four in five, answered: 'No, I would look for a better job', or 'I would buy a small business'. But even those who would not look for a job would say 'But I would have to do something, otherwise I would be finished'.

Asked whether they would enjoy staying at home instead of going out to work, only those who had a sideline or a very fascinating hobby would answer, yes. But the big majority would say that only during holidays or weekends it would be all right, but staying at home while you are supposed to be at work is boring and dissatisfying. 'I would prefer to put in time and get paid for it', they would say.

Asked what it was they liked most about the job, they would answer: 'Company', or 'Something to do', or 'Variety', while others said 'Security', or 'The money'. A working man who has been working with his hands from the age of fourteen or fifteen cannot stop working with impunity; he is an active man who must exercise his muscles. A sense of achievement was frequently referred to by craftsmen or by leaders of a team.

Even those who worked with obnoxious materials, with a great deal of dust and fumes, even those who had been disabled in the course of production or suffered from industrial diseases, rarely complained about their jobs. Moaning about the job is regarded as wrong; you have to take the rough with the smooth. Of course, in the evaluation of these answers a great deal must be discounted as a mere tribute to conformity, but sifting carefully all the evidence I would say that most men are reasonably happy about their work.

The ethos of work can best be seen in the image of a model man, as visualized in the mind of the worker. A model man must be a good mixer, with a sense of humour and wit, but also a good workman, a hard-working man. A dodger, a swinger, even if he is a good mixer, could never be popular with the men—I was told by workmen as well as foremen; men who talk too much are also not popular.

Record of Unemployment, Accidents and Industrial Health

The forty-plus group had suffered in the past from a great deal of unemployment, while the under-forties were practically free from unemployment, as can be seen from the following figures (total length of unemployment over the years) from my sample:

TOTAL

Forty-plus	Zero or less than one year	One to two years	Three to five years	Six to ten years	Over ten years
59	24	13	14	7	1
Under-forties					
45	44	1	0	0	0

Among the under-forties there were only four who reported unemployment of any length, one up to twelve months at various periods of his life and three others from four to nine months. We see here the strong contrast between two generations, which is especially true of Workington, and the older men often referred to this as the most outstanding differential in the mental make-up of the two generations.

Accident prevention was taken seriously at Workington. There was a main Accident Prevention Committee together with seventeen departmental committees. Every encouragement was given to employees to go to the Health Centre even for the most minor cut. In 1957 the number attending the Health Centre was 5,113. The number of accidents which resulted in a loss of employment was 128 in 1957 with a frequency rate of 1·86. ('Frequency rate' gives the number of accidents per 100,000 man-hours worked.)

The frequency rate varied from department to department—from 0·50 in four departments to 2·00/2·75 in five departments, while in Rail Bank it was 3·12.

Nevertheless, the accident record of the works was relatively good, standing in the top twenty for the iron and steel industry.

In my sample, out of 104 men, twenty-six had at one time or another met with a serious accident resulting in loss of shifts for more than one month. Let me quote these cases here in full as they may throw light on this side of industrial life:

No.	Age	Nature of Accident	Loss of Shifts	Compensation
1	56	Broken foot and burns	20 weeks	nil
2	47	Broken toe	9 weeks	nil
3	36	Hand crushed	3 months	nil
4	64	Broken leg	6 months	nil
		Finger tip cut off	3 months	nil
5	54	Fractured leg and collar bone	16 weeks	nil
6	31	Serious burns	9 weeks	nil
7	22	Ribs burnt	3 months	nil

No.	Age	Nature of Accident	Loss of Shifts	Compensation
8	32	Cut in the head	6 weeks	nil
9	45	Fractured skull	6 weeks	nil
10	42	Badly bruised	6 weeks	nil
11	33	{ One finger lost	13 weeks	£750
		{ Burnt face	3 weeks	£400
12	60	Lost one eye	8 months	£2 per week
13	64	Lost two fingers on railways before joining firm	11 weeks	
14	30	Lost sight of one eye as fireman on railways before joining firm	3 months	
15	47	Concussion	2 months	nil
16	55	Fractured kneecap	8 months	nil
17	29	Two finger ends broken	3 months	£50
18	53	Broken ankle	1 month	nil
19	31	Cut in ear: hearing affected	2 months	nil
20	46	Smashed foot	5 months	Pending
21	23	Smashed leg, lame	18 months	£1,500 plus £1 5s 7d per week.
22	54	{ Broken arm	2 months	nil
		{ Broken hand	1 month	
23	50	Two fingers lost	9 weeks	nil
24	63	Spine fracture	13 months	£1,500
25	52	One finger crippled	—	£100
26	31	Burns all over the body	3 months	£200

We see from the above list that sixteen men belonged to the forty-plus group and ten to the under-forties so the age differential was not very large (22 per cent for the under-forties compared with 27 per cent for the forty-plus); this may be due simply to the longer exposure to accidents of older men.

I enquired also into the record of ill-health. Six men suffered from stomach ulcers, out of whom two had had stomach operations, four suffered from arthritis or rheumatism, one from asthma, one from malaria spells. The pattern of age composition was, in this field, strikingly different from that in the field of accidents. Out of these ten men only one belonged to the under-forties.

As to industrial diseases in the strictest sense, in a year there were only a few cases of silicosis or pneumonocosis (about six in a year), rather more of carbon monoxide poisoning (about forty), but of a mild nature, and also a few cases of dermatitis (about ten). There were also a few cases of neurosis or nervous breakdown (about twenty a year).

Altogether, sickness absenteeism amounted to about 3 to 4 per cent (in September 1958—3·07), while accident absenteeism accounted for 0·11 per cent.

The works doctor reported an enormous improvement in health as well as in cleanliness. 'Before the war I used to see fleas on patients every day. I haven't seen a flea for seven or eight months. The sanitary arrangements in the works compared with pre-war have improved 200 per cent.'

The Social Life in the Firm

The social life of the firm centred round the canteen, sports and outings. There were four canteens, one for the top managerial staff, another for the senior staff such as departmental managers and senior clerical staff, a staff dining-room for junior clerical staff and foremen, and a self-service canteen for workmen. This division is fairly general all over industry and represents the hierarchical structure of the works community, which is composed of those four layers. To be promoted means passing from one canteen to another and the canteen is the main symbol of status in the works.

In contrast the sports club is the leveller of class distinction, as it brings together all grades including staff. The membership of the club in Workington was voluntary, with a contribution of 2d per week, and about 66 per cent of work-people belonged to it. The most popular sections were: (1) Football, which engaged about 200 to 250 men up to the age of thirty-five (all workmen); (2) Cricket, with 400 members, men playing up to the age of fifty; (3) The angling section with eighty members, both workmen and staff; (4) Netball, with 140 men, women and staff; (5) Hockey—fifty, men and women; (6) Badminton—sixty members, workmen and staff; (7) Rugby—fifty members, all workmen; (8) Swimming—200 men and women, workmen and staff; (9) Aviary culture—100 members, all workmen; (10) Choirs—seventy members, half workmen and half staff.

There were also small sections like rifle shooting or chess (nine staff and four workmen). Outings, children's parties, concerts for retired colleagues, old-time dancing were arranged from time to time.

III. VAUXHALL MOTORS LTD IN LUTON

January and February 1959

Local Background

Luton is a highly industrial town, rapidly expanding, prosperous, its people running after jobs and money more or less in American fashion. One could say that Luton is a slice of America in Britain, self-assured, beaming with vitality and go-aheadness, a cosmopolitan community, drawing its immigrant population from many distant areas, especially from South Wales, Ireland and Scotland, mainly under the allurement of high wages. As one probation officer in Luton remarked: 'The boys from Glasgow and Greenock who arrive here and often get into trouble with the police think that the streets of Luton are literally paved with gold'.

In the last fifty years the population of the town has more than trebled and nearly doubled in the period from 1931 (from 68,000 to 114,500 in 1956 and an estimated 120,000 in 1958). This rapid growth has resulted in the fact 'that the community has not yet had time to find itself', as is often heard. The community life could not be as integrated as in other old-established towns, for instance in Workington which forms a complete contrast to Luton in many respects. Cultural life is also less developed. As one welfare officer remarked: 'The Lutonians are too busy making money to bother about this', and as one workman who settled here from Liverpool put it: 'Luton is for making money but entertainment is poor. Those who can afford it go to London for entertainment.'

The main social activities centre around sport (Luton has a very good football team), brass bands and choirs (The Luton Girls Choir is famous), around churches, especially the Presbyterian, the Methodist and the Catholic (with a strong Irish contingent), and also around societies such as the Caledonian Society, the Buffaloes, the Freemasons, the Druids, etc.

One of the positive effects of the town's rapid development is the nearly complete lack of slums and poverty-stricken areas and the high percentage of home ownership.

The insured population in Luton amounts to about 74,000, among whom 22,500 are women. The rate of unemployment is usually below the national average, the wage rates above the national average. The biggest firm in the area is Vauxhall Motors, with its 23,200 employees [1] in two factories in Luton and Dunstable, but there are a number of other medium-sized firms in the range of 2,000 to 5,000 employees, such as the Skefko Ball Bearing Company, Commer Cars, George Kent, Electrolux, etc. If we exclude female labour the employment in Vauxhall amounts to about 45 per cent of the labour market in Luton and about 36 per cent if the Dunstable factory is excluded.

One can see from these figures the preponderance of Vauxhall in the Luton labour market, which presents serious problems both for the town and for other firms as well as for Vauxhall. In times of full employment and expansion Vauxhall has to fall back on labour imported from other areas with all its inconveniences, which become noticeable especially at times when overtime is dropped and newcomers cannot afford to maintain two homes or pay for newly acquired houses.

[1] 28,000 in 1960.

The preponderance of Vauxhall in the Luton labour market has meant that the population of Luton has grown mainly in response to Vauxhall labour requirements and the prospects of Vauxhall still control the fate of Luton to a large extent.

However, the rise of Vauxhall is such that it has to draw its labour force from a far larger area than Luton itself. From my enquiries I gathered that only about 60 per cent of Vauxhall work-people live locally and that one in four comes from areas as far as ten or more miles away, which presents serious problems especially in times of extensive overtime working. (Some men travel daily from as far as London or Oxford.)

The Vauxhall labour force has nearly doubled over the last ten years. It was 12,000 in 1948 and 23,200 in January 1959, of which 18,357 were hourly-rated men and 4,846 staff. The bulk of hourly-rated operatives (15,114, of whom 415 were females) was concentrated in the Luton factory, and the rest (3,243) in Dunstable. The staff in these two units included 452 foremen, the average ratio of foremen to men being in the region of 1:40, being higher on the production side and lower on the maintenance side. (In the Workington Iron & Steel Company the ratio was much lower, 1:27, which is due to the difference between mass production and the older types of work.)

The rapid expansion of the firm has produced certain features of the labour force. One of them is the relatively young age structure, as the average age of the newcomers is around thirty, and rarely above forty-five.

The other feature is a lower degree of social integration both in terms of Union organization and community life in the works. About half the men in my sample came from other districts, mainly from Wales, Ireland, Scotland and the North, or from London. (In Workington about 90 per cent were local men, the influx from other areas being insignificant.) The Union organization was also less developed, estimated to be in the region of 60 per cent, compared with 90 per cent in Workington.

Labour Relations

The reputation of the firm among its work-people was very high. I often heard remarks such as: 'That is the best Company in the district', or 'This is a very good firm to work for. They take care of you.' General cleanliness and tidiness and good working conditions were also mentioned frequently. Only in some departments the air pollution, draughts or excessive noise were complained of. Security of jobs was also stressed as a great attraction. 'They don't sack here', they said. In fact, dismissals were very rare, one could say exceptional, apart from during the first six months of probation. In case of redundancy the principle 'Last in, first out' was strictly adhered to, so that men with longer service, over, let us say, a year or two, enjoyed a high measure of security.

There had been no strike of any importance for thirty-eight years. Relationships were easy and free, and in most departments men, foremen and often departmental managers were on Christian name terms.

Vauxhall is a non-federated firm and officially it does not take part in collective agreements. The standing of the Trade Unions in the firm is not very high and most of the business in labour relations is transacted through the Management Advisory Committee, an elected body outside the Union, although most of its members are in fact shop-stewards of the A.E.U. or the National Union of Vehicle Builders. The position of shop-stewards is not recognized in a formal sense, in particular on the production side, though in fact they act as the men's representatives on the shop floor.

The rate of absenteeism from all causes was fairly low, amounting to 3·96 per cent as an average for the whole firm. Only in some departments, such as Factory Cleaning Services, with about 550 operatives, where labourers, mostly Irish, are employed, absenteeism had risen as high as 10 per cent, but there was a specific background to this.

The appreciation of the firm by the work-people is also expressed in the low rate of labour turnover. The annual separation rate including quits, discharges, redundancies, retirements and deaths was 19·4 per cent, while the annual quit rate was 14·7 per cent. Most discharges and quits occur in the first six months which are regarded as the probationary period. During this period about 10 per cent leave or are dismissed, as some men are unable to accept what is called 'the realities of mass production'. The relatively high rate of early quits or dismissals often has disastrous effects on home life as men take on commitments such as home ownership which they cannot fulfil later on.

The standards of selection are, generally speaking, high, but they depend primarily on the state of the labour market and the urgency of labour requirements. By and large, from one hundred applications, about sixty-five would be selected for interviews and out of these about fifty would be engaged; finally about forty-two or forty would in fact turn up for the job. But in some skilled areas like the electrical department, out of five applicants who were selected for interview only one would be taken on. The high level of wages offered by the firm attracts the cream of the labour force in the area and often draws skilled labour into semi-skilled operations, as the difference between skilled rates in Luton generally and semi-skilled production rates in Vauxhall is in favour of Vauxhall. From a sample test undertaken in different production departments I gathered that about 10 per cent of men on semi-skilled operations are in fact skilled men who had served their time in other firms, such as fitters, turners, carpenters, bricklayers, etc. (In my sample I had also a few who had been salesmen, commercial travellers, clerks and small business men.) I asked some of the skilled men now on semi-skilled operations how they felt about it, and their answers ran on these lines: 'At first it was a bind but I got used to it. It doesn't matter how the job is classed. Money comes into it. I get more money for my family as a semi-skilled worker than I would get in my own trade.' The pride of the craftsman was not too strong, especially among those who had left their own trade. Even in a skilled department like carpentry it was not too marked, as one could see from the fact that when overtime for cleaning was offered nearly half the craftsmen would accept it if there was no overtime in their own trade. 'It is the money', they would say.

The comradeship here was quite good, but somewhat below the Workington standard. Men when asked about it would say: 'A pretty good crowd', or 'Good sort of lads', or 'Pretty fair', or 'We muck in all right'. There were two main handicaps which hindered the development of a deeper sense of comradeship. One was the large number of outsiders with different habits and ways of life; the other was the frequent transfer of men from one department to another, and also the size of the firm.

The comradeship, moreover, was of a rather superficial nature, and was not always expressed in mutual help on the job (when a bonus was in operation more mutual help was given). Mates rarely went out together. In my sample about only one in three stated that they saw their mates outside work, and this included also those who saw them only occasionally.

Men on Production

About two-thirds of hourly-rated men were on production. The period of training for their jobs might be anything from a few hours to a few months. The operations in most cases did not require skill, but a certain alertness, dexterity, team spirit and resistance to the monotony linked with mass production. When they were completely 'green', they would start as trainee improvers with 6s 0½d per hour, but in most cases as grade 2 men with 6s 3d per hour.[1] After a few months, in most cases between six and twelve months, they qualified for grade 1, with 6s 8d per hour, having mastered different operations and become versatile, so that they could be used on most operations in the departments. The Company is at liberty to transfer men from one job to another in the department and from one department to another, and even from the Luton to the Dunstable factory, and there is no resistance from the Union side to such transfers. The transfers are frequent and occur nearly every month, with changing schedules, shifts, overtime, etc. Most men do not like transfers and that was the most frequent subject of complaint I heard. 'It is like an army camp here, the shifting from one place to another all the time', or 'You don't know half of your mates when the men are shifted about'. Most men acquire a certain confidence in their jobs and frequent transfers upset them.

[1] The rates were raised in April 1960.

They would often say to a supervisor announcing the transfer: 'Why, what have I done?'

On the production side about 70 to 80 per cent of men were grade 1; one condition of service in grade 1 is an understanding that the management can shift the men as they are required. There was also a small percentage of setters with three grades (up to 7s 4½d for special grade) and group leaders (with 3d premium), both subject to merit money up to 3d per hour, solely at the discretion of the Company. Both setters and group leaders were recruited from the line but sometimes the setters came to the department as already skilled men. The percentage of setters in the departments and group leaders varied between 3 and 5 per cent and in some departments setters acted also as group leaders. Group leaders acted in most cases as working charge-hands with simple supervisory functions and also as 'floats', able to take over any operation or help out in any operation.

On the production side the wage structure was very uniform, one could say not only of one piece but also of one standard rate. About 70 to 80 per cent of production men had one single rate, although the jobs they performed were most varied and in the most varied conditions. The Company's policy is primarily to secure easy transfer from one job to another, which is facilitated under one rate. However, not all departmental managers agree with this policy as some jobs are more strenuous, require more skill or are performed under more difficult conditions than others, hence the request for transfers from some departments. This wage structure is in complete antithesis to the principle of the 'job evaluation', as all production jobs are classed as one. I am not convinced that such a drastic reversal of the job evaluation principle is justified in most cases.

The 'promotion-mindedness' of production men was very limited, both in terms of interest and in the number of men who cared for promotion, which in most departments did not exceed 5 per cent. This is not surprising as the avenues for promotion for men on the line are very restricted. One man in twenty or so could become a setter or group leader and one man in forty or so a foreman, but when the foremen, group leaders and setters are in their young or middle years, the chances are even smaller. Most men, i.e., eighteen or nineteen out of twenty, ended their working life where they had started. After six months or so they became grade 1 and after two years they got another 1d per hour for length of service, and there they would stop for life. More men were interested in getting the grade of group leader, in spite of its limited premium which, with the highest merit money, could not exceed 6d per hour, than the position of a foreman, as foremen often lose the overtime allowance which can completely obliterate the premium for supervision.[1] Besides, the foremanship on mass production

---

[1] During 1959 the Company adopted a scheme of payment for foremen to cover approved and planned overtime.

involved a great deal of strain and became even more strenuous after the bonus scheme was withdrawn two years previously. It was considered a hard job involving a great deal of worry which is often taken home, affecting family life. I came across two cases of foremen who felt that they could not stand the strain of home worries and job worries as well. One potential foreman, when he got to know that his wife suffered from heart trouble, felt that he would not be able to stand the strain of foremanship, when finally the position was offered to him after two years of training. The other foreman, who had upsets with his wife, considered giving up his foremanship as the strain brought home added to the domestic upsets.

When the bonus scheme was in operation, the foremen regarded it as a help, although it brought in its wake a great deal of petty complaints and grievances. Most managers and foremen, let us say 90 per cent, stated that the job of supervision and the keeping up of schedules and efficiency were easier under the bonus system. Characteristically, most men (about 95 per cent), with the exception of group leaders and setters, liked and appreciated the withdrawal of the bonus scheme, preferring time rates to bonus rates.

The interest of production men in the work itself was rather limited. The most frequent answer to my question as to whether they liked their job was: 'Well, it's repetitive. The same thing all over again. It's monotonous.' In Workington I rarely heard the term 'monotony' but in Luton it was time and again brought up by men on the production side and also often referred to by managers and foremen. 'There is a certain feeling of resentment against mass production and you can feel it in many ways. Especially the more intelligent men resent putting in a screw or a bolt,' a manager told me. One can feel also a certain feeling of contempt in the term itself used by the men when the question of job attitudes was brought up. 'You should know, it's mass production', they would say. A carpenter who was three years on production before he was transferred to a skilled area, described his feelings to me: 'I am much happier now. It was a great relief to leave the line. It was soul-destroying work at high pressure, no scope for thought. Now, I would not wish for anything better.'

However, the degree of monotony varied from department to department. It was much smaller in the finishing stages where men could already see the finished product, or where men were on longer cycles of operation, or where a greater degree of skill was required.

The ability to stand monotony also varied considerably with individual character, attitude of mind and home life. By and large, men who were fond of day-dreaming and had something nice to think about did not complain of monotony. 'No,' they would say, 'I don't mind mass production. I think about home, sweetheart, music, or football.' But those who had home worries or who had had a bad experience of life complained that they had too much time to think and that this added to their worries. As one man put it: 'No one likes to have too much time to think: thinking makes for worry, feelings of guilt, regrets and doubts'.

Most men did not complain about the speed; they said that they could easily keep their station time. The strain of mass production comes not so much from speed itself but from the constant level of effort. In skilled jobs there is a rhythm based on concentration followed by relaxation or release, while on mass production the effort is continuous, on one level.

But the reference to monotony was rarely put in a form of complaint, and most men, once they had accepted the realities of mass production, were successfully dealing with it in their own way. As one operator put it: 'The job is sometimes boring and sometimes not. It all depends on your state of mind', or as another man said: 'If you are against it, it becomes hard. You have to tell yourself, this is your job and you have to do it.' One man who had broken service in Vauxhall related his experience to me: 'When I was younger I could not stand the monotony, it made me irritable and dull, sort of a scatter-brain, so I left it. Now I don't mind it—it doesn't affect me at all.'

Some men referred not only to the monotony of the operation but also to the monotony of the place as a whole, and that is in my view an even greater problem which can be dealt with successfully if tackled the right way.

Skilled and Ancillary Labour

About one-third of hourly-rated men were on what is called indirect labour. These were mostly skilled men, but also included some semi-skilled and labourers. The grades varied considerably with trades and departments but there was a similarity of grading as on production, grade 2, grade 1, special grade, with or without merit money. The general principle prevailed that analogous grades, grade for grade, are lower paid in indirect labour than on production. For instance, a semi-skilled man on production would receive 6s 8d, while a semi-skilled man as a material handler or storekeeper grade 1, 5s 6d, a crane or locomotive driver 5s 8d. General labourers form the bottom grades with 4s 9½d, grade 2, and 4s 11½d, grade 1. The rates were high in absolute terms, but the differentials between direct and indirect labour resulted in many requests for transfer from all those who could stand the pace and the monotony of mass production.

As for skilled trades on the maintenance side such as fitters, turners and electricians, the differentials were also comparatively low; grade 1 men got 7s 0½d, which, compared with grade 1 production men, represents a differential of 4½d. The premium for skill is roughly speaking only 6 per cent which is regarded as insufficient by many managers in the skilled areas.

The attitudes to and interest in the job in the skilled areas presented a complete contrast to those of production men. These men rarely referred to monotony. They were much more interested in the work itself and they showed also greater interest in promotion, especially in getting to the top grade—the special grade with the highest merit money—as each of them considered himself as well qualified for the grade. Their only complaint was that they were often being hurried by the production supervisor in cases of breakdown. Their concern for the quality of work and their sense of responsibility produced also their specific attitudes to overtime and shifts, different from those of the production workers.

Overtime

The standard hours were 42½ a week [1] but the motor trade is seasonal and, in order to avoid redundancy in the second half of the year, long spells of substantial overtime are often worked. From January 1959 an average 5¼ hours per week overtime was expected but the incidence of overtime was uneven and some men in my sample worked as much as 20 to 30 hours overtime. To quote a few examples, a fitter of thirty-nine, married with three children, actually worked 33 hours overtime in one week; a semi-skilled production man, twenty-seven, married with one child, 24 hours; a cleaner, fifty-eight, married, 22 hours; a janitor, thirty-nine, married with one child, 19 hours. The wage packets were swelled considerably in such cases, and I came across a case where a man earned £36 0s 0d in one week. In these cases long hours do not leave much time for family life and this has definite repercussions at home. I came across cases where excessive overtime resulted in disruption and breaking up of home life. Men busy making money do not realize that they are upsetting their wives and breaking up their personal relationships until it is too late.

The general attitude of men to overtime was very ambivalent, governed by a set of contradictory forces; on the one hand they clamoured for overtime, on the other hand they objected to it and tried to avoid it. Everyone struck his own balance between the two contradictory pulls. When I asked a man whether he liked overtime, he would grin and give an answer of this kind: 'I can't say that I like overtime but I take my turn', or 'In my case overtime is a necessity', or 'It means all the difference between the comforts and the drabness of living'. Practically everyone had his own reservations: 'I like it only in moderation', or 'Every third week', or 'When I have to pay for the car', or 'It is too much at present', or 'I take my turn but I wouldn't like to spend my whole life in the factory'.

The prevailing attitude can be best described in a generalization made by one foreman: 'If no overtime is worked they complain and some leave but if too long a spell of overtime is worked, they complain again. They claim the right measure of overtime at the right time.'

[1] In 1960 the standard week was reduced to 41½ hours.

Shiftwork

The incidence of nightshifts varied from department to department and job to job, according to the type of equipment and its scarcity, and from month to month with changing schedules, but roughly speaking, all over the factory it amounted to about one shift in four (in 1958 about 28 per cent of hours were worked in nightshift). There was a monthly rota and in some departments and jobs, nights were worked every second month, in others every third, fourth, fifth or sixth. Few men were on permanent nights because they preferred it and a few men were excused on a doctor's certificate for themselves or for their wives; men over sixty were similarly excused. In my sample about one in three were permanently on days by virtue of their jobs.

Two years previously the shift allowance had been raised from one-fifth to one-third and the effect of it was, as the standing joke went, that 'this has cured most of the stomach ulcers'. At the time of the enquiry most men did not object to taking their turn.

The Company's policy in regard to shiftwork was open to departmental variations; in some departments the worker could be replaced by a volunteer substitute, in other departments a strict rota was enforced.

The attitude of men to shiftwork differed significantly from that in Workington in many respects but we have to keep in mind that the system itself was different from that in Workington. In Workington there was a three-shift system with a weekly rotation, as a regular and strongly established practice, and with full support in the shiftworking area. In Luton shifts were rather the exception than the rule, less definite, more vacillating, with possibilities of escape, and the rotation was monthly, bi-monthly and so on. In Workington, shifts were a way of life, while in Luton they were only a peck of trouble. The cycle was too indefinite for men to get used to nights. The negative attitude to shifts was consequently much more pronounced in Luton than in Workington. In my sample about two to one among those who were on shifts said that they would prefer to work regular days and give up the night allowance.

I would say that where little shiftwork is done and the shifts are less regular and definite, negative attitudes to shifts prevail, with a higher measure of maladjustments, irritability and frustration. On the other hand, where the shift system is more general and more definite with little escape or alternative, the worker adjusts himself better, with a greater measure of tolerance for shifts and a greater percentage of those who enjoy shifts. I would venture here a more sweeping generalization, saying that where the demand is constant, firm and definite and the worker realizes that there is no nonsense about it, the response is better than where the demand is vacillating, less firm and less definite.

The other interesting difference between Workington and Luton consisted in the attitudes towards the period of rotation. In Workington practically everybody preferred the weekly rotation, adding, 'As it is'. In Luton everybody preferred the monthly rotation, again adding the same remark. We see here the result of habit forming. Men can adjust themselves, it seems, to practically anything—and every change needs a new adjustment.

Training

The Education and Training Centre provided for the training of young people between the ages of fifteen and twenty-one. There were various training schemes to suit different backgrounds and careers, for trade and engineering apprenticeship, for the office junior, for the sandwich degree scheme, degree students' scheme, commercial apprenticeship and traineeship. Here we are concerned with trade and engineering apprenticeships only. The school provided four to five years' intensive training with normal entry at sixteen to seventeen for candidates with four to five or more G.C.E. subjects at ordinary level. During the time of the enquiry there were 700 apprentices in the Centre. There were about 160 vacancies per year and the ratio of applications to vacancies was between 4:1 and 5:1. About 40 per cent of boys were *de facto* recruited from grammar schools, 10–15 per cent from technical schools, 35–45 per cent from secondary modern schools. The boys were accepted after a general test and dexterity test. The ratio of acceptance of grammar school boys was, in fact, in the region of 1:2, from secondary modern schools, 1:6. The secondary modern school boys were regarded as late developers.

About 80 per cent of boys came from fathers employed in the firm, mostly hourly-rated men. The contacts with fathers were very close and most fathers took a keen interest in the progress of their boys. Those who came from other areas were put up in approved lodgings which were supervised by the school authorities.

The first wage in 1959 was £3, rising to £4 10s 0d, £5 5s 0d, £6 10s 0d, £8 0s 0d with every year. So after the first year an apprentice coming from other areas could pay for his board (£3 to £3 10s 0d on the average).

The percentage of failures in the school was very small, amounting to about 1 per cent. Boys conscripted to the Army came back to the firm, and the loss of apprentices to other firms was very small.

Accidents

Accidents were on a much smaller scale than in Workington, as to be expected in an engineering firm compared with a steelworks. The frequency rate (number of injuries per 100,000 hours) was, in 1957, 0·69, about one-third that of Workington. The frequency rate had decreased from 0·88 in 1955 but had increased slightly from 0·68 in 1956.

Lost-time accidents (cases when men are away from work as a result of injury) amounted, in 1957, to 245, but 40 per cent of these only lost one or two days.

The interesting features about accidents in Vauxhall were:
1. A higher frequency rate for nightshift than dayshift. In 1957 about 30 per cent of accidents were reported for nights, while 24 per cent of the total hours were worked on nights. This, in itself, shows the different strain of work on nights.
2. One-quarter of all accidents occurred to men with less than twelve months' service, much above the percentage of such men in the personnel.
3. Falls, falling and striking objects, and burns, accounted for 61 per cent of all accidents, accidents with machinery only 10 per cent, with other equipment 10 per cent and with hand labour 19 per cent. The highest frequency of accidents was among material handlers. Lack of normal care was regarded as the prime cause of all accidents.

Welfare and 'Fringe' Benefits

The welfare and 'fringe' benefits were on the increase all the time and they played a big part in binding the men to the firm. They were very much appreciated by the men and they were often referred to during the interviews.

There was a group accident and health insurance scheme with the financial assistance of the Company, without medical examination, securing at a very low cost substantial benefits (2s 10d weekly contribution for most men with £6 per week benefit). There was a life assurance scheme, providing a cash payment in the event of death and a monthly allowance in case of a permanent and total disablement. There was a pensions scheme and a supplementary pension plan. There was a benevolent club for those who were sick for longer periods, with benefits up to £3 10s a week. There was a holiday advisory bureau, an overall service, providing overalls for 6,500 hourly-rated men, a lodging service for those recently recruited from outside, etc.

To give an illustration of the level of the welfare services I will quote here a case of a man interviewed by me, who stated that during his three and a half months' sickness he was actually better off than during a normal working week. He received £6 from the group health insurance, £4 15s from National Insurance, 35s from the benevolent club, 15s from the Union, £2 10s for Christmas, and in addition £24 income tax rebate. Those opportunities were very rarely abused by the men, as the low rate of absenteeism shows.

The Social Life of the Firm

The social life centred round the canteen, licensed bar and sports club. About 30 per cent of men, both hourly-rated and staff, made use of the canteen for their main meal, but practically everyone used it for teas and snacks. There were two tea breaks, each for ten minutes, 10 to 10.10 a.m. and 3.50 to 4 p.m. As in Workington, there were four canteen levels, one for senior executives, another for junior executives, the third for weekly-paid staff, the fourth for hourly-rated men; the outstanding sign of promotion was the passing from one canteen to another. Often those who felt that they ought to be considered of a higher rank would not attend the canteen until the new promotion took place.

The sports club had twenty-nine different sections, but active participation of members was small, amounting to about 5 to 6 per cent of the personnel. This was partly due to large distances and partly to the high percentage of newcomers to the firm.

The most active sections were:

Football. There were seven teams with about 100 footballers, with the strongest support from the staff. Age up to thirty.

Cricket. There were five regular teams with seventy to eighty players, both staff and men.

Rugby. Two teams with about fifty players. Seventy-five per cent of staff. Age up to twenty-eight.

Fishing. Two hundred and fifty regular members.

Dramatic Society. Fifty active members. Ratio of staff to men, 5:1. Three to four plays a year were performed.

Choirs. Two choirs, forty strong, mostly hourly-paid men.

Orchestra. Thirty-five strong, 50 per cent staff.

Tennis. One hundred players, mostly staff.

There was an Annual Sports Day and, once a year, a Wives' and Families' Week for visiting the works. Outings were arranged on a departmental basis.

IV. THE DUNLOP RUBBER COMPANY LTD IN ERDINGTON

March and April 1959

Local Background

Birmingham, the commercial and industrial metropolis of the West Midlands, is a very prosperous city with a rate of unemployment below the national average and a level of wages above. The labour force shows a fairly stable character in its composition and is firmly rooted in local tradition, but has a fair percentage of newcomers from other areas. In my sample of 115 men in Fort Dunlop, twenty-one came originally from other areas, mostly from Ireland, Wales and Scotland but also from other parts of the country; however, none of these had two homes, but were all living with their families in the district.

Since the war the population has spread considerably to new estates on the outskirts, which has added to the difficulties of transport. From sample tests undertaken by me in various departments of Dunlop I gathered that about 40 per cent of men lived within a three miles radius, 50 per cent from three to eight miles and 10 per cent over eight miles which, for shiftwork, presented considerable handicaps.

The area in which Dunlop mostly recruits its labour, covered by the local Employment Exchange in Waswood Heath, Erdington, with roughly speaking about 55,000 insured population, is a very highly industrialized centre comprising five to six big firms, mostly motor firms, such as Fisher & Ludlow with 6,000 to 7,000 employees, Nuffield Metal Products with 3,000, Morris Commercial and Tractor Transmissions, each with 2,500, Metro Cammell Carriage and Wagon Works with 2,000, etc. The prevalent system of working in the area is piecework as well as shiftwork, and mass production. The motor firms pay very high wages, higher than Dunlop, so they have the first choice of the labour market, especially for young and vigorous men who can stand the pace of conveyor work.

After the motor firms, Dunlop ranks as the best paying firm with the best conditions, so much so that it sometimes drew skilled men from other firms into semi-skilled operations. In my sample I had several semi-skilled operatives who were previously engaged in other firms as skilled men in various trades; they had found it more profitable to throw away their Union ticket as skilled men.

Before 1958 the area enjoyed full or even over-full employment and the competition for the right kind of labour among the firms was very fierce. The labour turnover could be at times as high as 60 per cent; men would leave their jobs for more money and better conditions, but primarily for more money. Since the recession the firms find it easier to recruit labour, though even now the choice of labour is fairly restricted in Birmingham. Prior to 1958, five interviews were necessary for engaging one man, the rest of the applicants would prove unsuitable; in 1958 this figure came down to two to three interviews necessary for one engagement. Prior to 1958 about 30 per cent (in 1955—40 per cent) of men already engaged would not turn up for work; in 1958 this figure came down to 20 per cent.

The Labour Force

The total labour force employed by Dunlop in Erdington was about 10,500 at the time of the enquiry, but only about 6,600 were hourly-rated men. The large percentage of staff is due to the extensive research and development departments, and also to the sales organization and other headquarters departments of the Dunlop organization. The factory goes back forty-three years and has undergone very considerable development and growth. However, in the last two decades (war development excluded) the manual labour force did not increase to any extent; it rose from 5,205 in 1938 to 6,851 in 1949 and it declined slightly to 6,640 in March 1959. The decline in the last decade is mainly due to the fall of female labour, owing to the transfer of some lines of production like golf-ball and tennis-ball manufacture, more suitable for women's work, to other districts (the female labour force fell from 1,439 in 1938 to 1,046 in 1949 and 759 in 1959). The general output per man also rose considerably both in quantitative and qualitative terms as a result of the introduction of new modern equipment. There is a strong drive towards constant technical improvement by introducing more automatic machines and this tendency was often referred to by operatives in the interviews. They talked about 'automation', showing concern about the prospects of future employment. One man who was emigrating to New Zealand with his young family justified his decision in this way: 'I get moving before my job gets caught up in the meshes of automation. There is a lot of this going on in our department.'

One of the results of this more-or-less static force is its relative ageing. Only 40 per cent of operatives were under forty while 11 per cent were over sixty. There was a pension scheme for men over sixty-five and even for those over sixty, but the compulsory retiring age for hourly-rated men was seventy and in May 1958 about 4 per cent of male operatives were over sixty-five.

The labour force was pretty stable, with relatively long service. About 47 per cent had more than ten years' service, about 21 per cent more than twenty years' service and about 14 per cent more than thirty years'.

The labour turnover was relatively low for the district and declined considerably during 1958. In 1958 the gross rate of labour turnover (males only), comprising all causes was 20·5 per cent, while 16 per cent left of their own accord. The leavers were mostly newcomers in their first year. However, the rate of turnover differed from department to department, depending on the working conditions and the pace of work, level of wages, the incidence of shiftwork, incidence of short-time or overtime. In some departments three out of ten newcomers would leave in the first six months, in other departments far fewer. However, the main reason for leaving was shiftwork, especially for those who had started shiftwork late in life. Actually the Employment Office tries to avoid engaging men who have previously had no shiftwork experience but shiftwork is a fairly established practice in the district. It is characteristic that most semi-skilled or unskilled men, when being engaged, do not ask about the nature of the work, but about wages, shifts, hours and overtime, and (less frequently) about pension schemes and other fringe benefits.

Interest in the Job

The labour force was divided into two main sections: the rubber workers and the engineers. The rubber workers formed about 70 per cent of the male labour force, while the engineers on maintenance and in the toolroom about 25 per cent; the rest were classed as labourers and ancillary labour.

The rubber workers are semi-skilled, their training lasting between a few days and a few months. Only very few jobs such as on moulding or aero-rerubbering or fabric preparation are regarded as more skilled, for which training would extend for several months. Generally speaking, a tyremaker can be as good in three months as the next man who has been at the job for years, but on some operations it takes nearly eighteen months to reach full productivity. Usually training is done through the T.W.I. scheme and the trainer is put on average earnings with an extra 1d an hour. Most operatives who are instructors enjoy this job of training as it breaks the monotony.

The engineering workers are predominantly skilled men who serve their apprenticeship or who in some cases have been upgraded by the Company; a fair number of semi-skilled men are serving their tradesmen.

There was a vast difference in degrees of interest in the job between the engineer, especially the skilled man, and the rubber worker. To my question as to whether they liked their job the most frequent answers I received from the skilled engineers ran as follows: 'I like it very much, something I took an interest in for life'; 'I like it. It's the variety. Keeps my mind active'; 'I like to be at work rather than at home, on a weekday, I mean. You never get bored'; 'I am interested in the new machines. There is always something new to learn.' 'I would say this is my work and my hobby.'

Only a small minority would complain about monotony or say 'It is just a job', and these were mostly those who had previously had more interesting jobs in engineering firms.

Attitudes among the rubber workers were strikingly different. Their interest in the job was limited. Some would say, 'Rubber runs in your blood', or 'If I left I would feel I am missing something', but these were mostly leading hands. Most rubber workers would say: 'It's just a job', or 'I like it reasonably well', or 'You get to like it', or 'It's a steady job and every job is the same', or 'Making a living for eight hours a day—no trouble', or 'It keeps you going. I like moving fast.'

The complaint about monotony was rarely heard. 'You have no time to get bored. It's piecework.' In fact, piecework adds considerable interest to the job.

To my question as to what it was they liked most in the job, the answers were mostly: 'Short hours, good money, nice atmosphere'; 'Good mates, nothing to worry about'; 'Security. I am as secure as a manual worker can be'; 'I like the fellows, the friendliness'; 'I like Dunlop's regular employment.'

However, some answers to the same question were more cynical: 'What I like most is picking up the wages at the end of the week';

'Knocking off at the end of the shift'; 'Money. We all work for money, don't we?'; 'The money is good. That is the biggest point.'

To my question, what did they dislike most in their job, the big majority answered: shifts. Some would say: dust or fumes. 'The smell doesn't enter into it although we are smelled out when outside. We call ourselves rubber-bugs from the fly which appears in summer.' Others would complain about the job being too tiring, or too fast, or too warm, especially in summer-time.

Those who had been previously on clerical or salesmen's jobs or on skilled trades definitely showed a certain dislike of the job. They would say: 'The job is not up to my standard of ability but I do it for my family', or 'I am looking around to see if I can find a more suitable job'.

The homeo-static principle in attitudes to the job is very striking, in the sense that it seems an attempt was made to maintain a balance in the mind between like and dislike of a job. Working conditions varied greatly from department to department and some jobs were really exacting, being carried out in strenuous conditions, such as in the mill where men were covered with carbon black, or on moulding or case-making in the big tyres department (Giant shop), or on gangwork for moving heavy machinery. Still, men on those jobs did not speak disparagingly about their work, or at least no more than men working in comfortable conditions, even in spite of the fact that the wage differentials to compensate for this were very small. Somehow most men come to terms with these conditions, and every job, even those with the most adverse conditions, creates in the minds of the men its own compensations. Actually those working in adverse conditions develop a certain sense of achievement, a certain satisfaction derived from adversity, a feeling of righteousness that they are able to stand these conditions and overcome the obstacles, and that they are doing all this for their family. Heavy and difficult jobs carry an element of self-respect, light jobs a certain element of contempt. This kind of balancing-up in attitudes has a more general background and can be seen even more clearly in attitudes to shiftwork.

Labour Relations

The reputation of the firm amongst work-people was fairly high. Men said: 'Good firm to work for; they care for you', or 'A well-organized firm, they are very fair', or 'Good conditions; the place is kept clean and tidy, very pleasant'.

Both human and labour relations were satisfactory, and were often referred to by men in positive terms. The firm operates, on the rubber side, through the National Joint Industrial Council, and on the engineering side it is a member of the National Federation of Engineering Employers, and so all agreements of those bodies with the respective Trade Unions apply in the firm. The main Unions are, on the rubber side, the United Rubber Workers and the National Union of General and Municipal Workers and, on the engineering side, the A.E.U. The Company advises the operative employees to join the respective Unions. The exact percentage of Union membership is not known to the Company but it is estimated to be in the region of 50 to 60 per cent, more on the skilled side and less on the rubber workers' side.

Wage System and Piecework

The average wage for the whole factory (hourly-rated adult males) was, in January 1959, £16 13s 0d for 46·2 hours. In the previous months the average for the whole factory (adults hourly-rated, both males and females) was lower, £15 9s 11d for 43·8 hours.

There were two separate wage systems, one for the rubber workers and another for the engineering side. The skilled engineers had their own rates according to their trades, with piecework in the machine shop and a small group bonus on maintenance. They were graded according to their skill, experience and merit, in some departments up to eight grades.

The rubber workers had four grades, with basic time rates from 3s 8d to 4s 0½d with piecework based on these rates as well as shift and night work allowance. About 80 per cent of rubber workers were on piecework and about 70 per cent on three shifts, which added considerably to their earnings. So piecework is the standard wage system of the factory and at the same time one of its main problems. It is reckoned that there are about 1,700 operations in rubber production and there are thousands of prices given for those operations. During 1959, 1,300 new piecework prices were issued. Under these conditions it is very difficult to keep consistency and balance in the rates issued and many managers believe that 'there is no wage structure to speak of' and that the whole wage pattern has 'got out of hand'.

The attitudes to piecework differed very considerably in the two main sections. Most rubber workers, a very large majority, liked piecework, and particularly individual piecework. I discovered that those on piecework, in fact, mostly preferred piecework and those on time mostly preferred time rates, those on individual piecework mostly preferred individual piecework and those on gang piecework mostly preferred gang piecework. Is it that those who preferred these arrangements were attracted to these systems, or does it merely show the effect of habit forming? Habit certainly plays a very big part in this process; the men had come to terms with the existing arrangements and they would say simply: 'It suits me'.

Generally speaking, the rubber workers on piecework would say: 'Time goes quicker when you are on piece', or 'You can please yourself. You receive only what is coming to you', or 'You can put your back into it', or 'You have something to work for'.

However, there were exceptions to this rule: those who could not adapt themselves, who were naturally slow, or who were getting on in years. Such people would say: 'It is all right if I can make the money', or 'Piecework is good for young men. It is actually a young man's job. After forty you are finished', or 'I suffer from dizziness', or 'My eyes are not so good'.

Generally speaking, elderly men, even if they find the speed satisfactory, care little for piecework, as their financial needs are dropping off and they can afford to ease off the pressure in their work. They would say: 'At my age I prefer a flat wage' or 'At my time of life a fair day wage would do for me'.

On the engineering side the rule that those on piecework like piecework also held good for skilled men, but not to the same extent. First, because piecework as a system was not firmly established on the engineering side (some are on time, others on piece, some are partly on time and partly on piece), the time rates were higher and the bonus earned formed a smaller part of total earnings. Second, because the skilled men were more concerned about the work as such, they took greater interest in quality and achievement and they felt greater responsibility.

A large minority of skilled men are critical about the piecework system, contending that they would prefer a fair flat wage. They would say: 'If the money is decent, better flat rate'; 'It's a worry if you have to do a good piece of work'; 'In my trade, piecework is a bad thing', 'In piecework it's one eye on the job, one eye on the clock'; 'Not much pride of work on piece as you can't make a good job of it'.

It was interesting to enquire about the target of output, whether the target is individually set or collectively agreed. We can distinguish here two groups of men: those groups where everyone sets a target for himself, and others where the target is collectively agreed between men on the same or similar type of work. Those in the first group would say: 'I set my own target', or 'I do what I can', or 'I have a target to suit myself'. Those in the second group would say: 'We try to work to a target agreeable to all'; 'We keep the same target. I wouldn't like to exceed it'; 'We keep to time and a half' or 'We keep to time and a third'; 'To exceed the target, it wouldn't be fair to men, even not to the foreman and the rate fixer'.

The groups were often interchangeable. Sometimes in a group with an agreed target, a man who needed the money badly would break away and set a higher target and the others would follow him. Or a strong personality would come along and persuade men in the first group to keep the same standard of performance so as to show better comradeship. By and large, young married men starting to build up their homes belonged to the first group.

On the whole the times given for piecework were regarded as fair and comfortable, the complaints only sporadic. The most criticized incentive system was the bonus system of the engineers on maintenance. The bonus was small, amounting to about 10 to 15 per cent of total earnings, and some of the engineers contended that the system slowed up maintenance work as such. Often more time is wasted on getting estimates, issuing tickets and clocking-in than on the work itself. The premium for skill was very small and existed only in rates but not in actual earnings.

Overtime

The attitudes to overtime puzzled me. Why was it that in some places like Sheffield or Workington there should be a nearly 'insatiable appetite' for overtime, while in Vauxhall a considerable appetite, but not an insatiable one, and in Dunlop a very moderate one? The valid explanation which I believe is the key to understanding these differences in behaviour is the actual incidence of overtime in different workplaces and areas. Where overtime is a long-established practice, the worker raises his standard of living, reckons the overtime earnings as part of his legitimate earnings and incorporates them as if of right into his expectations. If, in this, he is supported by the general practice of overtime in other firms in his district, he expects overtime, and demands it when engaging himself, and then resents not being granted a fair amount. The amount of overtime asked for would represent the difference between his standard wage and the standard of living to which he is already accustomed or to which he has pledged himself by buying his home or car or giving the children the education he would like them to have.

In Vauxhall overtime was seasonal, while in Dunlop during 1959 very little overtime was worked. So in Dunlop the most frequent answers to my question whether a man cared for overtime ran as follows: 'No, but I do it', or 'I don't mind but I don't ask', or 'I don't care but never refuse', or 'Up to a point', or 'A bit but not too much, within reason', or 'Only if necessary', or 'Only if I need the money for extras', or 'In winter, not in summer', or 'I am not over-keen—only if the need arises.'

Again the rule already referred to applies, that when a man has worked overtime for a long time, he affirms his liking for overtime as a consequence of habit forming. He would say: 'I have done it for such a long time, I am used to it as part of my job'.

Men on time rates would care for overtime more frequently than men on piecework, not only because as a rule they earn less but also because pieceworkers can make additional money by extra exertion when they need, and this may be an additional factor in overtime attitudes in Dunlop. As one pieceworker said: 'You know if you want a little bit extra where to get it'.

Only a minority of operatives were over-keen on overtime, and these were mostly the young married men who were building up their homes, buying a house, or men with large families, or labourers on small wages, and from these the comments were: 'I have to, I am buying a house', or 'I have to, I have three daughters', or 'The more overtime the better, I bought furniture for £200', or 'I am only a labourer and the wages are not enough'.

At the other end of the scale the small minority which objected to overtime consisted mainly of elderly men, or men not in good health, or those for whom piecework imposed strain, or men with sidelines or strong hobbies who knew how to make good use of their leisure time.

Most men did not object to Saturday mornings but objected strongly to Saturday afternoons. Sunday was appreciated because of its high rate and only one or two minded working on Sunday on religious grounds.

Shifts

About 70 per cent of rubber workers were on three shifts, the rest on two shifts or on regular days. They worked on a weekly rota and the sequence of three shifts was in most cases: mornings (6.30 a.m. to 2.30 p.m.), nights (10.30 p.m. to 6.30 a.m.) and afternoons (2.30 p.m. to 10.30 p.m.). Most men liked this sequence rather than the sequence mornings, afternoons, nights, because after a week on nights they could recover some of their lost sleep on afternoons. The official number of hours was 44, made up of six mornings, five afternoons and five nights, but actually when on full-time 45 hours were worked, with 1 hour counted as overtime. In the 8-hour shifts there was no break for dinner but only two 10-minute breaks for tea. The two-shift system consisted of days and nights on a weekly rota, each lasting 10 hours with a 1-hour break for a meal (actually working 9 hours per shift).

Before 1954 a two-shift system was worked by most operatives; then the factory switched over to a three-shift system, at first against a great deal of resistance from operatives. The resistance has since declined considerably, although judging from the material of my interviews a slight majority would still prefer two shifts. Of thirty-one men who were asked which system they preferred, seventeen declared themselves for two shifts, thirteen for three shifts and one said that there was little to choose between them. In fact, both systems had their good and bad points.

Those who preferred two shifts gave the following reasons: 'Less change about, you are not all the time on a swing, you get settled down more easily'; 'There are no afternoon shifts and I hate them more than anything else'; 'It isn't so tiring as there is a break for a meal'.

Those who preferred a three-shift system did so mainly because the hours are shorter and there is more leisure time. However, the big majority of men preferred daywork to shifts, but with reservations. Out of seventy-one men on shifts who were asked this question, forty preferred regular days with less money, while the remainder answered: 'No'. However, most of those who declared themselves for regular days made it dependent on not dropping more than a limited sum in their weekly earnings, mostly in the region of £2 to £3. Actually, what came out was that most men were prepared to give up the shift and night allowance but some only part of it, a pound or so. Only very few said: 'Money doesn't come into it, it's my health'. Those who preferred shifts to daywork were equally divided between those who liked the shift system as such and those who said that they could not afford to lose anything. The latter would say: 'I come to work for money, money is the main object'.

The most popular shift was the morning shift—though not with all men as for some it meant rising too early, between 4.45 a.m. and 5.15 a.m., and quite a number said: 'I don't come alive until 8 a.m. or 9 a.m. and I don't take breakfast before I leave'. For many men the afternoon shift was as unpopular as nights, especially in summer-time. The popularity of the shifts is best expressed in the figures of absenteeism. In January 1959, of those on three shifts, 894 were on mornings but only 826 turned up for afternoons and 791 for nights (in September 1958 the corresponding figures were: 840 on mornings, 788 on afternoons and 778 on nights). We see here a great difference in reporting for work between mornings and other shifts, but a much smaller difference between afternoons and nights.

Welfare and Fringe Benefits

Canteen. Only about 700 of the hourly-rated men used the canteen for their main meal. The number of canteen users has declined very considerably during the last few years, mainly because of the introduction of three-shift work where there is no meal break which allows men to use the canteen. In fact, the canteen users were those on two shifts or regular days. For three-shift workers there was a trolley service, providing tea and light snacks, and this service was very well patronized.

Sickness and Benevolent Fund. Membership of this fund is voluntary but, in fact, nearly 100 per cent of the operatives were members. A man pays 7*d* per week into the fund which entitles him to a sickness benefit, varying slightly according to the number of his dependants. The benefit ranges from 23*s* per week for a single man to 32*s* for a man with a wife and four children. Membership of the fund also entitles employees to use the Dunlop Convalescent Home at Rhos-on-Sea in North Wales, a home with accommodation for some sixty patients, which is used by Dunlop factories throughout the country. The fund also provides certain other benefits such as cash grants for members who have to purchase dentures or spectacles under the National Health Scheme.

Although the company makes a contribution for each member, the fund is operated by an executive committee. Nine members of this executive committee are nominated by the five Fort Dunlop consultative committees, and the company nominates the chairman, secretary and treasurer.

Pension Scheme. Membership of the scheme is obligatory for all men aged twenty or more with one year's service and for all women aged twenty-five or more with one year's service. The normal contribution for a man is 2s per week and his pension on retirement will vary according to the number of years in the scheme, but his maximum pension would be £2 0s 0d per week. If he wishes to increase his pension he can contribute an additional weekly sum, but this is not matched by the company as is the original 2s.

Accident Prevention. Very close attention is paid to accident prevention and awareness of accident hazards is encouraged in many different ways. There is a full-time safety officer and there is also an Accident Prevention Council which meets periodically to discuss safety matters which the members choose to bring forward. This council consists of shop management, elected representatives and other employees with an interest in the subject. The number of lost-time accidents during 1958 was eighty-two and this represents a decrease on the numbers during the previous year. The frequency rate for 1958 (number of accidents per 100,000 man-hours worked) was 0·56.

Social Life of the Firm

The social life of the firm centres around the social club and the sports club. For those who live in Erdington the social club in Dunlop is the main centre for gathering. It is reckoned that about one-third of operatives use the bar of this club at one time or another, and about 100 men who live locally use the bar as their 'local', spending about £15 per year per head.

Out of 10,500 employees at the time of the enquiry, about 7,500 subscribed 2d a week to the sports club, but only about 3,500 were active members, two-thirds of them operatives and one-third staff.

There were twenty-eight sections, of which the most popular were:

Tennis. 100 members, with 80 per cent staff.
Angling. 150 members.
Football. Six teams with eighty members, age up to thirty.
Cricket. Three teams with sixty members.
Hockey. Eighty members.
Rugby. One team, twenty members, mostly staff, age up to thirty.
Operatic Society. 100 members.
Choral Society. Twenty to twenty-five members.
Dramatic Society. 120 members, mostly staff, giving three public performances a year.

Various sections arranged day-outings.

The sports club derives considerable income from a popular draw arranged every week. About 17,000 tickets, 6d each, are sold every week from which 25 per cent goes to the club and 75 per cent to prize money, with eight prizes from £80 downwards.

V. THE MULLARD RADIO VALVE COMPANY LTD IN MITCHAM

May, June and July 1959

Local Background

Mitcham forms part of a larger area covered by the Labour Exchange in Croydon which serves also Beddington, Wellington, Carshalton, Sutton, Purley and Thornton Heath. The insured population in this area numbers about 123,000, among whom 49,000 are women. It is a very prosperous area with a rate of unemployment of about 50 per cent below the national average in the last ten years. However, the average level of wages is not very high as it is the centre of light industry with a very high percentage of female labour. The demand for female labour is very high and hardly ever met. At the time of the enquiry there were 500 vacancies in the Labour Exchange for 138 women registered, plus 106 part-timers. For men the ratio was not so favourable as there were 522 vacancies for 822 unemployed, out of whom 250 were reckoned as in fact unemployable, classed as the hard core of unemployment. But we have to take into account that the labour exchanges at present deal only with a fringe of the labour market, mostly with inferior grades of labour, and the figures of vacancies and placements form a very small part of total demands and supply of the labour market. The percentage of placements in Mullard from men and women sent by the Labour Exchange is about 5 per cent for women and also very small for men. The labour exchanges are losing very fast their character as a real Exchange, controlling a significant portion of the market, and become more and more agents for social insurance.

A number of large-scale and medium-size firms compete for labour in this area, the biggest being Powers-Samas (Accounting Machines), Creed & Co. (Teleprinters), Louis Newmark (Watchmakers), Philips Electrical Industries (Croydon), Bailey Meters and Control, A.G.I. (Aero and General Instruments), Hackbridge Cables, Briggs Motor Bodies, etc. Although the competition for labour, especially female labour, is very fierce, there is little trespassing on each other's preserves, and the general level of wages offered by these firms is fairly constant. The pressure of full employment has eased recently but has not disappeared.

In Mullard for one placement about three to four interviews are needed; the figure is higher for skilled men where approximately five to six interviews may be required. The unsuccessful interviews are equally divided between rejection and decline, though the borderline between them is often difficult to draw as in many cases both sides find the match unsuitable. For shiftworkers the number of interviews required for one placement is, generally speaking, higher than for dayworkers. If the applicant has no previous experience of shiftwork the employment officer advises him to discuss the matter with his wife, after which the applicant often does not come back.

The Company and its Labour Force

Like two previous firms, Vauxhall and Dunlop, the Mullard Radio Valve Company also forms part of a large organization, with international connections. The Mullard Group operates three main factories, in Mitcham, Blackburn and Simonstone, supplying (1954) about 60 per cent of the total trade in valves and tubes in the United Kingdom. Mitcham is engaged in small-scale valve production, Blackburn in larger-scale production and Simonstone is a new mass-production centre for cathode ray tubes.

The works in Mitcham on which the study was centred goes back to the early thirties, and has expanded rapidly since 1936. Part of its staff was transferred a few years ago to a new location with about 1,500 employees, which fact has a bearing on the average length of service of the remainder of the labour force in Mitcham.

At the end of June 1959 the works in Mitcham employed a total of 3,184, of whom 2,012 were hourly-rated operatives, 827 weekly staff and 345 monthly. Of hourly-rated operatives the majority, i.e., 1,100, were women, while 922 were men. In the previous two years there had been little change in total employment, the employment figures tending to rise slightly within a range of 5 per cent, more on the men's side than on the women's side.

The male labour force was divided into two groups: two-thirds were semi-skilled, one-third skilled, and among these a large number were highly skilled. A few labourers were engaged in service and cleaning. The female labour force was almost entirely semi-skilled, with a sprinkling of cleaners and similar grades. It was divided into two almost equal sections: full-timers and part-timers, on mornings, afternoons and evenings.

The labour force in Mullard is relatively young. In a test sample of 229 male operatives, 128 were under forty, ninety-one between forty and sixty and ten over sixty. There was little difference between the age composition of skilled and that of semi-skilled men (from 114 skilled men, sixty-five were under forty, from 115 semi-skilled, sixty-three were under forty).

There is no official retiring age for operatives at sixty-five; operatives who are able and willing to carry on are retained on an individual basis. However, there is a contributory pension scheme which entitles members to, roughly speaking, about £4 a year for every year of work.

The female labour force is even younger. In a test sample of eighty-nine full-time women operatives, only twenty-four were over forty. Part-time day operatives were mostly in the age group thirty-three to forty-five (in a test sample of ninety-three, forty-eight were in this age group). Part-time evening operatives were mostly in the age group twenty-five to thirty-five (in a test sample of forty-three, twenty-three were in this age group) and were often mothers with young children whose fathers returned from work to baby-sit.

Labour Relations

Labour relations ran very smoothly; the last strike had been in 1935 on the introduction of the Bedaux system. The reputation of the firm among its work-people was very high: 'This is the best firm I ever worked for' or 'A very good Company to work for', I often heard. General cleanliness, tidiness and the good overall service were appreciated. The work itself is not heavy; it is fine and small work with clean and light materials, generally speaking, although there are some departments with a more heavy type of work. The atmosphere was described by a very big majority as 'Pleasant and friendly', 'Good mates and helpful supervisors'. The speed was comfortable; only a few, mostly newcomers, complained about the excessive speed. In some departments men and women worked together and the contacts often resulted in lasting friendships and marriages. In my sample out of ninety-six married men five had met their future wives in Mullard., 'You can get to know the girl you are working with better under more genuine conditions', one of them said. Many more men, about one in five of married men in my sample, had their wives working in Mullard, some in the same department. Not all of them were pleased with this fact. 'Too much of a good thing', they said.

Both men and women operatives were very highly organized in their respective Trade Unions. The estimated percentage of organization amounted to 85 to 90 per cent. There were six Trade Unions operating in the firm with sixty-eight shop-stewards, but the majority of operatives, both men and women, belonged to A.E.U. and E.T.U. with a preponderance of A.E.U. which had sixty shop-stewards.

Labour Turnover, Length of Service and Absenteeism

Labour turnover was relatively small. Among the male operatives (for the period 26th April 1958 to 2nd May 1959) it amounted to 15·8 per cent (from all causes), among full-time female operatives to 29·8 per cent, and among part-timers to 37·1 per cent. It is interesting to note that the figures for labour turnover on the male side in all three of the last firms visited, Vauxhall, Dunlop and Mullard, came very close to each other (16 per cent for Dunlop, 14·7 per cent for Vauxhall, 15·8 per cent for Mullard).

As to the family status of the leavers, the rate of labour turnover was much higher for single men than married men. In the previous six months twenty-nine single men had left and forty-three married men (the overwhelming majority of men were married). Of the eleven men dismissed in the preceding six months as unsuitable or for disciplinary reasons, seven were single.

However, the average length of service was not very high, partly due to the fact that the factory is relatively young and has greatly expanded in the last decade, while a number of long-service men had been transferred to another location. The average length of service was much higher on the skilled side than on the semi-skilled—partly due to the fact that mass production employing men had only recently been developed. Out of a test sample of ninety-one skilled men fifty had given over five years' service, of whom nineteen had given over ten years'. In a test sample of eighty-nine semi-skilled men only twenty had given more than five years' service, among them eight more than ten years'.

It is interesting to note the difference in age composition between the skilled and semi-skilled as related to the length of service. Of nineteen skilled men with over ten years' service eight were under forty, while of eight semi-skilled men with over ten years' service one was under forty. Of fifty skilled men with over five years' service twenty-seven men were under forty, while of twenty semi-skilled men with over five years' service only four were under forty. Generally speaking, skilled men settled earlier in a job and remained with the firm.

Owing to the fact that mass production employing women operatives has a longer tradition in the firm, the average length of service of a full-time woman was greater than that of semi-skilled men. Out of a test sample of eighty-three full-time women operatives, thirty-four had more than five years' service and twenty-two more than ten years' service. The length of service of part-timers compared very favourably with that of full-timers. Out of a test sample of forty-one day part-timers twenty had over five years' service, and five over ten years'. However, some of those who were part-timers at the time of the enquiry had served at one time or other as full-timers. The length of service of evening part-timers was the shortest of all as this kind of work had been started recently. Out of a sample of fifty-seven part-timers only three had more than five years' service.

Absenteeism in the factory is very low as far as male operatives are concerned. It reached serious proportions only among female operatives. For single girls absenteeism amounted to 12·6–14·4 per cent, for married full-timers between 17·4 and 18·3 per cent, while for married part-timers it was between 19·1 and 21·8. Those with longer service tended to show lower figures of absenteeism in all those groups.

Travelling Distance and Housing Conditions

The population is strongly local in character, or comes from other parts of London as a result of rehousing or slum clearance schemes. In my sample of 101 men only eleven came from other districts, including Scotland, Ireland and Wales. The housing conditions are not very satisfactory. In one of the adjacent areas, Carshalton, only thirty Council dwellings (flats and maisonettes) a year are built, while 129 families are on 'A' List, 143 on 'B' List and 800 on 'C' List. Actually the new houses go mostly for slum clearance and a few for those on the 'A' List with special priorities, mostly for health reasons. Consequently the average couples, those on Lists 'B' and 'C', have practically no chance of getting a Council house.

The big majority live within a distance of five miles from the works but it is interesting to note that distance increases with the rise in status. The skilled men live further away, often in their own houses, with their own transport, while the semi-skilled dayworkers live much closer, shiftworkers closer still and women workers closest of all.

In a test sample of 123 skilled men twenty-nine lived at a distance over five miles and thirteen over ten miles. Out of 102 semi-skilled dayworkers only thirteen lived at a distance over five miles and four over ten miles. Out of fifty-eight shiftworkers only three lived at a distance over five miles and none over ten miles. Out of fifty women workers only two lived at a distance over five miles, none over ten miles. About one-third lived in such close proximity to the works (under two miles) that they could go back home for lunch.

The Wage Structure

The level of wages was on the whole somewhat above the Federation rates. The characteristic feature of the wage structure was the large gap between the wage earnings of skilled and semi-skilled workers. This was due not only to higher rates but also to the longer hours worked, generally speaking, by skilled men (as the supply of skill in the district does not cover the demand). In the Plant Department the average wage of skilled men in April 1959 (in a test sample of twenty) was £19 3s 8d for 57·49 hours; in the Machine Shop, for toolmakers and kindred trades, £16 1s 0d for 49·31 hours; the average wage of semi-skilled production men was £12 8s 7d for 46·67 hours; the average female full-time wage was £7 10s 3d for 42·72 hours, while part-timers received £4 9s 0d for 23·66 hours.

The wages of production semi-skilled operatives were based on a premium payment plan which was often described to me by the operatives as 'semi-piecework'. It has certain affinities with an unelaborated job-evaluation scheme. The jobs are grouped in four classes (A, B, C, D) according to the type and nature of the work, difficulty, responsibility, intelligence required, etc., and for each class, five levels of performance or tasks (calculated as M/hours values) are distinguished. In order to qualify for a higher bonus the M/hour associated with the task must be reached and maintained for not less than 40 hours a week for two consecutive weeks. This scheme thus creates twenty levels of wage rates for semi-skilled operatives. The lowest wage for semi-skilled male operative (Class A, task 1) for 44 hours was £9 5s 7d, the highest (Class D, task 5) £12 9s 5d. The lowest wage of women operatives was £6 19s 6d, the highest £8 5s 0d. At the bottom of the scale came the labourers with an average wage of about £8 6s 0d.

Most men and women who were on the premium payment plan accepted it and were satisfied, and to my question as to whether they prefer time wage, piecework or premium payment plan, the answer was, in the overwhelming majority of cases, simply: 'As it is'.

Practically all the skilled men who were on time rates, asked whether they would prefer piecework, answered 'Definitely not', often referring to piecework as a social evil. The answer amounted to the phrase 'As it is'.

Hours of Work and Overtime

The big majority of men, about 78 per cent, were on days, and their standard hours were 44, five days a week, from 7.30 a.m. to 5.15 p.m., with a break of 1 hour for a meal and two tea breaks of 10 minutes each. The remainder were on shifts, either on a two- or three-shift system. The standard hours for both systems were $37\frac{1}{2}$. The rotation was weekly. The two-shift system, which is called double shift, consists of mornings and afternoons, the three-shift system consists of mornings, afternoons and nights and the starting times are 6.30 a.m., 2.30 p.m. and 10.30 p.m. with a $\frac{1}{2}$-hour break for the main meal and two tea breaks.

The part-timers worked in three shifts, 5 hours mornings, $4\frac{3}{4}$ hours on afternoons and $4\frac{1}{2}$ hours on evenings. On evenings they received an addition of one-fifth on their basic rates.

Little overtime is worked on production; only maintenance and skilled men work longer hours. In April 1959 men on days worked an average of 45·3 hours, men on double shift 39 hours, men on three shifts 39·6 hours. Saturday mornings are mainly worked as overtime and this is welcomed and appreciated by most men; the weekday overtime is less popular, and least liked of all is what is regarded as irregular overtime.

Shiftwork

The incidence of shiftwork in Mullard is relatively small: only 22 per cent of male workers were on shifts, either on double shifts or three shifts. The two-shift system presented few problems, in fact no problem at all as most men preferred two shifts to regular days because of shorter hours and better wages. None in my sample of double-shift workers was willing to exchange two shifts for regular days and lose the shift allowance. Actually, most of them would have preferred the two-shift system to regular days irrespective of the shift allowance.

If the two shifts are excluded, the incidence of shiftwork amounted to only 18 per cent of male workers in Mullard, which is very small compared with other shiftworking firms.

By and large, shiftwork in Mullard was more tolerated than in the other firms visited because the incidence of shiftwork was very small and the work was light and not too strenuous. The selection of shiftworkers could be more carefully carried out, both on the side of management and men, as only a few shiftworkers were required.

In my interviews, twenty-two men on three shifts or who had recently been on three shifts were asked whether shiftwork affected their health, stomach, sleep or nerves and only seven answered this question in the affirmative. In addition, one man complained of a feeling of excessive tiredness when on nights. Of these seven men, two complained about lack of sleep, one about stomach troubles, two about stomach and sleep, one about stomach, sleep and nerves, one about sinus trouble which his doctor put down to shifts. Among those who reported stomach disorders, two attributed their peptic ulcers to shifts. Those who lived in blocks of flats or furnished flats, or fathers with large families and small babies, found it difficult to get their normal sleep.

The wives of Mullard shiftworkers seemed also to tolerate shiftwork better than in the other firms visited. Out of twenty-one shiftworkers, twelve said that their wives did not mind their shiftwork; eight wives disliked and even detested their nightwork, while one said his wife minded the afternoon shift more than the nightshift. The correlation between those affected in their health and their wives' dislike of shifts is very great. Practically all those affected in their health stated that their wives detested the shifts, giving as an additional reason that they were 'grumpy and irritable', easily upset when they came home from nights. However, the problems presented by shiftwork cannot have been too serious because when asked whether they would prefer regular days, with loss of the shift allowance, out of twenty-two, twenty answered 'No', saying: 'I need the money', or 'I couldn't afford it' or, as one man said, 'I have to stick to shifts now because I bought a car'. Some said that they preferred the shiftwork to daywork on account of shorter hours and greater variety, apart from money. A few had a sideline such as that of salesman, painting and decorating, breeding and racing dogs, breeding budgerigars. Only two men said that they would prefer regular days, one being willing to give up the whole shift allowance, the other only half.

Attitudes to Work

Attitudes to work follow status distinctions closely. Among nine foremen and charge-hands there was only one man who qualified his interest in, and liking of, the job; all other supervisors described their work as: 'Most interesting', or 'Very nice', or 'The best'.

Out of thirty-two skilled men, only five men regarded their job as 'dullish', saying 'I don't think any man can really enjoy it', or 'Means to an end', or 'Passing the time', or 'I can't say I enjoy it but I'm not annoyed'; ten other men described their job as 'Interesting', or 'Nice', or 'Enjoyable most of the time'; the remainder praised their job very highly in such terms as: 'Very interesting', or 'First class', or 'Bred and born into it', or 'Gets into your blood', or 'I know it inside out'. Thus the attitudes of skilled men can be described as very positive or tolerant; there was hardly a case of a forthright rejection of the job.

The attitudes of the semi-skilled men were stated in a different key; they were also positive in the majority, but the reservations were stronger and more numerous. Out of sixty non-skilled men (mostly semi-skilled with a sprinkling of labourers), only nineteen described their work as 'Very nice', or 'I like it very much', or 'Very interesting'; another fourteen said, 'Interesting', or 'Satisfied'; eighteen more, 'O.K.', but pointing out some snags, or describing it as 'Just the job', or 'A means to an end' or 'I can adapt myself to anything'; nine described their job as 'Monotonous', or 'Not of the right kind', or 'Soul destroying' or 'Not congenial' or 'Strenuous'. So, the positive attitudes of the non-skilled were those of a small majority (about 57 per cent of cases), 15 per cent of men had a negative attitude, while the remainder had developed a sort of good-humoured toleration.

Most striking was the relative lack of complaints about monotony. To most outside observers the work of semi-skilled operatives would appear monotonous. I often asked specifically about monotony but the hint was rarely accepted, only in about 10 per cent of cases. Good fellowship and comradeship were stressed by practically everyone; sociability at work is a great compensation even in the dullest and most repetitive job. The counter-balancing advantage of repetitive work was referred to by many in such terms as: 'It's easy', or 'No responsibility', or 'No worry', or 'You can have a chat'.

The social distance between skilled men (who, being electricians, belong to the top ranks of skilled men) and semi-skilled men was greater in Mullard than in the other firms I visited. This also is due to the fact that the premium for skill is higher in Mullard than in the other firms, and, combined with the long hours worked by skilled men, the gap between earnings of the two groups is considerable. The skilled men have greater stability of employment and greater security of job. A skilled man would, therefore, take on responsibility more readily and also acquire such symbols of higher status as a house or a car. This was confirmed by comparative figures of house and car ownership which were much higher for skilled men than for semi-skilled. About half of the total number of houses and cars in my sample in Mullard were owned by skilled men, although they formed only one-third of the total sample.

The Social Life of the Firm

The social life of the firm was strongly developed, more so than in Dunlop or Vauxhall. Though only a third the size of Dunlop the firm had ninety football players (in Dunlop, eighty), about eighty cricket players (sixty in Dunlop) and twenty rugby players (twenty in Dunlop).

Altogether there were twenty-one sections of the sports club with 55–60 per cent of operatives taking part. The most patronized sections were the horticulture section, with 200 members, the cinema section, with ninety members, the amateur dramatic club, with forty-five members, and the angling section, with forty-five members.

The sports club provides services for theatre tickets and holiday bookings, it arranges about twenty-four outings a year, and it arranges two draws a year with a £10 first prize for a 6*d* ticket. Having a younger mixed population, both men and girls, helps the social life of the firm. It is also helped by the greater social integration of the work-people in Mitcham.

Index

Accidents etc., 219, 232–4, 244–5, 256
Acquisitive tendencies, 65ff, 71–3, 206
Agnostics, 146, 149–50
Atheists, 148–9

Bach, 90ff
Bachelor types, 159–63
Beethoven, 90ff
Behaviour, mechanism of, 195–212
Birmingham, see Dunlop Rubber Company Ltd
Buddha, 89ff
Byron, 89ff

Catholics, Roman, 18, 49, 73, 146, 148, 152–3, 187
Children, adopted, 15
Chopin, 90ff
Class-consciousness in men, 133ff; in women, 187
Communists, 209
Compensation schemes, 232–3
Concubinage, 49
Confucius, 89ff
Cultural opportunities, 89–95, 211–12

Darwin, Charles, 89ff
Dickens, 90ff
Divorce, 46ff
Divorce and remarriage, 48–9
Domestic troubles, 85–8
Dostoievski, 90ff
Drinking, 96, 106, 129ff, 159, 201
Dunlop Rubber Company Ltd in Erdington, Birmingham, x, xiv–xvi, 246ff

Earnings, male (average), 2–5; deductions from, 3–4; family, 4; of wives, 12–14; see also Wives, working
Einstein, Albert, 89ff
English Steel Corporation Ltd, see River Don Works

Family allowances, 11
Family planning, 14–19
Family planning and women's employment, 39ff
Family statistics, 11–13, 14, 19
Father–family relationships, 20–25, 203, 206–7; see also Husband–wife relationship
Fourier, Charles, 196
Freud, Sigmund, 79, 89ff, 192

Gambling, 96, 106, 201
Gandhi, 90ff
Goethe, 192
Grouping of workers, 155ff

Hire-purchase, 121–2
Hobbies of men, 59–60, 74, 96ff, 158–9; of women, 186
Home equipment, 8–10, 123, 183, 206
'Homeo-stasis', definition and application of, 189ff
House-ownership, 124ff; and mobility, 129; as social index, 126, 128

Index

Housekeeping relationships, 33–9; statistics, 34, 37
Housing, 5–8, 16, 62
Husband–wife relationship, 31–32, 59–60, 74, 173, 177, 179–83

Interviewing technique, xiii–xvii

James, William, 192

Kipling, Rudyard, 89ff

La Rochefoucauld, 32
Labour–management relations, 219, 226, 236–8, 250–1, 259
Le Play, Frédéric, 30
Life insurance, 121, 123, 124
Luther, Martin, 89ff
Luton, see Vauxhall Motors Ltd

Marriage, early, 10–14
Marx, Karl, 89ff
Michelangelo, 89ff
Mitcham, see Mullard Radio Valve Company
Mobility, 129, 197–8
Mohammed, 89ff
Money-incentive, 68, 71, 76, 199
Mortgages, 121–2
Mother-image, 23–5, 207–8
Motor cars, 44, 60, 65, 96, 100; as social index, 104ff
Mozart, 90ff
Mullard Radio Valve Company Ltd in Mitcham, x, xiv–xvi, 171ff, 257ff

Neighbourly contacts, 116–17, 184–5, 200
Nightshifts, 217–18; compensations of, 189

Outdoor sports, 97–8, 158
Overtime and family life, 75; for and against, 70ff, 242, 253–4, 262

Part-time jobs for pensioners, 170
Pastimes, see Hobbies
Paternal trades, following, 139ff
Personal contacts at work, men's, 81–3; women's, 183–4
Personal contacts in family circles, men's, 111–15; women's, 185
Personal contacts outside work, men's, 107, 116–19, 194; women's, 184–5
Picasso, 89ff
Piecework v. time rate, 196, 251–3

Radio, 91, 98; see also Home equipment
Reading by men, 100–103; by women, 186–7
Recruitment of labour, 224
Refrigerators, see Home equipment
Religion, 146ff
Religious belief, shades of (men), 150–2; (women), 187–8
Rembrandt, 89
Retiring-age problems, 167ff
Riesman, David, 210
River Don Works (Sheffield), ix, xiv–xvi, 213ff

Savings, 121ff, 168, 206
Scott, Sir Walter, 89
Schopenhauer, 193
Schweitzer, Albert, 90ff
Security of employment, 203, 205–6
Seneca, 193
Separation (marital), 48–51
Shaw, Bernard, 90ff
Sheffield, see River Don Works
Shelley, 89
Shiftwork, age-factor in, 61; and family relationships, 63–4; problems of, 53ff, 229–30, 243–4, 254–5, 262–3; wives and, 55–6, 63, 64
Sidelines, 99

Socrates, 193

Temperance as status index, 130–2
Tolstoy, 90ff
Training schemes, 225, 244
Television, 8–9, 90–1, 93, 96, 106, 108–11, 117, 119, 183, 194–5, 206, 207

Unemployment and self-respect, 78–9
Union influence, 71–2, 82, 203, 208, 226, 237

Vauxhall Motors Ltd in Luton, x, xiv–xvi, 234ff

Wage differentials, 2

Wage scales and structures, 2, 218–19, 228–9, 251–3, 261–2
Welfare and social services, 31, 219–21, 225, 234, 245–6, 255–6, 264–5
Wells, H. G., 90
Wesley, John, 89ff
Widowers, 163ff; remarried, 163–5
Wives, working, 12–15, 39–46, 74, 127, 171ff, 202
Women workers, 171ff; attitude to work of, 172; economic motives of, 175–6; mothers as, 174–5
Work, attitudes to, 65–9, 77–80, 172, 230–1, 263–4
Workington Iron & Steel Company, ix, xiv–xvi, 223ff